RECORDS TRULY IS MY MIDDLE NAME

by
John Records Landecker

Produced by Rick Kaempfer

*To Jack,
Hope you enjoy
the book!
Rick K*

Copyright © 2013 by John Records Landecker and Rick Kaempfer

Published in the United States by

Eckhartz Press

Chicago, Illinois

Cover and interior design by Kelly Hyde

Cover photos from the personal collections of John Records Landecker, Rick Kaempfer, and John Gehron

All rights reserved.

No part of this book may be used or reproduced in any manner whatsoever without written permission except in the case of brief quotations embodied in critical articles and reviews.

ISBN: 978-0-9848049-8-6

First Edition

DEDICATION

This book is dedicated to:

My parents, Werner and Marjorie Landecker

My daughters, Tracy and Amy

My brother Tom, his wife Sharon and my nephew Will

My soul mate, Nika

Judy Landecker, the mother of my children, her sister Bambi and their brother Joe

My granddaughter, Lola

Paula and Laura

Grandpa Records and all my relatives in Indiana

Angela and Lyndon Welch, who helped me in more ways than they will ever know

And the three people who helped get my first radio job: Lucy Dobson, Ted Heusel and Tom O'Brien

I love you all,

John

ACKNOWLEDGEMENTS

It took several years to write this book, and it definitely wasn't done in a traditional way. My coauthor and former producer Rick Kaempfer came out to my house in Michigan City, Indiana, and asked me to start telling him stories about my life. He recorded and transcribed them, and then came back out to my house again and again to ask me to tell some more. When we had finally finished, he sent me the transcripts, and I began to write some additional stories myself. Rick then cobbled all of that together into its current narrative form.

Rick also conducted the interviews of the other people quoted in this book. I can't tell you how grateful I am for the kind words from people like Tom O'Brien, Art Vuolo, Joey Reynolds, John Gehron, Jonathon Brandmeier, Bob Sirott, Fred Winston, Alan Rosen, Turi Ryder, Bill Zehme, Jim Martin, Spike O'Dell, Jim Smith, Eddie Webb, Kevin Matthews, Eric Ferguson, Greg Eckler, Catherine Johns, Leslie Keiling, Greg Brown, Len O'Kelly, Vince Argento, Kipper McGee, Mary June Rose, Don Wade, Jan Jeffries, Jim Bohannan, and Rick himself.

Thanks to all the people that helped put this book together, including my publisher David Stern from Eckhartz Press, my editor Bridget Kaempfer, and my excellent book designer Kelly Hyde. Thanks also to the people that provided some of the photos contained in these pages, especially John Gehron, Scott Childers, Tony Lossano, and Paul Natkin.

    I would like to thank everyone who listened. I would also like to thank everybody I ever worked with — but if you're one of those people who made my life a living hell — go fuck yourself.

INTRODUCTION

A few years ago I was at a party and the subject of "John Landecker on WLS" came up in conversation. Someone said to me: "You know, you're a celebrity on some level."

I said "A what?"

I guess it's some kind of semi-compliment. Sort of a "some may know you, but some don't." If you are in a certain age group, lived in a certain area of the United States, and listened to radio or worked in the industry, you might know who I am. To others I would ask: Are you a Baby Boomer? Were you around for the birth of rock and roll? Did you ever wonder what was happening behind the scenes at those radio stations you did listen to? Do you remember where you were when JFK was shot, when the Beatles were on Ed Sullivan, when John Lennon died, when O.J. got off? Did you get married, divorced, have children, face job loss, drugs, alcohol, illness or death? Did you refuse to join AARP because your parents belonged to it?

OK, maybe that last one is just me. But if you answered yes to any of the other questions, maybe I'm not a celebrity on some level, maybe I'm just a guy writing a book about the times we all lived through together.

John Records Landecker

CHAPTER ONE
WHAT'S IN A NAME?

A short description of my father Werner Landecker's life gives you an idea of the truly profound and memorable things he must have experienced between his Berlin birth in 1911 and his Ann Arbor, Michigan death in 2003. He grew up a Jew in Nazi Germany — the last Jew to earn a law degree in Berlin before the war. He eventually escaped and immigrated to the United States, became a sociology professor at the University of Michigan, married a farm girl from Indiana, fathered two boys, and lost his sight early in his adulthood.

Dad obviously had some great stories. I wish I knew more of them.

WERNER LANDECKER IN HIS OWN WORDS
Shortly before my father died, my brother Tom managed to videotape him telling a few. This is one of my favorites: Family history down the toilet... *I was very close to my mother's family, and especially my grandmother Sophie Kahn. When I was an adolescent and visiting Grandmother in Berlin, my cousin and I became interested in our family history. Nobody seemed to know much about the earlier generations of Kahn's, but they remembered there was an old abandoned Jewish cemetery in town that might offer a few clues. So, we took along someone that could read Hebrew, and we found several gravestones. My cousin*

took meticulous notes and wrote down all the names and dates from the gravestones, and he promised to do more research when he got home.

Unfortunately, that cousin lived in Hanover, and had to take a train back to his hometown. The bathrooms in those trains in the Weimar Republic days were notoriously bad, and this one was no exception. When he went into the bathroom stall, he noticed that they didn't have any toilet paper. Well, this was an emergency, and my cousin had only one piece of paper that would solve the problem; the piece of paper with all the notes about the family's history.

That Kahn family history was literally flushed down the toilet on a train to Hanover.

A JEW IN NAZI GERMANY

My father didn't talk about those days in Germany very much, unless we really pulled it out of him. He told us that when he was young, a kid was following him around one day, throwing matches at him. Dad responded by punching him.

Another time when he was a college student, he intentionally visited a library he knew was run by the Nazis. I asked him why in the world he would do that, knowing that as a Jew, he wouldn't be allowed to study there.

"I just wanted to see what it felt like," he said.

I think that describes my father perfectly.

He stayed in Germany longer than it was safe for Jews to stay there because he really wanted to finish his doctor of jurisprudence degree at the University of Berlin. He was the last Jew to receive that degree in pre-war Germany, but because he was a Jew, his dissertation was never published.

That 1936 dissertation is a story unto itself.

After he left Germany, Dad never gave it another thought. Then, in the mid 1990s, when Dad was in his eighties, an old German colleague of his, Professor Guenther Luschen, called up to say that he really wanted to publish it because he thought it was a historically important document. I can see why Professor Luschen felt that way. 1936 was no ordinary year in German history. It was the first full year the Nuremberg Laws were in effect.

The "Law for Protection of German Blood and Honor," made it illegal for Jews to marry non-Jews. The "Reich Citizen Law" stripped German citizenship from anyone that had any Jewish blood — they became known as "subjects of the state." And in 1936, Jews were banned from all professional jobs once and for all, officially ending any influence they may have had over politics, education, academia, and industry.

And what was my father's dissertation about? The importance of international law.

I'll say.

If you go looking for it on the internet, you'll need to know what it's called. In German it's a mouthful. Try this one on for size: *"DIE GELTUNG DES VOLKERRECHTS ALS GESELLSCHAFTLISCHES PHANOMEN: EINE RECHTS- UND SOZIALWISSENSCHAFTLICHE ANALYSE AUS DEM JAHR 1936; HERAUSGEGEBEN VON GUNTHER LUSCHEN."*

I put it in capital letters because I can't picture anyone saying it without shouting. The English version isn't much better: "The Importance of International Law as a Social Phenomenon: A Judicial and Sociological Analysis from the Year 1936."

When it was finally published in 1999, 63 years after he originally wrote it, Dad was still alive to hear about it. Alive, but quite frankly not doing too well. He was 88 years old. He had fallen and hit his head and it had a lasting effect.

Plus, becoming published was already old hat to him. To remain a tenured professor at a major institution you had to "publish or perish." Teaching was not enough. My father had written countless papers for journals, and two textbooks: *Class Boundaries* and *Class Crystallization*. The idea that his work as a student in Germany would finally be published did not excite him.

I found it to be a fantastic story. I envision a modern day German classroom referencing this book as part of their course work. Maybe Dad was fine with leaving those things behind in Germany, and grateful those things didn't make it out.

That's really all we know about Dad's time in Germany. Although he did tell my brother Tom another good story on that videotape. Werner Landecker in his own words regarding a family heirloom… *When my parents were fleeing the Nazis in 1939, the Nazis were still allowing Jews to ship their belongings — but not anything valuable, like artwork or jewelry.*

My mother had a diamond pin that she really loved, and my father decided to take a risk to keep it. He bored a hole in some dining room furniture he was shipping, inserted the pin, and covered it up again. If this had been discovered, he almost certainly would have been imprisoned or killed. But he got lucky, and the furniture was shipped to Newark, New Jersey, and put in storage there.

When Marjorie and I were married, my mother decided she wanted Marjorie to have the pin, so she sent us to Newark to retrieve it. All of the furniture had been left out to rot on a dock somewhere, ruined by water damage, and picked apart by scavengers, but the pin was still there — hidden in the furniture.

So we went out to dinner with the pin to celebrate. We had a nice dinner and were walking away from the restaurant when Marjorie suddenly realized 'Oh no! I left the pin at the restaurant!'

It was still there when we went back for it, but we found it pretty funny that it got past the Nazis and the New Jersey dock workers, but we had managed to lose it in less than an hour.

HOOSIER MAMA

Mom was an Indiana girl through and through. How stereotypically Hoosier were my mother's parents William J. Records and Ione Records? William was a farmer, and Ione was a grand champion blue-ribbon winner at the Indiana State Fair. I have an article about my grandmother in the local paper, and the reporter wrote: "If you took all her ribbons and stretched them from end to end, they'd go from here to waaaay out there." She won 'em all: pies, bread, baking, and sewing. Multiple awards — year after year after.

My mom, Marjorie Victoria Records, grew up on the farm along with her three siblings Marvin, Virginia, and Jeannette. In some ways Mom was a typical Hoosier, but she was also unusual for her era. Mom reached out beyond the agricultural stereotype and went to college at Franklin College in Franklin, Indiana, and then to graduate school at Indiana University.

That was incredibly atypical for her time. Her parents didn't go to college. The great majority of her Indiana relatives never went to college. (Only one of her sisters, Virginia, did.) The two Records girls that went to college really left the Indiana farmland behind. Virginia married a doctor and moved to South Carolina.

Mom met Dad. And according to urban legend, this is how it happened.

They were driving in separate cars in Brown County, which is in downstate Indiana — a beautiful vacation area about thirty miles from Bloomington. He was in one car, and she was in another. They came to a stop at an intersection, gazed into each other's eyes, and decided to go for coffee. The rest, as they say, is history. They were married for fifty years.

I can only imagine what it must have been like when my mom brought my father (a liberal, intellectual, German Jew and member of the NAACP and ACLU) to her farm in the heartland of conservative, Christian, rural Indiana, but if there were any stories of the Records clan not accepting Dad, I never heard one. In all the times we came to Indiana, there was nary a peep, hint, innuendo, or aside from anybody.

AND BABY MAKES THREE

There's an old expression about the month of March; in like a lion and out like a lamb. Not necessarily. At 5:14 pm on March 28, 1947 in Ann Arbor, Michigan, the lion was roaring.

Outside their small apartment on Washington Heights in Ann Arbor there was a white-out blizzard accompanied by sub-zero temperatures. Inside, Werner & Marjorie contemplated their situation. Marjorie's water had broken.

After clearing a path and walking very cautiously, Werner got Marjorie safely into the front seat and then prayed to the ignition gods that the car would start. It did. Since the weather was so bad, traffic was extremely light. That gave Werner the luxury of using the entire road to travel the relatively short distance to St. Joseph Hospital. With his right hand on the wheel, he used his left to open the window and reach out to help the overburdened windshield wipers keep the snow off the windshield so he could see where he was going.

Even though the temperature was below zero and the wind was howling, a small line of perspiration formed on Werner's forehead. As was her way, Marjorie was calm and reassured her husband that he was doing a great job getting them to the hospital and all would be well. When the car finally came to a stop at the entrance to the hospital, things began to move rather quickly. At approximately 7:40 pm on the evening of March 28, 1947, Werner Sigmund Landecker and Marjorie Victoria Landecker had a son.

That son was me.

I came out face first; a metaphor for how I would live the rest of my life. My face was covered with deep bruises, and my neck was grotesquely out of alignment. The bruises would fade, but the neck treatment required me to be placed between two sandbags until the neck and head assumed the proper position.

When they were sure I was healthy, they realized I needed a name. John was their choice for the first name and obviously Landecker for the last. In a nod to my mother's upbringing, they chose her maiden name, Records, as my middle name.

They had no way of knowing that their son would become a radio disc jockey, or that this name they had chosen would become my unlikely calling card.

But it is an absolutely true story. One that I have had to tell many, many times. One that my mother and father had to tell many, many times. (*The full transcript of Mom and Dad telling it on WLS Radio is in the appendix.*)

Even though nobody believes it: *Records Truly is My Middle Name.*

CHAPTER TWO
A BABY BOOMER'S CHILDHOOD

In the 1950s, Dwight D. Eisenhower was the U.S. President, and Elizabeth was the brand new Queen of England. The Cold War was at its nadir, and Senator Joseph McCarthy was conducting anti-American hearings in Washington, exposing alleged Communists. Even though Rosa Parks refused to go to the back of the bus, and schools were ordered to integrate, America was still a very segregated country. The average American family earned about $5,000 a year. Most historians consider the official beginning of the rock and roll era the release of Bill Haley's "Rock around the Clock" in 1955. The next year, Elvis Presley became the biggest star in the world, Alan Freed became the first famous rock and roll disc jockey in America, and every parent in the country was against everything all of that stood for.

If the stories I've been told about my childhood are true, some of my strengths and weaknesses were there from the very beginning. For instance, I had an aversion to taking responsibility for my actions. When I was very little, whenever I was going to be confronted or scolded for something I shouldn't have done, my immediate reaction was to say: "Look at the birdie! Look at the birdie!" As in, let's take our mind off our problems. (Years later my mother was diagnosed with cancer and I purchased a small wooden bird and gave it to her so that she could "look at the birdie." It was still on the kitchen table when she died.)

My poor mother also tried to teach me math, which is another of my lifelong weaknesses. She had to get creative to get through to me. Across the street from my school, Bach Elementary, there was a neighborhood store that sold penny candy and was run by a guy we called Johnny Gyp. He didn't really gyp people, but I suppose if you have an onslaught of elementary school people descend on your store after school every day, five days a week, you might turn into a "Johnny Gyp" too.

My mother would try to teach me how to add and subtract by telling me to go to the store and get penny candy. She would say, "let's say you have five pieces of penny candy, and three pieces that cost a nickel, how would you know how much to spend?"

My answer was: "Ask the man."

Who says a half-Jew needs to haggle?

Just as my weaknesses were there from the beginning, so were some of my strengths. I had a very early interest in performing. When I was really young I was in a play called *The Ugly Duckling*. I still have the program from that performance: It was Sunday, December 6, 1953, at 2pm. General admission was sixty-three cents plus tax, for a total of seventy-five cents. In a really strange twist of fate, the two ladies who put that play on were later married to two men that would have a very big impact on my radio career: Ted Heusel and Joel Sebastian.

It was also very important to me when I was in elementary school to be part of the cool crowd. There were a few fashion trends that came and went, and I had to be part of them. One of the odder ones was when all of the boys wore white nylon jackets, or windbreakers. I have no idea why those were considered cool, but they were, and I had to have one. We also wore these shirts that were designed to look like a shirt with a sweater over it, like a cardigan.

They were actually just sewn that way. I have no idea why. They say that everything eventually becomes cool again, but we're still waiting for that white nylon jacket and fake cardigan look to come back in style.

1950s Ann Arbor was a very typical American experience in a lot of ways. The first time McDonald's came to town, it was a huge deal. Everybody had to ride their bikes over there to see this cool new hamburger place. I remember the menu distinctly. A hamburger was fifteen cents, French fries were ten cents, and a chocolate shake was twenty cents. I don't want to say this was very early in the McDonald's dynasty, but if you had a photograph of the McDonald's sign when it first debuted in Ann Arbor, it probably said: "150 sold."

INDIANA MEMORIES

Because we lived in Ann Arbor, and Mom's family was in Indiana, we spent every vacation of my childhood in the Hoosier state. I loved going to Indiana, I loved going to my grandparents' farm, I loved going to the Indiana State Fair. It's where I discovered bumper cars and snow cones. But my favorite moments came when my blue-ribbon winning grandmother was baking at the farmhouse. Everything was made from scratch, no mixes. That meant homemade icing. I still love icing, probably because my grandmother always left a little bit in the bowl for young Johnny to scrape up with a spatula.

My grandparents' farm house didn't have central heating. In the winter, the upstairs was closed off and everyone slept on the first floor, which had a large gas furnace in the living room. When we visited for Christmas, my mom would sleep on the couch, and Grandpa Records set up three cots in the front room for Tom, Dad and me. On Christmas Day my grandmother would have to make a huge turkey for the all the relatives. You can imagine how big of a bird that required and how long it took to cook it. One year I woke up in the middle of the night on Christmas Eve, and saw my grandmother passing in front of that huge gas heater as she was making her way from the bedroom to the kitchen. I can still smell that delicious warm turkey.

The animals on the farm were just a part of life, although sometimes that wasn't quite so pleasant. I had to hold the male pigs while they were neutered by a vet. If you've never seen it done, it's pretty quick. You prop up the pig's legs, the vet comes in, and zip zap, off they go. The pigs don't even seem fazed by it. I watched my Aunt Jeannette kill a chicken too. She put her foot on the chicken's head and yanked. The head came off, but the rest of the body ran around the yard for a while before flopping down. Of course that's the origin of the expression "running around like a chicken with its head cut off."

There was also one really mean rooster on Grandpa Records' farm that would run after my brother and me and peck at our legs. So, I devised a plan. I convinced my brother to be my bait, and I got a good hiding place. Tom came running down the driveway with this rooster in full pursuit. I waited until Tom passed me and then I made my move, hurling rocks at the angry bird. It was all very dramatic and exciting. I hit the little bastard a few times, and he never bothered me or my brother again.

THE SILVER SCREEN

We were visiting my grandparents in 1959 when *Ben Hur* came out. It was showing at this huge ornate movie palace in downtown

Indianapolis. One day the whole family got in the car to drive the thirty five miles from Grandpa's farm. I was just enthralled by that whole experience; the theater, the city, the surroundings. It was just the best.

If you've seen the movie, you probably remember that lepers are a side story — and if you're anything like me, you remember that as the really scary part. It was creepy. You could feel the tension building in the theater. It was ramping up and up, and suddenly as the music swelled, one person stood up in the middle of the movie theater and screamed.

"I can't take it. I can't take it. I can't take it anymore!"

And he ran out of the theater.

I thought "WOW! This movie is really something!"

Every time I've watched it since, I've watched to see if that leprosy scene has the same effect on me, and it still does.

There was another movie memory from that year that wasn't quite as grand, but it also left a lasting impression on me. One day, for reasons I still don't understand all these years later, my mom decided to take me out of elementary school to go to the movies. I don't remember why, but I remember the movie: *John Paul Jones* starring Robert Stack. John Paul Jones was the great naval hero from the Revolutionary War, and this was one of those old fashioned "could have been done by Walt Disney himself" interpretations of the American Revolution.

Fast forward fifty two years later. It was 10am on the 4th of July, and Turner Classic Movies was showing patriotic films in honor of Independence Day, and I just happened to stumble onto the channel just as they were showing *John Paul Jones*. I hadn't seen that film since 1959, the day my mom took me out of school, and I have to admit, I got a little emotional as the memory came flooding back to me.

FUN WITH BLINDNESS

But as typical as some elements of my childhood were, there was one thing that was totally different. My father was blind. He wasn't blind yet when I was born, but I don't have any memory of him being able to see. Maybe it was just because it was all I knew, or maybe it was because he handled it so well, but it was never a problem for us — never an issue. He still managed to support the family as a professor of sociology. Granted, it would have been extremely difficult for him to do it without the help of my mother, who handled absolutely everything else — if anything needed to be taken care of, she took care of it — but there were never any stories of strife in dealing with being blind.

I never heard a hint of "boo hoo, woe is me." Never. When I was a little kid I asked my father why he wore glasses if he couldn't see anything, and that was the last time he ever wore glasses.

"You're right! I don't know why I wear them. Why, thank you, John."

He had a great sense of humor about it. Occasionally my brother and I would pump whip cream from a can onto his cake, and pile it up a little higher than usual, because we knew that when he bent down to eat, he would stick his face right in it. (Of course, he knew it was coming — he just played along.)

We weren't shy about ribbing him, and he wasn't shy about ribbing himself if the subject came up. Years later a rock club opened up in Ann Arbor called "The Blind Pig." One day I came home and checked my answering machine for messages. I heard my Dad's voice with a bunch of noise in the background. He said: "John, I don't know if you can hear me. I'm at the The Blind Pig, and I'm having a great time. I just wanted to let you know where I am."

My parents were not above turning the tables on Tom and myself. At one point Tom decided to get his ears pierced. He was an adult, he was married, he had a kid, and he lived in California, yet he still had some reservations about how his parents would react. Tom, his wife Sharon, and my nephew Will came home for Christmas. My father took two of my mother's gaudiest earrings and put one on each ear. He then greeted Tom at the door like everything was totally normal.

> **TOM LANDECKER** *REMEMBERS*
> *This vision issue did affect my brother Tom… Sometime in the mid '80s I noticed that I had a dark spot dead center in my left eye's field of vision. I went to see a specialist in Berkeley who injected me with a dye and then looked into my eye with a scope and saw there was a leak in the back of the retina. He told me this was technically a detached retina. Given how much this affected me (I'm a photographer), it was decided to treat it with a laser. They took a detailed medical history from me in preparation for the laser surgery, asking if I had experienced anything such as stroke, heart disease, previous vision problems, etc., which I told them I hadn't. Then they asked about my family history, wondering if there were any vision problems.*
>
> *I said no.*
>
> *All of a sudden I realized what they meant by vision "problems," a term that really didn't fit in Dad's case, because by no stretch of the imagination did he have a problem. He had*

been blind all of my life, and for most of it he walked to work with a series of leader dogs at a pace that required me to do a light jog to keep up. Nonetheless, I decided to mention his retinal detachment and blindness. The doctor just looked at me for a long time.

> He clearly thought I was out of my mind.

GIRLS, GIRLS, GIRLS

The day my father told me the facts of life is a story right out of a 1950s Norman Rockwell painting. Imagine if you will, a professor/father with his pipe, wearing his suit coat and tie in his study at home. He calls for his boy to join him.

"Young John, come in and sit down."

Then he explained to me in clinical detail about the penis and the vagina, and exactly how sexual intercourse worked. Direct, and to the point, without any embellishment. No vernacular, no slang.

"This is how it works — the man inserts the penis into the woman's vagina."

OK, thanks Dad. Sounds good. I think I'll give it a try.

By then, I had definitely already taken note of the opposite sex. Watching television had a lot to do with that because *The Mickey Mouse Club* was on every day after school. One Mouseketeer in particular had an impact on me; Annette Funicello. Yes, she was beautiful. Yes, she was talented. But more importantly, as time went on she developed breasts right before our very eyes. The Mouseketeers wore sweaters with their names spelled out, and as the years progressed, Annette's "A" and "E" grew farther and farther apart. I'm telling you, it was a sensation. I finally got to interview the girl of my childhood dreams when I was working in Toronto in the '80s. It was fabulous. If you can believe it, she told me that she felt very self-conscious when she was on *The Mickey Mouse Club* because she was the only "ethnic" one, and how did she put it? I believe she said she looked a little bit *different* than the others. Yeah Annette, I think we know what you mean.

So first there was Annette, but then there was Nancy. Nancy March was my first girlfriend in elementary school, and it was all very innocent. I literally carried her books home from school. When I had a birthday party at the local YMCA, she gave me a 45 RPM record of the Fleetwoods song "Come Softly to Me." Many years later, the subject of first girlfriends came up during a radio show I was hosting, and I told that story, and brought up the name of Nancy March. Wouldn't you know it? Somebody listening to the show knew Nancy. That led to a telephone conversation with her, and a lunch in Chicago with Nancy and her husband. It was great reconnecting with her all those years later. I'm happy to report that she went on to live happily ever after. Nancy was, and always will be for me, part of the holy trinity of girls that sparked my discovery of human sexuality.

Who is the third part of the holy trinity of girls, you ask? Well, for this young American lad, no female represented sexuality more than Ann Margret. I still have my *Bye Bye Birdie* soundtrack, and if you know anything about me, you know I don't normally go for musicals. But if it had Ann Margret in it, that was good enough for me. In one movie called *The Swinger* (with Tony Franciosa), she played a writer who had to prove to a publisher that she was sexy by writhing around the floor covered in paint. Oh boy. Still, the quintessential all-time Ann Margret experience as far as I'm concerned is in the rock opera *Tommy*. So what if she plays Tommy's mother? In one scene Ann Margret slid around the floor as baked beans washed all over her, and

28

then the baked beans turned to chocolate, and chocolate was spewing all over Ann Margret's body, and she was writhing and grinding all over the floor. That's how I'll always remember her — rolling around the floor covered in various liquids. It sure works for me. Years later I was able to have a brief telephone interview with her and the first thing I did was thank her for that.

NOT EXACTLY NORMAN ROCKWELL

After Bach Elementary School, I went to Slauson Junior High School. At those schools I was hanging out with typical blue-collar kids whose parents were milkmen and plumbers, even though we were in a university town.

Slauson was an integrated school, but there were very few instances of racial tension. I moved well in every circle because we all played football together, and that was an equalizer. But there was one occasion where I was accused of stealing a nickel from an African-American kid in the locker room. I didn't do it, but the kid didn't believe me and said "I'll meet you after school."

I have to admit, I was nervous about it, but I showed up in the alley on the side of school. I showed up alone, and he showed up with thirty of his friends. I knew a lot of these guys from football, so I said: "I'll fight him, but I won't fight all of you."

The guys I knew from football agreed that was fair, and they formed a circle around us. We were just about to start the fight when the athletic director of the school poked his head out of the window, saw what was going on, and broke it up.

This athletic director is another story. I didn't know anything about pedophiles or molestation when I was in junior high, but this guy was a pedophile. I didn't have the slightest idea at the time, but looking back, there were a few clues. For instance, he made us swim nude in swimming class, which was a little odd. I also have a memory of him sitting with a few of his favorites surrounding him during recess. Years later when I heard what he had been doing, that image immediately came to mind. Our very own Jerry Sandusky.

SCOUTING A CAREER

Other than my brief acting gig as a boy, I got my first real taste of performing in scouts. We did skits at potluck dinners and things like that. I got a lot of my material from a comedy team that was on Ed Sullivan all the time, Wayne and Shuster. I also got a lot of material from Bob Newhart. I remember at one point I had literally memorized most of *The Button-Down Mind of Bob Newhart* comedy album, and I would do his routines to entertain my fellow scouts.

I don't think the Boy Scouts would have advertised my troop as a good example for Boy Scouting in America. Our troop leader bought us cigarettes, which I'm guessing most troop leaders didn't do for their scouts. We also went on a campout at Point Pelee National Park that wouldn't have made the Boy Scout brochures. It was a peninsula with a beach that was reputed to be big make-out area for local teens. So, one night we hid in the bushes, and sure enough, there were couples on the beach doing their thing. In the morning we found used condoms where they had been the night before. We put those used condoms on the end of sticks and went to campsites that were going to be used that day, and placed them amongst the burnt embers of previous night's charcoal briquettes and burned twigs. When the next unknowing victims would come and cook their wieners over the fire, we would wait in the bushes and watch them, and giggle about the special seasonings they were getting from what we had planted in their ashes.

Were we not the poster children for Boy Scouting in America?

Something else we did as Boy Scouts was a Christmas wreath fundraiser. I believe I ended up with $15, and let me tell you, I had to sell a lot of wreaths to end up with $15 in those days. I credit my mother for her help — she drove me all over the city so I could sell them door-to-door. She knew I was highly motivated to earn that money. I wanted an upgrade for my first radio, a crystal diode radio in a cigar box with copper wiring wrapped around a toilet roll. It had no tuner. It had no on-off switch. It had no battery. And whatever it was you faintly picked up in your headphones, you faintly picked up in your headphones.

My plan was to go down to the store and buy a fancier crystal diode radio, but my parents — exhibiting one of the traits that remained consistent throughout their lives — always consulted the experts before making any decision about anything. Doing the research, they found out that crystal radios were basically toys, so they surprised me by saying they would match my money (and then some), and buy a $36 transistor radio. At the time, that was a huge amount of money. It got a six-transistor Channel Master AM radio. I brought that Channel Master home and my father listened to all of his newscasts that night, and that was a big deal for all of us. I don't think he realized at the time just *how* big of a deal it was for me. It was instrumental in directing me into my career.

The other thing that did it for me was my father's Dictaphone, which was a very elementary device used to record the human voice. Because he was blind, Dad used the Dictaphone to take notes. I remember being allowed to play with it a little bit. I pushed the buttons, and recorded my voice. The first time I heard my voice come back out of that tiny speaker, I experienced an epiphany or revelation of some kind.

After that, I went to the library and took out books about announcing. I remember one was called *This is Your Announcer*. (I looked for that book again while I was writing this book. I'm not 100% sure, but I think it was written by Henry B. Lent in 1945, and the full title of the book is *This is Your Announcer: Ted Lane Breaks into Radio*.)

I *really* got into this. I set up a fake little radio station in my closet. I think I called it WXXV. When I finally got a tape recorder of my own, I would start up a record, and talk over the intro just like the real DJs. I also got sound effect records including sound effects of a screaming crowd, and would pretend to be a sports play-by-play guy. Can you picture it? A youngster sitting all by himself in his bedroom closet, pretending to be on the air on a completely fake radio station? Now that I've admitted that to you, I can claim to be a lot of things, but I can never again pretend that I wasn't an absolute radio geek.

ROCK AND ROLL

Anyone that was there in the early days of rock and roll will tell you that it had two sides; the Elvis side and the Pat Boone side. Ed Sullivan wouldn't show Elvis' lower body on TV because it was too suggestive. Pat Boone was the preppy all-American boy. Elvis' trademark was his greased-back hair. Pat Boone's was his white bucks. (Those are shoes, by the way.) I suppose it was a little bit like the difference between the Beatles and the Stones. If you asked me, I was an Elvis guy. On the other hand, I also knew the lyrics to "Love Letters in the Sand."

At that time I would visit my father on campus, go up to his office, and spend the day reading my Hardy Boy books and drinking a couple of Coca Colas as he went about his business of being a college professor. He always loved the academic life, but there was one thing he couldn't stand: rock and roll music.

    He didn't consider rock and roll to be a legitimate art form, or even legitimate music. That's probably why I have such a vivid memory of the one time he managed to put that aside, at least for one night. I had written away for an album that had all the hits on it (remember those ads — "The original hits with the original artists!") Unfortunately, on this album they *weren't* done by the original artists. Oh well; they were still the hits, and as far as I was concerned, there was no reason to send it back. On New Year's Eve, my parents were having a party, and even though they supposedly hated my music, they actually borrowed my record player, and borrowed my records, and played them downstairs for the grownups. That was a big deal to me. It showed that my music wasn't so illegitimate after all.

    There was a bit of good cop/bad cop going on with my parents. When my father was not around all sorts of bizarre cultural events could occur. OK, so I'm exaggerating a little bit, but I had a bookshelf and a little desk at home in a hallway on the second floor, and I was sitting there doing my homework one day, when I suddenly heard music come blasting up the stairs. My mom had the radio on and was cranking Johnny Horton's "The Battle of New Orleans." Why, the nerve! Listening to popular music! Listening to loud music! Interrupting your son's homework!

    We didn't have a lot of options for rock and roll radio at the time. We had two stations in Ann Arbor: WPAG, and WHRV. The biggest jock on WPAG was Dave Pringle. On WHRV it was Ollie McGlocklen (who later went on to produce the Capitols and their hit "Cool Jerk"). Eventually I discovered Detroit radio. There was a station that was technically across the border in Canada (though it boomed into Detroit) called CKLW and an air personality named Tom Shannon. He was huge.

But the station I really loved at that time though was WXYZ, the station that originated the Lone Ranger back in the day. They were at 1270 on the AM band and didn't have much of a signal but I found the FM simulcast fooling around with my dad's Zenith radio. It was a great radio station! A ton of great personalities. The two I liked the most were Joel Sebastian (yes, the same Joel Sebastian whose wife directed me in the play when I was boy) and Lee Allen. These guys had style. They had attitude. They were cool. The music was cool. I figured if I listened, that meant that I was cool too.

There was one other station that influenced me in those early days of rock radio, and that was WIBC Indianapolis. As we drove down to visit Grandpa Records, I would press my transistor radio against the window to listen. I put a sleeping bag over me so my father couldn't hear the music, but when we got to Grandpa's farm I knew I wouldn't have to cover up anymore. WIBC was also a big farm station. In the morning they had all the important farm news. We all listened to it together.

WIBC! Rock and roll, and the price of corn.

CHAPTER THREE
THE HIGH SCHOOL YEARS

> The early 1960s was the Kennedy era, a time that has become known as Camelot. President Kennedy was the first television president. We asked not what our country could do for us, but what we could do for our country. The early 1960s introduced us to Sean Connery as James Bond. Comedies started to overtake Westerns on television, with huge hit shows like *The Dick Van Dyke Show*, *The Andy Griffith Show*, and *The Beverly Hillbillies*. Elvis Presley got out of the army and went into movies. Chubby Checker had everyone "Twistin" and Phil Spector's Wall of Sound was a hit factory. And in Detroit, a little record label named Motown started to become a powerhouse.

My parents moved across town when I was in eighth grade, and I refused to go the other public school (Tappan Junior High School), because they were Slauson's arch rival. We hated those guys! There was no way I was going to go that school. No way. So, my parents enrolled me in University High School, which was a full K-12 school. University High was run by the University of Michigan, smack in the middle of the University of Michigan campus. (If you've ever been to Ann Arbor, it was right by the engineering arch.) To go to school I had to pass by fraternity and sorority houses. All of us really felt like we were a part of the university.

I made some great friends at University High. One in particular, Dave Pearson, was a real character. As far as I'm concerned, he was the person that invented the term "beaver." At least he's the first person I ever heard say it. He also coined the term "updock beaver." (An updock beaver is when a girl bends over and you catch a glimpse of her boobs.) Another Dave Pearson original: When the cheerleaders did the splits, he always said the same thing: "Boy, I'd like to be the floor on that one." Dave also made farts by blowing into his hand and flapping his armpits, and when it came to farts, he also had the rare ability to light them — which I witnessed firsthand. He was an adolescent artiste.

I'll never forget one day a special meeting was called by our high school homeroom teacher Mr. McKelsky. Some official from the high school came into our class.

"Alright, we need to talk to you boys," he said. "There's been graffiti inside the boys bathroom, and it's signed 'Dave Pearson.' Now, we know it's obviously not Dave Pearson, because he wouldn't sign his own name, so which one of you other boys is responsible?"

Nobody said anything, because it *was* Dave Pearson.

And he *did* sign his own name.

NOVEMBER 22, 1963

I remember exactly where I was on November 22, 1963. This is a milestone in the memory of all Baby Boomers. There are only a few select moments in life that you can remember with such vivid clarity, and I can tell you every detail about where I was. I was at University High School in Hope Chipman's geometry class.

Just to give you an idea of what Miss Chipman was like, I need to set the stage. Rock and roll was starting to become an important part of our lives, and it was more than just music — it was an attitude. It was a fashion. It was a way to dress; and the girls were wearing things like mini-skirts, and go-go boots. If a female student was up at the blackboard to do a geometry problem, and Miss Chipman felt that the hemline was a tad too high, she was not above quietly reaching up with her hand and tugging the hemline down in front of the entire class. I'm sure everyone in that era had a Miss Chipman. She was a spinster, if you will.

We also had a lot of student teachers because we were on the campus of the University of Michigan — they were like teacher-interns — and on this particular day, our student teacher saw what was happening on the television in the library. She came running into the classroom in tears, and breathlessly announced to the whole class: "President Kennedy is dead!"

The classroom was totally silent for a moment as we processed the news. After a long pause, Miss Chipman turned to us and said: "I think he would have wanted us to finish the class."

LOUIE LOUIE

Another Baby Boomer cultural milestone is the moment we discovered that the lyrics to "Louie Louie" by the Kingsmen were dirty. How dirty? At one point the state of Indiana banned the song, which really did nothing, because kids in Indiana heard the radio stations booming out of Chicago anyway — and there was nothing they could do to stop that.

At any rate, I can tell you exactly where I was when I found out: in a 1952 Ford with a friend of mine named Rick Bolgis on Norway Street in Ann Arbor. It was night, and we were going to pick up our friend Greg Nelson, who had been busted for buying alcohol with a fake ID. Our plan was to get there and pick him up before the police came.

The song "Louie Louie" came on the radio on our way over to get Greg, and Rick informed me that the lyrics were dirty, told me what they were, and then said I should listen closely. I think you can convince yourself of anything if you're listening for it, especially the way they sort of slurred the words. As far as I was concerned, I heard the dirty words perfectly: "A fine little bitch, she waits for me, She gets her kicks on top of me, Each night I take her out all alone, She ain't the kind I lay at home."

Now, of course, it turns out that the dirty lyrics were really just an urban legend, it was just a cover of a Richard Berry song about the sea, but I bet that urban legend didn't hurt the sales of "Louie Louie." By the way, in case you were wondering, we did get Greg out of there before the cops arrived.

WATCHING THE BEATLES ON ED SULLIVAN

The third Baby Boomer cultural milestone from this era certainly had to be the arrival of the Beatles to the United States of America. Mr. Berg, my choir director and the music teacher at University High, totally pooh-poohed the Beatles. He insisted that anybody could write a Beatles or rock and roll song. Mr. Berg's reaction was the stereotypical parental reaction to the music we loved. Everybody's parents felt the same way.

I remember stickers appearing on lampposts. Four heads of hair with no faces and the expression "The Beatles are Coming!" They were already on the radio, but this hype from Capitol Records made us even more excited. The Beatles were the quintessential rock band. They were a group, but they also had separate identities as individuals, and each of those individuals had a distinct personality. Paul was the teen idol, the cute one. George was the introspective quiet one. Ringo was sort of the silly one. And John was the deep thinking rebel.

So, it was a huge deal when the Beatles appeared on *The Ed Sullivan Show*. I watched, and everybody else watched. But honestly, what I remember the most about their appearing on that show wasn't that first night — it was their second appearance on the show, the show from Miami a few days later. And what I remember isn't what the Beatles or Ed Sullivan did. What I remember most was the guest right before the Beatles — Mitzi Gaynor. She was a pop singer, the kind of singer that existed before rock and roll, a female crooner, if you will. It was really hot that night — this was Miami — and she was wearing a low cut dress that showed a little bit of cleavage, and I could see her sweating. Oh yeah, I tell ya, I remember seeing that sweat.

The Beatles were great, don't get me wrong. I've played them on the air many, many times and still love their music, and I've never played or owned a single Mitzi Gaynor record in my entire life. But oh boy, I sure do remember Mitzi Gaynor on that Ed Sullivan show.

THE SPORTING LIFE

As a senior, I cut school to go to Detroit for the Tigers opening day, but even though it was considered the national pastime, baseball was never really my game. As an egomaniacal, self-centered personality, if I wasn't good at it, I didn't like it. And I wasn't good at baseball. I was on a little league team and took a fastball in the gut, and when I came back to the bench, the coach's son made fun of me. But when we got into Junior High, and began to play football it was a different story. And the thing I loved most about football was bashing into people. And guess who was on the other team in one of my junior high games? The same coach's son. Need I say more?

I was a pretty good football player. I played fullback and linebacker, and I also did a little bit of kicking off and played on the kick return team. It was a tiny school — class D ranking in the state. I'm not sure how I would have done at the big high school (Ann Arbor Pioneer) — probably pretty well because I did well every time we scrimmaged against them — but I really thrived at University High. I ended up being MVP, co-captain, and All-City by the time I was done.

The coolest thing about football, in retrospect, was not really about playing the game (although I loved that too); it was about the kind of people I encountered. One of them was Bob Ufer, who was the legendary U of M play-by-play guy for 37 years (1944-1981). Legendary! He used to honk a horn during the games. He called it the "Bo 'General Patton' Schembechler Horn," because it was the actual horn from General Patton's jeep. He would honk it three times for a touchdown, twice for a field goal or safety, and once for an extra point. He was spectacular. And when I made the WPAG 20th Anniversary Ann Arbor All-City team, Bob Ufer introduced us, and interviewed us. I can't describe how of a big of thrill that was. I wish I had a tape of that.

The other guy I met through football was Herb Deromedi. He was a U of M student at the time, and coached our team. Herb left after my sophomore year, and went on to coach Central Michigan University (an assistant coach from 1967-1977, and the head coach from 1978-1993). He turned that into a pretty darn good program, winning three Mid-American Conference titles and MAC Coach of the Year twice, with a record of 110-55-10 in his 16 seasons as a head coach. They even upset Michigan State a few times. He was eventually inducted into the College Football Hall of Fame.

I called him about two or three years ago. He remembered me, and remembered things about the practices that I didn't even remember; methods of coaching he said that would be banned today. I remember we got beat 36-0 once and he made us run wind sprints on the field after the game. He took film of the game, and we went over to his little apartment, and watched it. He said — "Landecker, look at you. Every time the ball is snapped you take a step or two backwards!" And he was right. I was like a freshman or a sophomore, and that really taught me something. Why in the world was I doing that?

The next year we went down to the same school that had beaten us 36-0 the year before. It was probably about an hour ride away. We dressed in our uniforms at the high school and drove over there in a bus, and I remember Deromedi at the front of the bus doing a pep talk. He got so fired up and so worked up, there was spittle coming out of the side of his mouth. We were motivated. We won. The score was 66-6. Total wipeout. To give you an idea of how well we played, we were ranked in the state after that game. At our next home game, there were actually fans in the stands! (Now, we didn't sustain that, and eventually it turned out that one of our players shouldn't have been there, and we had to forfeit the entire friggin season, but who cares?) That was an amazing time.

In life, how many of us get to experience something like that? I don't mean sitting on a school bus waiting to play football for Herb Deromedi, I'm talking about the motivation to achieve. In this case, Coach transmitted so much of his desire to us, that we actually got outside ourselves — forgot about our fears and shortcomings — and achieved above and beyond our usual level. When you read about former athletes that are beat up and have health problems but still say if they could to do it all over again they would, this may be the reason why: the intangible, almost spiritual, out of body experience of being caught up in someone's energy to be motivated to achieve. Believe me, it's something that once you experience it, you'll never forget it.

Today football is very concerned with head trauma. The NFL has made drastic rule changes concerning hits to the head, and players are all tested for concussions now after severe hits. And for good reason too — suicides, dementia, and other mental problems in former players have been attributed to numerous hits to the head. Of course, none of that was around when I played high school football.

In the final game of my high school career we were playing against Ypsilanti Roosevelt, (my buddy Greg Kershal played for them). I remember thinking: "Final game, John. All out, all the time." I was playing fullback, my number was called for a run off-tackle, but there was no running room anywhere, so I just put my head down and ran into that line with everything I had. I remember a sharp piercing pain in my head. (Don't let it be said that John Landecker didn't hit hard!) The next thing I remember is waking up in a hospital room.

But here's the thing — I was not knocked out during that run into the line. I continued to play, and I have no memory of that at all. I'm told my behavior became bizarre. I started calling the wrong plays on defense. I berated injured players on the sidelines for not playing. I repeatedly asked what the score was. They diagnosed me with a concussion and made me stay in the hospital a few days, but I never did recall anything that happened during that black-out time.

I wish the same were true of an incident that happened on the basketball court; my most humiliating sports moment. My grades had been a little lower than they should have been, so my parents had forbidden me from participating in basketball. Well, that was just not going to fly with me, so I lied to them and said I was staying after school to do extra credit work while I was actually going to basketball practice and playing on the team.

My father had no interest in sports, so I figured there was no way they were going to find out. I'm still not sure how they did; I think somebody made an off-handed comment about seeing me play, but this led to the aforementioned incident at a game. I was sitting on the bench, and as I looked up, I saw my mother come walking into the gymnasium. She walked under the backboard in front of everybody, and planted herself in front of the coach.

"John does not have our permission to play basketball," she said.

And she yanked me out of the game in front of everyone. My parents were so concerned about this they sent me to the school psychologist. I must be crazy, right? Any boy that didn't follow orders from his parents, and lied to play sports, must be crazy. I talked to the shrink for like fifteen minutes. He told me to get back on the basketball team, and that was that.

EDUCATING DAD

The Oxford English dictionary states that the ultimate entomology of the word "FUCK" is uncertain, but that the word is probably cognate with a number of Germanic words that mean striking, loving and having sex. (The German word for having sex, by the way, is "Fick.") There clearly were Germanic influences running through my family — literally centuries of history. It would seem that the meaning of the word "Fuck," while perhaps a word that was not used in polite company, would still be a well-known fact. I was in high school and was standing in the hallway outside my bedroom when my father summoned me.

"John," he said, "Your brother Tom (he always referred to him by name just in case some new sibling had secretly entered the picture) has used a word, and I'd like to know what it means."

"Sure Dad, I'll help you. What's the word?"

"Fuck."

Raise your hand if you had to explain the meaning of the word "fuck" to your father. Since I used the most scientific terminology I could think of, my father seemed quite satisfied with the explanation. Not knowing the Beatles? Fine. Not knowing Ann Margret? Fine.

But not knowing "fuck?"

MY FIRST LOVE

Nancy March was my first crush, but my first wife Judy was my first real love. (Look, I've been married four times — I've got categories for everybody.) I started dating Judy in the middle of 8th grade. We were in the same class in University High School. We were attracted to each other, and here's how I remember it happening. We were in the back seat of someone's car. They were driving, while we were making out like mad. I made a move and put my hand on her breast.

She didn't remove it.

I was in love!

We dated all the way through high school. Everybody knew us as a couple; "There go Judy & John!" Leslie Gore had a song called "It's My Party" about a girl named Judy and a boy named Johnny, and followed it up with "Judy's Turn to Cry," and both of those songs were significant to us. They were a big deal in our early romance. All through high school Judy and I were inseparable. We were together all day at school, we were dating and going out at night, and I was hanging out with her family on the weekends.

I really connected with her family; her brother Joe and sister Bambi, and her parents, Angela and Lyndon. I love them to this very day (though, sadly, Angela passed away a few years ago). Judy's family had an open house every Sunday, and it was always quite a production, with a huge spread of food. Relatives and close friends would come in and out, and I was invited over every week. I was really treated like part of the family from the very beginning.

Judy's grandfather was the head counsel for the United States Army while it was under investigation by Joseph McCarthy's Senate Permanent Subcommittee on Investigations for Communist activities in the 1950s. His name was Joseph Nye Welch and he famously said the line that turned public opinion against McCarthy: "Have you no sense of decency, sir? At long last, have you left no sense of decency?" He also occasionally hosted a television show called *Omnibus*. The walls of Judy's parents' rec room and bathroom were covered with old *Omnibus* teleprompter scripts. There was no need to bring along newspapers when nature called, if you know what I mean. Plenty of reading material on the walls.

My life with Judy in Ann Arbor was a like a scene out of the film *American Graffiti*. I'll give you an example. Judy's parents had these unbelievably cool Pontiac convertibles. One day Judy and I were on a date at the A&W drive-in. You know the kind I'm talking about — with the speakers, car hops, hot dogs, French fries. We had the top down on this powder blue Pontiac Bonneville convertible. I was wearing loafers and white socks — and I squealed the tires coming out of the parking lot.

I got a ticket.

NONNIE AND NOOKIE

They called Judy's grandmother "Nonnie," and she was quite a character. Nonnie was famous for driving a pink Thunderbird and a purple Lincoln Continental convertible. Imagine a grandma driving around in one of those cars. She was like the "Little Old Lady from Pasadena" in the Jan and Dean song.

Nonnie lived with one of her sons and a grandson, but for some reason they weren't going to be home one night, so they asked me if would spend the night at Nonnie's house. When I got there, the phone rang, and I picked it up. The voice on the other end of the line said: "We're gonna get you and the old lady!" I didn't recognize the caller's voice, but something clicked, and I somehow knew it wasn't for real. It turned out to be Judy's cousin Steve, who I also knew and went to school with, just having fun with me.

On another occasion Judy and I were alone in her grandmother's house, and were doing what youngsters do upstairs in the bedroom when we heard a car drive up. Her grandmother was home! I opened the window on the second floor, jumped onto the roof of a screened-in porch, jumped down on the ground, walked around the front of the house, and rang the doorbell.

"Hey, how you are doing? Nice to see you!"

There were a few other close calls. One time her father came downstairs while we were "watching TV" and we had to scramble like crazy. If Judy had turned around, her father would have seen that her dress was unzipped. Another time I had my hand down her blouse, and when I looked up, her younger brother Joe was standing right there looking at me.

Judy and I also spent a lot of time at the drive-in movie theater. At the time drive-ins had the reputation for being a perfect place to make out, but the drive-in also hired security guards to walk around the parking lot with flashlights and shine them into automobiles they suspected of hanky panky. I'll admit that Judy and I were in the backseat with the windows steamed up on more than a few occasions, but we also really did want to see the movies. They usually showed a very fine double feature.

    It was a win-win situation.

MY FIRST RADIO JOB

Judy had an aunt that was the woman's editor of a local radio station. When I was a junior in high school, she set up an interview for me with a guy named Ted Heusel. (His wife was the other woman put on the theater production I was involved in a decade earlier.)

    Ted was the program director of the local radio station WOIA-FM Ann Arbor and WOIB-AM Saline ("Your American family station serving southern Michigan and northern Ohio.") This was a middle of the road (MOR)/big band/talk station located on a dirt road in a little hut opposite a dairy farm. Ted Heusel wasn't just a well-known talk show host and program director; he was also the Ann Arbor School Board President. (The annual season ending football game between the two rival high schools, Huron and Pioneer, is now named after him; "The Heusel Bowl.") I went out to the radio station after school one day, and talked to Ted. After I told him I was interested in working in radio, he gave me a bunch of papers, and told me to read them when the ON AIR light came on. Just like that.

    He started making a big deal about a local high school kid: "He wants to be on the radio, so let's see what happens."

    The light went on, I read the newscast, and I guess I was sufficiently impressive for someone that had never been on the air before.

I never forgot Ted Heusel for putting me on the air on WOIA, and giving me a job as the janitor. When I worked in Philly or Chicago, whenever I came home to visit my folks, I would also just walk into the radio station and hang out with Ted. He never left Ann Arbor. He received offers to go to big markets like Detroit, but he had no interest in leaving. He was born in Ann Arbor. He lived there his whole life, and he was there until his dying day in 2007.

Tom O'Brien is another person I'm forever indebted to, because he eventually allowed me to be his newsman on the station's only rock show (9-Noon on Saturday morning). I'll never forget him either.

TOM O'BRIEN *REMEMBERS*

Tom O'Brien, now an attorney with Miller Canfield Paddock and Stone in Ann Arbor, remembers those early days too, when he was a disc jockey at WOIA… *I was working there in high school and college, and one day Ted Heusel said to me, "There's this high school kid that reminds me a lot of you. He's really interested in working in radio just like you were at his age. Could you find him something to do?"*

Well, I was doing a weekend dedication show at the time and I put him on the air doing the news. Here was this kid, I don't think he was much older than 15 or 16, and he sounded great! He was such a natural, not affected at all, with this nice voice and professional delivery. I remember one time he was doing a newscast, and I played all these sound effects and clips and stingers to try to get him to crack up, but he didn't lose it at all. Very impressive.

We used to have so much fun on that show. There was no format, no rules. We would do things like play the same song on different turntables, starting one just moments after the other, so that it had this harmonic sound. When I got another radio job in Flint, and left the station, John was given the show.

ANN ARBOR RADIO

Those early radio days were a blast! Ann Arbor had a huge summer event called the Ann Arbor Art Fair, and the city merchants would put on "Bargain Days" to coincide with it. The downtown area was divided into three parts; Main Street, State Street, and South University. I would join Ted Heusel in the WOIA remote van starting at 7 am on Main Street. We would broadcast from there until midday, and then move out onto State Street, and after a few hours there, move to South University in mid-afternoon. Eventually Ted would leave and go home, and I would finish the last few hours on my own. I got to sit on top of the truck with a microphone in my hand, and totally ad-lib what was going on during the Art Fair and Bargain Days. The Ann Arbor bank clock rotated on the other side of the block, conveniently telling me the time and temperature whenever I needed it. I never had so much fun in my life.

When Tom O'Brien moved on to Flint, Michigan, I took over the 9-Noon Saturday morning rock show. Remember, it was the only rock show on the station, and because of that, and the fact that we were such a small station; we couldn't get music from record companies. Tom had solved the problem by going to Discount Records, a record store in Ann Arbor, and making a trade deal. He got to borrow their records, in exchange for free commercials. Well, after he left, I kept up the practice until one of the 45's broke and the store suddenly didn't want to cooperate anymore. My high school friend Billy Byerwaltus had a huge 45 collection and I played those until I found another record store. It wasn't in Ann Arbor, it was in Ypsilanti, Michigan, and it wasn't rock or pop, it was R&B.

I'll never forget the day I hopped in my parents' Dodge Dart and drove over to the store. The building's paint job was peeling, and the proprietor was outside on the sidewalk reclining on a folding chair. He was dressed in an undershirt and sipping whiskey out of a paper bag when this white high school kid arrived.

"Hey there, can I borrow some tunes?" I asked.

"Absolutely, help yourself."

We had a great relationship.

Another person who was very influential in my radio career, before it was even a career really, was Art Vuolo. He was fascinated with everyone who did radio anywhere, and he went out of his way to make contact with them, take pictures of them in action, and put those pictures into a scrapbook. Since that time, he has made a career out of his fascination. His slogan is "Radio's Best Friend," and he really is. Art has the most definitive historical collection of radio recordings in America from 1965 to the present, better than any museum in New York or Chicago or anywhere else. Everything from small-market radio to Rush Limbaugh. He's got it all on video or audio, including, believe it or not, a tape of me taking a request on the air during that 9-Noon rock show on WOIA in 1966. In fact, Art's the caller on the phone making the request. *(The transcript of that call is in the appendix. By the way, if you don't believe me about Art's video/audio collection, go to his website at www.vuolovideo.com. He's got tape of every radio personality you could possibly name there, including nearly every single radio person mentioned in this book.)*

Art and I became very good friends (we remain very good friends to this day). One New Year's Eve, the station decided they wanted to stay on the air until three in the morning, and I was brought in to do the show. Now remember, we weren't a rock station. We played nice middle of the road music (like Perry Como). Well, I could only take so much of that, so when Art called and informed me that he could bring in a whole bunch of 45 RPM records, and if we played them on the air, we would be the only FM radio station playing rock and roll music on the air in southern Michigan and northern Ohio, I jumped at the chance.

We spun his records all night.

CHAPTER FOUR
COLLEGE

> The mid-to-late 1960s were a pretty tumultuous time. The Vietnam War was going on. Malcolm X, Martin Luther King Jr. and Robert Kennedy were assassinated. After the Summer of Love, the term "hippie" became part of the lexicon. Student protests were occurring all over the country. The Great Society came and went, and Richard Nixon became the President of the United States. Mid '60s pop culture was hip. Television shows like *Get Smart* and *Man from U.N.C.L.E.* were big hits. Movies like *The Graduate* and *Guess Who's Coming to Dinner* were being nominated for Academy Awards, and in the music world, we were in the midst of the British Invasion. Nearly every major band came from England, but more importantly, nearly every teen or young adult in America was forming a band too.

My main interests in high school were sports and girls. I was never an accomplished student, so when it came time to pick a college, there weren't a lot of options. First of all, my father informed me that there was no way I was going to a school outside the state of Michigan; in-state colleges only. So that narrowed it down. Then there were my grades and SAT scores, and that narrowed it down even further.

A group of my friends (Dave Pearson, Sam Sturgis, and Terry Ward) all decided to go to a small liberal arts school called Grand Valley State College in Allendale, Michigan. It's now known as Grand Valley State University, and has 24,000+ students, has won seven national titles (Division II) in four different sports, and is a widely respected school. At the time, it wasn't. It hadn't graduated a class yet (the first class had 138 students), and wasn't even fully accredited. So of course, that's the school I chose.

I obviously didn't go there for academics. I went there because I could get in, and because my friends were going there. I knew we were going to have a good time.

PLANTING A BUG

There were no dorms at Grand Valley State, so they housed the students in apartments. The four of us all lived together in an apartment. Now, remember, we were freshmen and didn't know anything, yet we were suddenly responsible for food and many other things. I don't remember what happened with money, but I do remember Dave deciding to use mayonnaise with his cereal one time because we ran out of milk. And when we ran out of napkins, we just used the curtains over the kitchen window. We were young delinquents and ne'er do wells; jolly pranksters if you will.

I was working in radio on the weekends, and I took my tape recorder with me everywhere. One day the extremely religious students across the hall from us asked if they could borrow it to listen to tape recordings of their pastor's sermons from their small Michigan hometown. Well, you can imagine how this went over with the frat-wanna-be, skirt-chasing, illegal-drinking, skateboarding, Euchre-playing Bozos that we were. It led to one of the most elaborate practical jokes of all time.

The ground floor apartments in this building had sliding glass doors that opened up onto makeshift patios of gravel, grass, etc. VWs and compact cars were popular at that time, and there were a ton of them in the parking lot. One night after a few beers (of course after a few beers — always after a few beers), it was decided that after the religious guys went to sleep, we would go into their apartment through the sliding glass door, rearrange the furniture in the apartment to allow space, then go around to the parking lot, pick up a car (there were enough of us to lift one), and carry it into their apartment.

Now, I have to say, we did put paper down on the floor. We were delinquents, but we weren't barbarians. So we papered the floor, and brought a Volkswagen into their living room, snapped a picture, went out the door, closed it, turned off the lights, and waited. They got up and contacted the resident advisor, and as I remember it, we didn't cop to anything.

"I have no idea how that car got in there. What are you talking about? A car? Really? That's impossible!"

And not only that, I think the resident advisors were having a very difficult time keeping a straight face. I don't remember any real fallout from that. I think even the religious guys marveled at the ingenuity and depth of this practical joke.

PANTY & THE RAIDERS

We also formed a band at Grand Valley State College. "Panty and the Raiders" consisted of Dave Pearson, Bruce Nyland who was from Flint, Sam Sturgis and me. They all knew how to play guitar. I didn't know how to play anything, so I played drums. I bought these really cheap drums for like a hundred bucks, and we sort of banged away on our instruments.

Our first "gig" was in a garage. We were *truly* a garage band. We played for all the beer we could drink. We didn't have visual effects or anything — we didn't even have a sound system. I did some singing and fashioned a coat hanger around my neck and taped the plastic microphone from my tape recorder and stuck it into one of the open jacks of a guitar amp, and that was that.

I don't know how we perpetuated ourselves because we couldn't play jack shit, but apparently, if you wanted to get drunk and have a good time, we were the band to have. We went to Ferris State University once and played a private party. Somebody actually paid us to do it — in beer and McDonald's. Eventually we even did a couple of college mixers. (There must have been a *huge* shortage of bands in Allendale.) It really was the American essence of rock and roll.

Our band name was obviously inspired by Paul Revere and the Raiders, one of our favorite bands at the time. If you go back and listen to the early Raiders stuff, that's some great rock and roll. Back in those days they were the house band on the television show "Where the Action Is." Their guitarist was named "FANG," and the bottom of his guitar had his name written on it with masking tape. He would flip it over on camera so everyone could see it. We thought that was so cool. They were a pretty raunchy rock and roll garage band. And so were we.

One night we bought beer at a package liquor store, and a few couples went out on this country road. Wouldn't you know it? We saw the sirens in the rear view mirror. Busted. When the cop pulled us over, he got a look at me.

"Hey, you're in that band!" he said.

I thought, "Phew, this is going to be great! He knows Panty and the Raiders!"

Not so much. We were all arrested.

We had to appear before a Justice of the Peace. He fined every guy in the car $30, and even though the girls were exactly as guilty as we were, he let the girls go, scot-free. This was my first glimpse of injustice in America. I really should call Bill Kurtis and have him do and A&E Special on it.

THE RAIDERS AND THE STONES

My two favorite bands from this era were the Raiders and the Stones, and for my money, these are their best songs…

Top Five Paul Revere and the Raiders songs
    5. "Just Like Me"
    4. "Stepping Out"
    3. "Hungry"
    2. "Kicks"
    1. "Oo Poo Pah Doo"

Top Five Rolling Stones songs
    5. "Street Fighting Man"
    4. "Sympathy for the Devil"
    3. "Little Red Rooster"
    2. "It's All Over Now"
    1. "You Can't Always Get What You Want"

TASTING THE "BIG" TIME

One day between my freshman and sophomore year of college, I was working as a stock boy at Ulrich's Bookstore on the Michigan campus to make a little extra money, when I had a brush with radio greatness. I'll never forget it. I was wearing an apron, and sweeping the floor, when I looked up to see who was coming in the door. It was Joel Sebastian! (Once again, the husband of the woman who put on my childhood play.)

Though Joel was a rock jock, he also had a number of other intellectual interests. He had a degree in psychology. He was interested in architecture. And on that particular day, he was trying to buy a protractor, of all things. I walked up to him, and mentioned the one thing I knew would instantly connect with him.

"Excuse me," I said, "do you know Ted Heusel?"

"Of course," he answered.

I went on to explain that my name was John Landecker and I wanted to be in radio, and he was very gracious and friendly. At the time I was still working with Ted, doing the weekend show at WOIA in Ann Arbor.

Tom O'Brien, my former WOIA colleague, had since become the night jock in Flint at WTRX. He gave me a call shortly after that to say that he could get me a job at his station as a weekend jock for the summer. "Are you kidding? A real rock and roll station?"

I was there!

WTRX was known as "The Home of Jones Boys." Everybody on the air had to use the last name of Jones. There was John Paul Jones and Casey Jones, and virtually every other famous derivative of Jones. The weekend jocks didn't have to use the Jones name, but I wanted to do it anyway. So, I became Dow.

TOM O'BRIEN REMEMBERS

I was happy to get John that job. He was great on that station too. I went to law school after that and lost touch with him, but years later when he was working at WLS in Chicago, I heard him on the air. I called him up, and he put me on the air doing an intro to a record. I always thought John was a great guy, and someone that had a God-given gift to do what he did.

LONG DISTANCE ROMANCE

The toughest thing about Grand Valley State was that Judy went to Wheaton College in Norton, Massachusetts, many miles away from me. I missed her and decided I was going to fly standby to see her. It was called student standby at the time, if I recall correctly.

It was a nightmare to get there — I flew from Grand Rapids to Lansing, Lansing to Detroit, Detroit to Toledo, had a layover for four hours, and then finally flew from Toledo to Boston. I landed in Boston and had no idea where I was going. I got in a cab and only had so much money, so the cab driver drove me as far as that money would take me. I got out, and walked the rest of the way to the school. I spent one of the nights at Harvard because Judy had friends there (that's as close as I'll ever get to Harvard).

But then one night, Judy and I went to Boston and got a hotel room. Let me tell you, I was paranoid beyond belief. It seemed really, really wrong, and I worried that if we got caught, it would somehow be considered a crime. In the movie *The Graduate*, there's a scene where Dustin Hoffman's character has to sign in for his room with Mrs. Robinson. If you've seen that movie, and seen how ridiculously nervous his character was, that's how I felt in Boston that night. In those days getting a hotel room was not like it is today. It just wasn't done unless you were married… or naughty.

So, we walked into the hotel and pretended like Judy was getting a room and that I was only there to help her carry her things up to the room. When we got up to the floor of "her" room, I walked to the end of the hall and opened the window by the fire escape so I could climb in later. Then I went back downstairs, through the lobby, and walked around to the side of the building to the parking lot, climbed onto a parked car, jumped up to the fire escape, climbed the stairs, went through the window, closed it behind me, and went back into "her" room.

Every sound I heard that night made me jump. I thought they (whoever "they" were) had found us, and were coming to get us.

MARRIAGE AND PARENTHOOD

Around this time, Judy became pregnant. When we got the news, there wasn't a second of consideration given to anything other than getting married. We always assumed we would eventually get married anyway. She flew from Massachusetts to Grand Rapids and we got married at a Justice of the Peace behind a hamburger stand. It wasn't exactly the wedding or wedding reception of our dreams. The Justice of the Peace had a plastic waterfall on his television. When we left, I forgot to pay him, so he ran out to get me.

After the ceremony, we stopped at a grocery store and bought a cake and had our "wedding reception" with a few friends at the Mr. President Motor Lodge, where we watched Star Trek and ate cake. It wasn't a sleaze ball sex inn, just a regular motel, but it did have one of those vibrating beds. (Put a quarter in a slot and the bed would vibrate — not exactly a turn on.) The next day we borrowed a car and drove from Grand Rapids to Ann Arbor, and called both of our parents.

"Hi," we said, "We're in town, and we'd like to come over and talk to you."

First we went over to my parents' house, sat everybody down, told 'em we were married, and pregnant, and gave them a due date. There was a long pause.

My father finally said: "I've always wanted a daughter."

Isn't that sweet? Then we went to her parents' house. Now remember, I had been going out with their daughter since the 8th grade, so it wasn't like this was some sort of one night stand. We sat *her* parents down and told them we were married, and that we were pregnant, and again, there was a long pause. But her father didn't say anything.

Instead, he crushed the Schlitz beer can he was holding with one hand.

A little different take on the situation, if you get my drift.

After the announcement of our pregnancy, our parents had a meeting to decide the financial implications of our situation. Very rational — both sets of parents. Judy's parents were well-off and Republican. My parents were not well off, and Democratic. Yet, there wasn't any acrimony. I was never told the details of that financial planning (for their knocked up kids), but it wasn't "Hey your son knocked up my daughter, you pay!" Or "The Hell I will! Your daughter is a well-known slut and seduced our son, you pay!" If anything, Judy and I were both surrounded by emotional and financial support. We both had fantastic parents.

My parents agreed to buy us a car. Their only proviso was that they got to pick it out. They decided on an Opel Cadet. Stick shift. Small. No Radio. (When I was at WERX I finally got a car radio and a WERX engineer helped me install it — AM only, of course.) The car had one unique feature. If you were driving in the rain and a passing truck spread water all over the hood, the engine would stop running. But at least we had a car.

And we were about to become a family.

I have two specific memories of the week my oldest daughter Tracy was born in Grand Rapids. Right after she was born, I drove to a hamburger stand called Sailor's. I had a burger, coke, and fries, and looked across the parking lot at the Meijer's Thrifty Acres across the highway. I remember thinking that my life would never be the same. I was pretty anxious.

In those days the baby and mother stayed in the hospital for a while, and that's where my second memory took place. I was walking down the hospital stairs, and who did I run into there? My mother. Despite the circumstances of our situation, and the tension it had caused, Mom had driven all the way across the state to help out and do whatever she could with the new baby. That meant a lot to us.

I'M A HAPPY FELLA AND I GOT A PLATTER POLL

At the time I had a job doing an afternoon radio program making a whopping $1.50 an hour on this little station in Wyoming, Michigan; WERX. It was a daytimer — meaning they were only licensed to broadcast from sun up to sunset. WERX was located in a small, narrow building, almost like something you'd see at a trailer park.

One of the great perks of working there was that I got free passes to the drive-in movie theater. I used *a lot* of drive-in movie passes back in the day, because we were able to bring Tracy in the backseat. The drive over there would put her to sleep, and Judy and I could enjoy the film. We had no money, and no baby sitters, and there really weren't many places you could go with an infant.

It's also about the time I met John Leader Alfenito. He went on to a great career in radio and a gigantic career in commercial voice over work. (If you've ever seen that classic YouTube video of the five voiceover guys in a limo, he's one of those guys.) He and his girlfriend Pam, who eventually became his wife, would get together with Judy and me quite a bit. John would cook Russian burgers (hamburgers mixed with Russian dressing) and we'd drink beer and obsess about radio together. That's really how it was. Radio was all I ever thought about. I loved TV. I loved the movies. I loved rock music. I loved football. But I *obsessed* about radio.

As we were putting this book together, I found an old 1530 WERX survey *(in the photo section)*, and it brought back lots of memories. Tom Ambrose was the program director who hired me. For a while, I was the music director. Record companies sent the station new 45 RPM records every week. (This station wasn't borrowing from local record stores anymore. No sir, this was the big time!) I would listen to the new releases and use my expert ear to pick the hits of the future. You can see on the "Platter Poll" survey that my WERX Wax of the Week was… "The Loser" by Gary Lewis and the Playboys.

Never heard of it.

I'm also a little foggy on some of the other "Happy Fellas" that comprised "Kent County's Friendliest Pepper Uppers." I do remember Dr. Soul had a show on Sunday afternoons. John Leader was already my friend before he worked there, and Bill Adams was from the high-strung school of broadcasting. When he became the PD, I remember him writing a manual on the dos and don'ts of his format. Bill's wife was with him at the station a lot. They got into some yelling matches that I thought would get on the air when I had the microphone open. One time I was on the air, and I heard this popping and snapping sound from the back of the studio. I turned around and there was Bill's wife, popping her chewing gum, and snapping the tops of her garter belts.

"Don't you see that giant red 'ON AIR' sign?"

VIETNAM

The Vietnam War was in full swing at this time, and I was classified as 1A, which meant I was eligible to be drafted. But because I was still in college, I had a chance to qualify for a student deferment. I remember taking a national standardized test to see if I qualified, and the day I took it, it was unbelievably hot in the gymnasium. I was so uncomfortable, I finally just said screw it, and started answering the multiple choice questions willy-nilly so I could get out of there. Needless to say, I did not pass the test, so I was still rated 1A.

I was told to go to the Greyhound Bus Station in Ann Arbor at like four in the morning, and get on a bus to Fort Dearborn to have a military physical. The highlight of that experience was being in a room with a bunch of other naked guys, forming a line, bending over, and spreading my cheeks so some Army medic could take a look at my anus.

What a thrill.

Even though I had failed the standardized test, and passed the Army physical, I still had one more chance for a deferment. Students in the top 50% of their college class could appeal their status to their local draft board. Fortunately for me, thanks to the quality of Grand Valley State at the time, I was (just barely) in the top 50% of my class. So I appealed my draft status to the local draft board in Ann Arbor.

What happened after that is pure conjecture on my part, but as I look back on it, I think I know why that draft board gave me a deferment. Because they were in Ann Arbor at the University of Michigan and my father was a professor there, I can only assume my father's position influenced them. I do remember one of the members of the board asking me if my dad was a professor, and I said yes. I did legitimately qualify for the deferment because I was in the top 50% of my class, but plenty of guys in the same position were denied.

I never had any guilt about not going to Vietnam — I felt my deferment was legitimate — but in retrospect, my situation does sort of describe what it was like, doesn't it? If you were a student in college, you had an opportunity to get a deferment. If you were just a high school grad, guess what? You went to Vietnam. It really was a class-based system, as to who served and who didn't serve in Vietnam (other than the people that volunteered). That's why you heard stories about protestors burning their draft cards, or running away to Canada, or causing violence in the streets. I wasn't one of the protestors. I was a student. A husband. A father. And I was given a deferment. But let me tell ya, when I went to that military base and got that military physical, I really thought I was going to be shipped off to Vietnam. I couldn't stop thinking "What am I going to do about my family?"

I was one of the lucky ones. Millions of men in the same boat as me thought the same thing, and they still had to go. I can only imagine how difficult it must have been for them.

By the time I got out of college, the whole draft situation had changed sufficiently that I was no longer likely to be drafted, although I still had to have a selective service card.

It would later come in handy for something completely different.

MICHIGAN STATE

I probably never would have gotten out of Grand Valley State College if Judy didn't get pregnant. She had to drop out of her exclusive girl's school on the East Coast and live with me at Grand Valley in married housing. As soon as she started living with me, my grades got better overnight. I'd just bring the homework home, and she'd give me the answers. She also wrote all my papers, so I scored some really good grades. My grades were even good enough to transfer to Michigan State University, which had a really good Communication Arts program.

So Judy and I packed up the car, loaded up our possessions, and left Grand Valley. I had not secured a place for us to live in Lansing yet, so we headed to my parents' house in Ann Arbor. Just to make the trip a little more interesting, I ran out of gas in the middle of nowhere. We were saved by the Michigan State Police. A state trooper actually siphoned gas out of his own tank so we could make it to the next gas station.

It wasn't an ideal situation at first, to say the least. We lived with my parents in Ann Arbor and I commuted to East Lansing for my classes and unsuccessfully looked for a place to live. Michigan State offered married housing; furnished apartments including a phone and utility at a ridiculously low rent, but there was a waiting list at first. We were thrilled when I finally heard from them that there was an opening for us — Apartment 1447K, Spartan Village. We didn't hesitate to grab it. Judy took care of Tracy, and I went to school and worked at the campus radio station in the basement of the student services building, WMSN.

It was a very exciting time for a couple of reasons. Michigan State had to be the coolest place for college radio in the country. Not only was there a campus station, but there were individual stations in most of the dormitories. MSU also had a television studio and a great faculty. The music scene in Michigan was really happening around this time too. Ted Nugent and the Amboy Dukes had a hit song called "Journey to the Center of the Mind." They played regularly at the local teen clubs, where you didn't have to be 21. The big club in town was only for people 21 and over. I don't remember the name of the place, but I do remember who played there. I was still at WMSN, and not yet 21, when Kenny Rogers and the First Edition came to town. Their first hit was "Just Dropped In (To See What Condition My Condition Was In)." I was a huge fan, and met with the owner of the club, pleading with him to let my wife and I see the show even though we weren't quite 21 yet. Somehow, it worked. We were seated at a table far away from the main floor, sectioned off by a velvet rope. It wasn't the front row, but the band was outstanding. (They later had a huge hit with "Ruby, Don't Take Your Love to Town," before Kenny Rogers went country.)

After I turned 21, Sly and the Family Stone came to the same club. This was one of my favorite rock groups of all time. They tore the roof off the Mutha! (This was obviously before Sly started slipping away because of drugs and other distractions. A few years later at a concert outside Philadelphia, I was the emcee, and Sly wouldn't come out of the bathroom.)

RECORDS

I did so well in my radio, TV, and advertising courses that I made it on the Dean's List. So, I started looking around Lansing to see if there was a radio station that would hire me. I applied at WILS, an AM rock station, and they hired me to play religious tapes on Sunday mornings followed by a one-hour show. That led to my own show, from 10pm-1am, every Monday through Friday. The school year was wrapping up, and I had to make a certain amount of money to cover expenses, so I went to WILS management and said: "I have to get $125 a week or I have to leave and find another job."

Luckily for me, they agreed.

At that time I listened to all those great AM radio stations booming in from Chicago; especially WCFL. I loved that station. Not only did the personalities have a name, they had a hook that went with it. There was Jim Stagg. He had something called the Stagg-line, where you would call for requests. There was Barney Pip. He had "Pip People" and had this phrase that was something like "Pip People turn into Peanut Butter." There was a guy named Ron Britain, who I think was the best of all of them, and he called himself King Bee. His show was a stream of consciousness. Insanely good.

I wanted something like that for my show. I needed a hook. So, in my typically overboard fashion, in one big flash I became the John Records Landecker Radio Leviathan Program. That was the first time I ever used my middle name on the air. As soon as I did, people immediately didn't believe that Records really was my middle name. So, WILS's program director Eric Forseth published my Selective Service Card on a survey. It had my middle name right on the card. The Army doesn't play along with wacky radio bits, so I honestly thought that would end the controversy immediately. Needless to say, it hasn't turned out that way. To this very day, all these decades later, I still get that question at least once a week: "Really? It's your *real* middle name?"

Yes, really.

The local newspapers in Chicago still insist on publishing my name with quotation marks around Records, which insinuates that it's a nickname or slang or something, and of course, it's not. Let me see if I can be very clear about this again. It's on my birth certificate. It's on my Selective Service Card.

Records Truly Is My Middle Name.

AMERICANA PANORAMA

At WILS-Lansing I started doing a bit I called "Americana Panorama," which consisted of talking into a megaphone with some goofy music playing behind me. It eventually morphed into something else entirely — a long story that ended with a pun that was a record title.

My father was always a big fan of puns, so I guess I have him to blame for that. Dad wasn't actually as serious as he seemed on the surface, and one of the ways that manifested itself was through puns, or wordplay. There was one he particularly enjoyed to tell. An Iranian president's name was Rafsanjani and he liked to say that he had a "rough son Johnny."

Get it?

Anyway, this punny bit caught on somehow. I think it's because it was intriguing once the listener realized it was going to end in a pun, so they followed along to see if they could figure out what song it was going to be. It was up to me to come up with the record title in such an obscure way that the listener had no idea what song it would be until the musical intro began, as I said something like "Sold Your Bowie" ("Soldier Boy") or "The Girl with Colitis Goes By" ("The girl with Kaleidoscope eyes"). I did this bit for many years, and for some reason it became a fan favorite.

Recently a friend of mine sent me a CD containing a bunch of these "Americana Panoramas" he had recorded over the years. I was cringing when I listened to it. I wouldn't play this stuff for anybody. You know, some things just do not hold up well over time.

STEVIE WONDER

I can tell you the exact date of my most memorable experience at WILS. It was April 4, 1968. We had a very special guest in the studio that day; Stevie Wonder. Stevie was a big star at the time for Motown Records in Detroit, but he also supported a local school for the blind in Lansing, so he came to town semi-regularly. The music director at WILS (Craig Dudley) knew Stevie, and knew that he loved playing disc jockey, so he invited him to come to our station, sit at the control board, play records, and talk on the air.

I was there that day, and was lucky enough to watch him in action. It was just an amazing sight. He cued up the records, turned the knobs, turned the microphones on and off; you name it. Even though he couldn't see a thing, he knew exactly what he was doing. There were a few Motown Records employees with him, but he was doing it all by himself. I was standing in the back of the studio watching the whole thing, in awe of his abilities.

That's when the news came across the wire that Martin Luther King Jr. had been shot.

At first it wasn't clear if King was dead or not, but we all suspected he was. An instant tension filled the room. The Motown executives didn't say a thing. None of the radio station employees (including me) responded, and neither did Stevie. But we all knew we were experiencing a significant moment.

Even though this clearly affected him, Stevie was a total pro. He finished the show.

THE BALL GETS ROLLING

Jim Donahue and Dave Alberry were fellow Michigan State students, and huge radio fans. They contacted me at WILS one night when I was on the air, and we hit it off. They were radio geeks just like me. I started hanging out with them at their apartment after I got off the air at 1:00. Another person that hung out with us was future actor

Robert Urich. He was an MSU student too. I met Bob when I directed him in a Fresca commercial that we made for directing class. At the time he had already done some actual paid commercial work. He was in a Frito Lay commercial and a couple of other things, but he hadn't broken through yet. I believe he eventually became the most watched actor in television history because of the many, many shows he starred in — everything from *S.W.A.T.* to *Vega$* to *Soap*, to *Spencer for Hire*, to *Lonesome Dove*, to *Love Boat*. He was a great guy. (I reconnected with him many years later, after he was diagnosed with cancer, and we talked all about those days in Lansing. He died in 2002.)

Radio was a favorite topic at Jim and Dave's apartment. They had gotten enamored with a radio consultant named Bill Drake, who was one of the most famous Top 40 programmers in radio history. I never did the "Bill Drake" format per se, but I did do similar formats, and it's safe to say that the things I later did at WLS like "Boogie Check," "Can I Get a Witness News," and "Americana Panorama" would never have been allowed at a station programmed by Bill Drake. He was a strict format disciplinarian.

Well, somehow, and I'd still love to know how they did this, Jimmy and Dave got their hands on the control room phone numbers of the Bill Drake consulted radio stations across the country, and began calling up disc jockeys, pretending to be Bill Drake. Take it from me, when the hotline rings in a radio studio, it can stop your heart. Anybody that has ever done a radio show knows what it means. It means you're in trouble. And when these poor unsuspecting jocks picked up the phone, they'd hear…

"This is Bill Drake, who is this?"

Followed by Jim or Dave bitching at these poor saps for doing the format incorrectly. It was actually pretty hilarious. They had it down. They knew how the format worked. They knew all the tricks. All of these jocks fell for it.

One of the Drake guys that Donahue and Alberry called was named Mike Rivers. Mike was doing afternoons on CKLW in Detroit (actually Windsor, Canada — just over the border). Without my knowledge, Jimmy and Dave gave a tape of my show to Rivers. Rivers gave that tape to his boss, Paul Drew, shortly before Drew left Detroit to program WIBG in Philadelphia. All of these balls were rolling without me having the slightest idea.

So, I was more than a little surprised when I got a call from Paul Drew. He said he wanted to fly me out to Philadelphia to interview me.

"Are you kidding me? Of course I'll come."

When I got there, he offered me the job.

Now, as excited as I was by this turn of events, I also knew that if I took this job, I had to do something else. I had to drop out of college. My father was on a sabbatical overseas teaching in Germany when I got the job offer from WIBG in Philadelphia. I knew he wouldn't understand the implications of this offer, but I sure did. This was a leap into market number four from market number nowhere. It was the #2 rated rock station in Philadelphia — this was a huge deal.

I talked to my professors about the job offer. They all told me to take it. I also talked to my in-laws, my father-in-law had gone to Harvard and MIT and my mother-in-law had gone to Vassar, and they supported the move too. Everybody pointed out to me that this was the reason I was going to college — to get an offer like this. So, I leaped at the opportunity and informed my parents overseas that I was dropping out of college my senior year to take the job.

I'm sure there was disappointment on their end, and I guess deep down there is some on my end too. Every once in a while, I remember that I never graduated, and I have fantasies of going back to Michigan and getting a diploma. I even went so far as calling up University of Michigan's admission office once looking for my high school transcripts. I told whoever was on the other end of the phone that I had attended University of Michigan High School, and needed to get my records. Her response?

"What town?"

CHAPTER FIVE
A PHILADELPHIA STORY

> The late '60s and early '70s was an exciting time. Neil Armstrong walked on the moon. The Woodstock Music Festival might have been the most important concert event in rock and roll history. The voting age was lowered from 21 to 18. But the Vietnam War was still going on, the Chicago Seven trial became a spectacle, and protesting students were shot dead by National Guardsmen at Kent State. The early 1970s was a transitional time in pop culture. Edgy television shows like *All in the Family* were on at the same time as the old guard shows like *Bonanza*. At the movies people were flocking to the first disaster film *Airport*, and the big war movie *Patton*. It was the beginning of the post-Beatles era of rock and roll, and totally different styles of music were becoming popular, from the sensitive singer/songwriters like Paul Simon and James Taylor, to the heavy metal bands like Deep Purple and Black Sabbath.

The jocks that were on the radio in Philadelphia at that time were real characters. Jerry Blavat (The Geator with the Heater), Joe Niagra (The Rockin' Bird), Hy Lit (a guy who once had a *71* share). Huge names. Real characters in the history of Philadelphia radio; larger than life.

But I had a slightly different style. Ted Heusel, Tom O'Brien, and Joel Sebastian were my influences. Ron Britain in Chicago. Dave Pringle and Ollie McGlocklin from Ann Arbor. I was different than what they were used to in Philadelphia, and I knew it.

I have never been as nervous as I was the first day I went to work at WIBG. It was the big time — no question about it. I had arrived. But when I arrived, I also discovered something else. I was no longer John Records Landecker.

Paul Drew had changed my on-air name to Scott Walker.

Scott Walker? Really?

I had been in radio for only a few years, and this was already my third name. But unlike "Dow Jones," I never cared for this one. It made no sense at all to me. They had hired the John Records Landecker Radio Leviathan Program. Why on earth would they put generic old Scott Walker on the air instead?

At first, WIBG was an absolute nightmare. Paul Drew was a micromanager's micromanager. He would wear an earphone wherever he went to constantly listen to the station. It seemed like he listened 24 hours a day. There was a spotlight in the corner of the studio connected to the studio hotline, and it went off all day long. Paul called to correct every jock every time he did something wrong, even if he was in the middle of a sentence. The joke at the station was that we all had sunburn on one side of our face because of that studio hotline light.

It's not that Paul mistreated me — he didn't at all. He was a very nice guy. In fact, he was incredibly generous in retrospect because he didn't fire me — and I gave him plenty of reasons. I even screwed up a countdown once.

I mean, I was just not gelling with this format at all.

I really thought I had made the biggest mistake of my life by going to this station. I had dropped out of college and moved across the country with a wife and kid, and came to a part of the country that wasn't comfortable to me — I wasn't an East Coast guy. I remember being in this hotel room one night, studying this ridiculous manual about the format — and breaking down because I believed there was no way I was going to be able to do it.

I didn't know it at the time, but everything was about to change.

BUCKLEY BROADCASTING

The station was sold to Buckley Broadcasting and Paul Drew was let go. I remember going over to Paul's apartment after I heard the news.

He asked me: "What do you want to do with your career?"

"Well I'd like to go back to being John Records Landecker," I said.

"You're never going to make it with that name," he said. "Why don't you go down to a medium market, somewhere like Atlanta, and get it out of your system? There was no way I could have used a John Records Landecker here, but in the end, I could have used six Scott Walkers."

He was trying to compliment me, trying to tell me that I did a great job executing the format, but being Scott Walker never felt right to me. In his defense, after I became a big success in Chicago, I did get a letter from Paul mocking himself for saying that to me. He wrote, "I guess what I should have said was 'I could have used six John Records Landeckers.'"

The day that Buckley Broadcasting took over WIBG, Philadelphia changed for me overnight. Rick Buckley, the son of the owner, was the new GM after the ownership change. When I met him, he asked me what I wanted to do.

"I want to be the John Records Landecker Radio Leviathan," I told him.

"OK," he replied.

And just like that I had my name back.

Rick also brought in another personality that I'm still friends with to this day. At the time he was a revelation to me — probably the most talented guy I ever worked with — his name was Joey Reynolds. Joey came in and totally changed the place. We went from a tightly-run super-strict format to absolute anarchy. It was unbelievable.

Joey was just fantastic. He was doing 6-10pm, and I followed him at 10. One night I was Scott Walker, and the next night I went on the air as John Records Landecker and ripped Scott Walker a new one. I got a couple of calls of outrage.

"How dare you? We love Scott Walker!"

"What are you talkin' about?" I retorted. "He's horrible."

I never addressed the fact that I was the same guy. Scott Walker was dead and buried as far as I was concerned.

JOEY REYNOLDS *REMEMBERS*

Joey Reynolds on our relationship... *John and I hit it off immediately. The two us had a few important things in common. My fight, similar to John's, was always on behalf of the listeners. We both have a great respect for the listeners. John was very sensitive — he knew when people were being genuine, and when they were just kissing his ass — and that requires a sensitivity — an ability to understand people. That's how he tapped into what the kids wanted. That's how he understood their needs.*

WIBG EXPLODES

With Rick Buckley and Joey Reynolds, WIBG became one of the wildest radio stations I have ever seen. We had dune buggies. We had our own dragster, complete with a garage and driver! We'd go to New York with clients at the drop of a hat. We took listeners to the Concert for Bangladesh. I was there for that. I was at the premiere of the movie *Woodstock* and arrived in the bus with The Who, and Joe Cocker, and Santana. It was wild.

A month or so after the Concert for Bangladesh, we put on a free concert with Leon Russell. We didn't even say where it was, we only gave out clues. Every clue brought the listener closer to the location. They found it, alright. 30,000 people packed into a little park in a Philadelphia suburb called Conshohocken.

We were having an absolute blast! At that time the rock and roll record business in Philadelphia was loaded with characters. Everywhere you went, you ran into somebody that had a record, or knew someone that had a record. Jim Croce's record was brought into the radio station by two nuns, who I think were his actual sisters — or the sisters of the guy that produced him. I would go over to Joey Reynolds' house, and people like Wayne Newton or Minnie Ripperton would walk in the door.

I became the music director for a while and we were very open about playing stuff that most AM rock stations wouldn't touch. We played Joe Cocker's Mad Dog and Englishmen off the album. We played the Overture from The Who's *Tommy*. Hearing that song on WIBG inspired local musicians to get together, form a group (they called themselves The Assembled Multitude), record it, and release it as a single. It was a radio hit across the country.

Philadelphia radio was happening, man.

WIBG had a competitor named WFIL, and they were our arch enemies at the time. We never missed an opportunity to needle them, to stick it to 'em. They were the station with the "boss jocks" and did this contest they called the "boss garage giveaway," which was just like *Let's Make A Deal*. The listener would choose a garage door, and get what's behind the door as their prize. Well, to make fun of WFIL, we did a boss garage giveaway too — but we gave away actual garages.

WIBG and WFIL fought over songs too. We had one guy who heard that the Beatles were coming out with something new, so he drove up to New York to get the test pressing so we could say we played it first. We had a button in the studio so we could listen to WFIL, and if we were playing a record that they were playing too, we'd say "You heard it here first!"

> **JOEY REYNOLDS** REMEMBERS
>
> Joey Reynolds has written a great memoir himself (*Let a Smile Be Your Umbrella, But Don't Get a Mouthful of Rain*), and remembers that time well… *WIBG had been a #1 radio station in the past — it had the best ratings in the country for years, but in the years before John and I arrived, WFIL had come in and cleaned their clock. We were supposed to be the restoration of that former glory. The shift was painful, new thinking is always painful, and we stepped on a few toes, but we kicked up so much sand that people started checking us out again.*
>
> *John and I would go around to the schools in these dune buggies and hand out record albums. I know that sounds a little Woody Allen-y, ("come here little girl, want some candy?") but what we were doing then was like the social networking of today. It worked too.*

PHILADELPHIA DAYS AND NIGHTS

Joey left the station shortly after that, and I was moved into his timeslot. I worked my butt off during those years. I hooked up with a guy named Richard Akins from Rick Trow Productions. They provided high schools with educational assemblies. Normally high schools had to pay for assemblies, but our hook was that the radio station would pick up the tab as long as I got to come out at the end.

The show was called "The Marvel of Sound." My part of the show was doing a track breakdown of a record to show the kids how the recording process worked. The Native-American band Redbone ("Come Get Your Love") had a song called "Maggie," and no other radio station was playing it except us, so they gave me a track breakdown to use. After I presented the song to the kids, I would tell them I was going to dedicate an hour of my show that night to their high school. It had a huge impact on the ratings.

I've never worked harder in my life. I was on the road every single day bustin' my ass. But you know what they say: "All work and no play makes John a dull boy."

And thanks to the way we ran things at WIBG, I was not a dull boy.

DON WADE REMEMBERS

Fellow WIBG jock Don Wade (and future colleague at WLS in Chicago) remembers those days fondly... *When I worked with John in Philly at WIBG, I was doing mornings and John was doing evenings. Our schedules were opposite, but we saw each other at weekly meetings that were a complete waste of time. We'd eat pizza and try to be serious, but nobody was. Before or after the meetings a bunch of us would go to this par-three golf course and drink beer, and hit balls. We didn't fit in at all at the golf course — we didn't know how to golf, we all had* long hair, and got dirty looks from the real golfers, the business executives.

When we weren't "golfing," we were playing softball. Rick Buckley, the son of the owner, would get a keg, and would show up wearing sweats, and we would go out and bat the ball around. We all loved working for Rick. All he wanted to do was have drinks and have a good time. He was one of the guys.

THE HIGHEST HIGHS

My second daughter Amy was born in Norristown, Pennsylvania. We were the perfect little family for a while; the DJ, the mommy, and now two little girls. We looked like a Norman Rockwell painting, and we were very briefly.

Unfortunately that perfect little family unit didn't last more than a few years thanks to me, and the temptations I didn't resist. Philadelphia was my first foray into the big time, and it brought things with it that weren't necessarily supportive of being a responsible family man.

Namely: Women and alcohol. Together. At the same time.

Every Friday afternoon we'd pool our money together, get some liquor, and have a party *at the radio station*. That was the first time I was exposed to being able to drink AND go on the air at the same time. And I found that to be a lot of fun. Unfortunately, that sort of atmosphere also gave me a lot of opportunities to be irresponsible. I still loved my wife and kids, but I was also just 21 years old when we arrived in town, and had never experienced anything like this before. I hadn't sowed my wild oats, if you will, between graduating high school and having kids. I'm not using that as an excuse. I'm not proud of what I did and I knew it was wrong, but it was like I had the devil on one shoulder and an angel on the other. When I drank, the alcohol seemed to remove my morality. I didn't limit myself to alcohol either. During this time, I also started using some psychedelic drugs like LSD and mescaline.

On one occasion, I took mescaline and went on the air. Something happened on that show, and the only reason I can still remember it today is because a listener was taping it and sent it to me. I was playing a song on a cartridge or cart (a tape that played over a playback head — if you remember 8-tracks, carts looked very much like that). Unlike a record, however, when a cart got damaged or dirty, it didn't skip. It slooooooowed down and the music wavered and wobbled. It didn't happen often, but it did happen while I was high that night. Instead of stopping the tape, I turned on the mic and talked, wavering and wobbling along with it. When it slowed down, I slowed down, and when it sped up, I sped up.

But believe me, I wasn't the only one having adult fun at that radio station. One time I was the victim of a practical joke played by one of the other jocks on WIBG — Don Cannon. I was working the 6-10pm shift, and everything seemed normal that night. I put a 45 RPM record on the turntable, put the needle on the record, and it began playing on the air. But as I was talking over the intro, a hand reached over and picked the needle off the record. There was suddenly nothing on the air but my voice. When I turned around to see what happened (with the microphone open), Don Cannon was standing there with a woman wearing a fur coat. When she saw me turn around, the woman opened her coat, and revealed that she was totally naked underneath. I was speechless. And Don Cannon laughed hysterically. To this day that is the only totally naked woman I've ever seen at a radio station.

Emphasis: *Totally* naked.

By the way, here's a little trivia about Don Cannon. If you watch the first Rocky movie, in the scene where Rocky is drinking the raw eggs, the radio is tuned to WIBG, and the jock on the air is Don Cannon.

CHICAGO CALLS

Unbeknownst to me, balls were rolling behind my back again. I didn't find all of this out until after the fact, but here's how it happened. See if you can follow along.

When WLS had an opening, they checked with corporate in New York to see if they had any recommendations. Someone at WABC-New York was friends with the PD at WFIL-Philadelphia, and asked him if he knew of anyone. The WFIL program director recommended me because he wanted to get me out of town.

So, the New York guy came to Philly to check me out, liked what I was doing, and dropped my name to Mike McCormack, the program director of WLS-Chicago. McCormack came to check me out (needless to say, this was before online streaming), liked what I was doing, and sent me a letter requesting a tape and resume, which I sent to him when I was home for Christmas visiting my family in Ann Arbor.

One day during that vacation I was out seeing old friends, and when I got back to my parents' house, my mom said to me: "You just got a call from a guy at WLS in Chicago."

I called him back, got on a plane the next day, and took the job.

CHAPTER SIX
THE BIG 89

> The early to mid '70s had high highs and low lows for President Nixon. He won the biggest landslide in history in 1972, but the Watergate burglars were caught, and eventually he was forced to resign. The Vietnam War finally came to an end, and Gerald Ford became the unelected Vice President, and then unelected President of the United States. The early to mid '70s brought us gritty movies like *The French Connection* and *The Godfather*. Television was gritty too, with shows like *Hawaii 5-0*, *Kojak*, and *The Streets of San Francisco*. But the music was anything but gritty. Singer/songwriters like Don McLean, Roberta Flack, and Carly Simon were big stars, and one-hit wonders like Paper Lace, and Terry Jacks were creating some of the worst music of all time.

I got off the airport bus at the Executive House, just down the street from the radio station, and got a taste of the howling December wind coming down the canal from the lake on Wacker.

Welcome to Chicago.

I got my first pleasant surprise as soon as I walked into the radio station doors. I knew Joel Sebastian worked at WLS (there's that name again!), but I had no idea he would be on the air when I came into the station that very first day. I walked into the studio and used the same line I had used years before in the bookstore.

"Excuse me," I said, "do you know Ted Heusel?"

WLS already had an all-star lineup when I came aboard in 1972. Superjock Larry Lujack was the morning man, Fred Winston was doing middays, and J.J. Jeffrey was the afternoon man. I was hired to fill the evening slot.

I met Larry before I was on the air a single time. The program director Mike McCormack called me into his office because he wanted me to sit in on a Larry Lujack aircheck. In the radio business we call them "airchecks," but they're really just critique sessions with the program director. The disc jockey brings in a tape of his or her show, and if the program director likes it, he praises it. I suppose this has happened once or twice in radio history. Usually it goes the other way. Usually the program director picks it apart.

McCormack started Larry's tape, and we listened to a bit Lujack had done that morning. It was reality radio. Larry was pointing out that you could hear the garbage trucks in the alley through the air conditioner in WLS's main air studio, and he held the microphone right up to it, so the listeners could hear it too. After the bit ended, the program director turned to me.

"What do you think of that?" he asked.

"I thought that was pretty funny," I said.

I didn't know what I had done, but after the meeting I was walking back to the jock lounge with Larry and he turned toward me.

"Thanks, kid," he said.

Apparently before I came in, the program director had been telling Larry he hated it, and Larry was defending it. When I backed him up by saying I thought it was funny, it defused the criticism, and Larry thought the new guy was alright.

On the other hand, not too long after that, I may have turned the tide in the other direction at least for a day. We were in a jock meeting, shooting the shit, and someone asked the seemingly innocuous question: "Who was more important to music — Elvis or the Beatles?"

"I don't think Elvis was that great," I said.

Well, I had no idea that Larry Lujack was a *huge* Elvis fan, but I found out pretty fast. Larry glared at me. And then he nearly spit the words at me, in his patented Lujack delivery.

"You don't know anything about music, you… Phil… a… del… phia… FUCK!"

ALAN ROSEN REMEMBERS

Alan Rosen was a production engineer at WLS throughout my stint at the station. He recalls the day we met… *Gil Gross (WLS newsman at the time) and I were just ending a double date, had just dropped off our girlfriends and were driving home listening to WLS. It was 2am and I heard an unfamiliar voice on the radio.*

"Who's that?" I asked.

"Oh," Gil said, "That must be the new guy from Philadelphia. He's starting the night show next week. They must be breaking him in on the overnight show tonight. I think we need to mess with him a little bit to welcome him to the station, don't you?"

"But of COURSE," I said and we drove over.

Gil and I walked into the studio while John was reading a live commercial. We were weaving around and I was holding an empty Budweiser bottle in my hand. John turned off his mic, and talked to the engineer.

"What's going on???"

"Oh damn," engineer Bob Ferguson (who was in on this) said through the intercom. "I forgot to lock the door. The London House must have just closed for the night." (The London House was the famous Chicago nightclub located on the street level at 360 N. Michigan Avenue.) "Sometimes drunks wander upstairs. Just don't make them mad!"

John turned his mic back on, and continued reading the commercial while keeping an eye on us. I stumbled to the floor and banged my beer bottle softly on the base of his chair. Gil got behind John and placed his chin on John's shoulder looking at John's commercial copy, his long beard dropping over John's chest. Landecker ad-libbed something like "Well, I guess I'm not in Philadelphia anymore!"

After the next song started, Gary Gears, who was the regular host of the overnight show popped back in the studio.

"John," he said, "I want you to meet Gil Gross, your newsman, and Alley Rosen, your engineer. You'll be working with them starting next week."

I think that set the tone for John at WLS.

TRANSITIONING TO CHICAGO

As much as I was loving this radio station, there was one thing that bothered me right away. Mike McCormack wouldn't let me use my middle name again.

I had been John Records Landecker in Philadelphia — that was the guy that they hired — but when I came to Chicago they lopped the Records off my name. (I eventually was allowed to use it again when a new program director came aboard.)

Even though I couldn't bring my whole name to Chicago, I did bring one thing from Philly: the high school assembly program. I started doing it right away. I learned quickly, however, that Chicago was a little bit different than Philadelphia.

I had no idea how segregated Chicago public schools were, so I naively chose the schools based on enrollment. I remember walking into Englewood High School, and realized pretty quickly that every single kid in the school was African-American. Two kids, in particular, were staring at me.

"What's goin' on?" one asked the other.

"Aw," the other replied, "just some honky with a tape recorder."

They weren't exactly interested in my presentation. But I had an epiphany that day while I was bombing on stage. Bill Bailey, the guy on the air after me every night, was an African-American. So, after that one time, I made sure to check if we were going to an African-American high school, and if we were, I brought along Bill, and had him wait in the wings. I'd come out and do my spiel, and they'd be as apathetic and disinterested as they were at Englewood High, but then I'd say, "Let me bring out another WLS jock to give me a hand. Please give a big round of applause to the guy that follows me on the air every night, Bill Bailey!"

At first he would be greeted with the usual polite applause, but the second they made eye contact with him, the place would go insane! I'm sure that the high school assembly program had a lot to do with the gigantic teen numbers we got in those days. There was a time at night when we had over a third of all teens listening to us. We had the highest nighttime ratings in the entire country.

Unfortunately, the high school assembly program wasn't the only thing that followed me from Philly. I got a call at the station one day shortly after we arrived in town from my very upset wife. She had just gotten a call from a woman I had been having an affair with in Philadelphia. That woman was so upset I had broken off our affair that she paid me back by calling Judy and telling her all about it.

I was forced to go into Mike McCormack's office and tell him what happened, and tell him that I had to go home *immediately.* It was only two hours before I was supposed to go on the air, and I had only been in Chicago for a very short period of time. I was shaking in my boots when I told him. Surprisingly, he was very cooperative and understanding, and let me leave work for a few days.

As you might imagine, Judy was justifiably less understanding. We tried to patch things up, and we did for a while, but I don't think the marriage was ever the same after that.

PRESIDENT NIXON

In my early years at WLS, I did an impersonation of President Nixon, calling him "The Big Guy in the White House." Needless to say, political satire was not exactly the norm for a nighttime teen rock show, but the kids seemed to respond to it. I recorded a parody song called "Make a Date with a Watergate" which was done to the Lou Reed song "Walk on the Wild Side," and a Dickie Goodman/Flying Saucer record called "Press My Conference." (Flying Saucer records featured an announcer "interviewing" famous people, but they only "answered" the questions with clips from a song.)

Both "Make a Date" and "Press My Conference" were big hits with the listeners, *(the full lyrics of "Make a Date" can be found in the appendix)* but ABC corporate headquarters yanked "Make a Date with a Watergate" off the air because it made fun of the Nixon administration. At the time an ABC television station in Florida was up for their FCC license renewal. ABC was scared to death of the Nixon administration, and worried that this song would create a stumbling block for them.

The timing couldn't have been worse for me. Before they made me pull it, Harry Nilsson was ready to present the song to the A&R department of RCA Records, and Lou Reed had agreed to go into the studio and really record it. (The version we played on the air had been produced at WLS by Alan Rosen, who simply chopped up the original song. He discovered that it repeated itself over and over, and as long as we got the "Doo Doo Doo Doo Doo Doo Doo" part in the right spot, it would work.)

Well, after the license was renewed and Nixon was thrown out of office, the song became even bigger. The radio station printed up 10,000 promotional 45 RPM records. I was totally excited about it until I looked at the records themselves. Would you believe they spelled my name wrong? On the label it said: "John Records Laudecker.'"

To fix it, they didn't print 10,000 new labels; they printed 10,000 itsy-bitsy tiny little stickers with my correctly spelled name that we had paste over each and every existing incorrectly spelled name. Welcome to the big time! *(An example of a misspelled 45 is in the photo section.)*

We almost produced a video for the song too. Second City was doing a special for Channel 11 (PBS in Chicago), produced by Ken Ehrlich (one of the biggest producers in Hollywood today). He asked if I would come to the Channel 11 studios and lip-synch the song for the special. I did and it was a total disaster. In the first place, I looked nothing like Nixon, and that was distracting. Secondly, I couldn't even lip-synch my own damn song. They obviously never used it.

WLS NEWS & POT

It seems almost impossible to believe today, but at the time WLS had seventeen people on the news staff. There were more people in the news department than there were jocks, and I worked with some great ones like Lyle Dean and Gil Gross and Catherine Johns and Jim Johnson. Every newscast began with "Good evening, I'm _____ and this is WLS News." There wasn't really any banter back and forth like you hear today. It wasn't encouraged.

During the night slot, I had a newsperson named Linda Marshall, and she followed our standard format every time. I knew that, so I set her up a few times with a lead-in like this: "You know, I was walking down the street one day and there was this really drunk woman coming down the street towards me, and I said 'Hey, how you doin', what's your name,' and she said…"

"Good evening, I'm Linda Marshall and this is WLS News."

She was a great sport about it. She knew I was just bending the format in ways that no one had imagined. All of us did. We weren't going out of our way to be shock jocks or do something that was purposely outrageous; we were just looking for loopholes to create something a little different. That was my approach to everything. I talked over jingles, I talked over commercials, and I talked over music. If anything, I was over-integrated with the format. Now, it didn't happen all the time with the news people. I didn't push it so much that I damaged their credibility. And I didn't do it when their lead story was overly serious or tragic. But when circumstances were right; stuff happened.

On the air, and off the air.

At night when management wasn't around, some of us liked to smoke pot, although not everybody. I would tell a certain engineer (who shall remain nameless) to play "Layla" followed by "American Pie." That would give those of us involved fifteen minutes to get completely stoned before coming back. If you were ever listening to the radio station and heard "Layla" and "American Pie" back-to-back, rest assured that something — I'm not saying exactly what — was definitely going on behind the scenes.

There were times I would go on the air completely rocked out of my mind. Was it just me, or did it make the music actually sound better?

"Dig it, man, 'Muskrat Love.'"

BOB SIROTT REMEMBERS

Bob Sirott came to WLS a few years after I did, and he was a kindred spirit. We hit it off right away. This is how he remembers that time... *There really wasn't any competition at all — not friendly or otherwise at WLS in the '70s. No rivalry. Not sure why, but we were all just into doing our own thing. J.J. Jeffrey, John, and I used to hang out with each other on weekends, as well as many times during the week after John would get off the air. (What we did is still classified, but will be released to the public after we're all dead!)*

J.J. and I used to drop little hints on the air that John was black... a little inside joke just to amuse ourselves, "Of course tonight at six, our Motown man John Landecker will be here." The inside jokes that made it on the air usually came out of the Saturday night dinners we had together. I also used to promote John by giving him shit about his fast talking over high music levels... "Good luck understanding what he says, but John Recordings Landecker will be here at six." I think we all kept each other in line — nobody could get a big head or become too serious about what we were doing on the station because the rest of us would just heckle that person back into his senses.

WORKING AND PLAYING TOGETHER

I thought we all got along great at WIBG in Philadelphia, but I haven't worked at a radio station before or since that had the kind of camaraderie we had at WLS in the 1970s. It was like one big non-stop party. We did all sorts of things together inside and outside the workplace.

The whole staff would play basketball and softball against local fire and police departments and various other organizations, and then after the game, all of our families would go out for pizza together. It usually ended up like Thanksgiving dinner, with two big tables — the grown up table, and the kids' table. Superjock Larry Lujack, the biggest star of all of us, would always, and I mean *always*, sit at the kids' table.

On the air we treated the radio station as a tool for our amusement. We would show up on each other's shows unannounced. There was nothing phony about our on-air kidding around. Everyone genuinely liked each other. Bob Sirott, J.J. Jeffrey and I had our own little language when we spoke to each other — code words and phrases that meant things only to ourselves. (For instance, a "W.A." was a "weak anecdote," an "S.A." was a "strong anecdote," and watch out that you don't get "T.T.F.O." or "thrown the fuck out.")

Bob and I ended up doing a lot of stuff together on the air at WLS, but we also did telethons (more than one) for the Muscular Dystrophy Association, photo sessions and promotional shoots together, and we hung out all the time. J.J. was one of the most unique characters I ever worked with in radio. He had this unbelievably great laugh, and that was all we ever wanted to do — get him to laugh on the air. J.J. was also a bit eccentric. For instance, he had nothing but blow up furniture in his apartment, he walked to and from work even though he lived at Belmont Ave, quite a long way from Michigan and Wacker, and he smoked cigarettes in a cigarette holder. There was no one else like him. In the mid '70s Pat O'Brien joined our clique too. Pat went on to work at CBS Sports, and then *Access Hollywood*, and *The Insider*, but at that time he was a Channel 5 news reporter.

One day I had the worst toothache of my life, and the dentist told me that I had four impacted wisdom teeth. He asked me what I needed to do that night. I told him I had to work, and then we were planning to go out drinking in Greektown.

He said, "Look, you can't work. That's out. You can go out and drink, or I can give you some painkillers, but you can't do both."

So, I picked Greektown. Now we could start even earlier!

Once again I brought my ever-present hand-held tape recorder, and recorded our whole night out. The recording began in the cab with Pat, Sirott and I listening to whoever was doing my show, and providing our own commentary. The tape continued in the restaurant — at the table while we were all drinking and getting crazy, and it ended with me passed out on the floor of my apartment. Bob Sirott did the final play by play, holding the microphone up to my mouth.

"This is John Landecker passed out on the floor," he said.

You can actually hear me snoring.

I don't think I played that tape on the air until many years later… and even then it was an edited version. I remember thinking that the tape, and probably this explanation, didn't do justice to that actual experience. It was such a great time.

BOOGIE CHECK

A lot of the bits that we did on WLS came out of something spontaneous, just making lemonade out of lemons. "Boogie Check" started because I was bored. I was playing the same songs over and over again and I wanted to shake things up a bit.

A lot of people ask me where I came up with the name. Well, I called it "Boogie Check" because of something J.J. Jeffrey did before he went out on dates. He used to conduct a sixty second "booger check" to make sure he didn't have any boogers in his mustache. I figured, if you could have a sixty second booger check, why not a sixty second "Boogie" check? My competition at WCFL (our arch rival station) was a guy named Dr. Brock, and his calling card was the word "Boogie." I figured I would tweak him, and have some fun, so I just started answering the phones live on the air by saying "Boogie Check. You talkin' to me?" (the last line taken from Robert DeNiro's character in *Taxi Driver*). If the person on the other end of the line didn't respond quickly, I hung up on them, and went to the next line.

That's it. That's all "Boogie Check" was.

What made it work was the combination of teenagers on the phone, and my spontaneous ad-libbed reaction to whatever they said. Nothing like this had ever been done on rock radio before — the only time any jock took calls was strictly for song requests. This was just a free-for-all; spontaneous, interactive, stream of consciousness. When a caller said the word "Fuck" on the air, though, it also became clear that there was no delay system at WLS. News of this spread like wildfire throughout the Chicagoland teen community. Eventually WLS engineers Carl Nelson and Ed Glab did design a delay system, but by then, "Boogie Check" was off and running.

ALAN ROSEN *REMEMBERS*

Alley was there for many "Boogie Checks," running the board… *One night when I arrived at work, the engineer before me told me that the delay system wasn't working. I told John that we'd have to scrap "Boogie Check" for the night. But when the regular time for "Boogie Check" rolled around, John told me to play the opening theme music anyway. He opened his mic and said on the air, "My engineer Alley has told me that the delay system is broken and that we'd better not do "Boogie Check" tonight. Now THAT'S the kind of thing that your PARENTS would say because they don't trust you. I know that I can treat you all like adults and that you'll be responsible and we can do this just like we always do."*

John punched up the first caller and said: "Boogie Check."

The caller responded: "Fuck you!"

Most of it got on the air before I could turn it down. John just stood there with this expression on his face that I had never seen before. He said nothing for several very long seconds. When John opened his mouth, he was mad.

"I TRUSTED you people!" he yelled on the air. 'I thought I could treat you like adults! I guess I was wrong. I have a wife and two girls and I'm not going to lose my job because of YOU."

He was yelling at the listeners! It was a surreal moment, but a totally John Landecker moment.

BOOGIE CHECK CHARACTERS

All sorts of eclectic characters emerged on "Boogie Check." A kid that hung out around the station was dubbed "The C-Kid" (because he always wore a Cubs hat). He would call in, sound a horn, say

"Good evening, John," and then offer his observations about the world. Other kids called up and flushed toilets, burped, asked weird questions, or told corny jokes.

One "Boogie Check" contributor turned into one of the biggest rock stars on the planet; the lead singer of the Smashing Pumpkins, Billy Corgan. I met him a few years ago and he told me that when he was a kid he used to call into "Boogie Check" and claim to be Maurice White, the drummer from Earth, Wind & Fire.

> **JONATHON BRANDMEIER** *REMEMBERS*
>
> WGN-Chicago morning man Jonathon Brandmeier was also a "Boogie Check" devotee... *When I had my first radio job, I was 16 at WFON in Fon du Lac, and my boss at the time said "Do whatever you want." I loved "Boogie Check" so much I wanted to do my version of it. So I called it "The Loon Line," and just took random calls. But the problem was that I didn't get any calls. So I called my brothers and asked them to call, and I called my buddies and asked them to call. And they did until people started to get it. But when they did, they could also tell there was no delay. Then they started calling up to say stuff like, "I just saw your mother at the A&W sucking a cock!"*

THE BOOGIE NETWORK

I've heard a lot of stories over the years from people that called into "Boogie Check." Apparently, there were so many calls coming in at once, it would tie up the phone lines, and if a kid called and got a busy signal, but stayed on the line anyway, he or she could talk to the other kids calling in between the beeps.

Can I take credit for the first social network?

In the end, "Boogie Check" was remarkably simple. The kids had to be kids and I had to be funny. It worked. I loved it. It came easily for me. It required no preparation. I just answered the first line, and away we went.

I'd like to thank J.J. Jeffrey and Martin Scorsese for their contributions.

JOHN GEHRON REMEMBERS

John Gehron did a spectacular job as the program director of WLS. He allowed things I'm sure that no other program director at any other radio station would have allowed. This included the mayhem that was "Boogie Check"... "Boogie Check" was great, but there were times it would go a little long, so I came up with a visual cue to let John know that his time was up. We played a cartridge when "Boogie Check" started, and all of our cartridges had a cue light that would come on when only five seconds remained. It was a way for me to give him the flexibility he wanted, but allowed me to gently edit him, without having to hotline him. Of course, John being John, there were times he ignored the cue light. But for the most part, it worked out very well.

LARGER THAN LIFE

I didn't really realize how big we were in the 1970s while it was happening. A few years ago I talked to Marty Greenberg, who was the general manager at WLS for a while, and he said: "We were the New York Yankees and we didn't even know it."

"It's probably a good thing we didn't know it," I replied, "because we probably would have been even bigger egomaniacs!"

Radio today is dominated by huge companies that own hundreds of stations, syndicate their personalities, and share staffs within each market. None of that existed when WLS ripped a ratings hole through the 1970s. We were owned by ABC, and they only owned a few select stations. We had a full staff — everything from general manager to program director to music director, promotions director to news director to sales and engineering. Hell, we had an advertising agency. We had a PR agent!

I went out to lunches that were set up by the PR department. I remember one lunch with a newspaper columnist named Maggie Daly from the Chicago Daily News, Buddy Rich, and Marty Feldman, the guy with the eyes in *Young Frankenstein*.

There were parties at the Playboy Mansion on north State Parkway. Somewhere there's an Elton John book that has a photograph of Elton John and Bernie Taupin playing foosball in the mansion game room against Hugh Heffner and Barbie Benton. I am in the middle of the shot doing play-by-play into my little tape recorder.

Me: "Elton, you came from behind to win."

Elton: "I usually do."

We called ourselves The Big 89 because everything we did was BIG!!! We did a promotion at Great America and we didn't just show up and broadcast. We flew a helicopter out there. We transported the entire control room, complete with engineers. It was astounding. (*Some photographs of those remotes are in the photo section.*) The contests were huge. We gave away a house. The concerts were huge. We did the first concert that was broadcast live on the air (with Styx). Nothing like that had been done before.

There was no way that anyone was going to beat us.

We were unstoppable.

BILL ZEHME REMEMBERS

In the 1970s we had a viewing window at the WLS studios, and kids could take a look at the DJ on the air through a window across the hallway. Bill Zehme was one of those kids. He later became the bestselling author of books about big stars like Frank Sinatra (*The Way You Wear Your Hat*), Johnny Carson (*Carson the Magnificent*), Hugh Heffner (*Hef's Little Black Book*), and Andy Kaufman (*Lost in the Funhouse*)... *I think of my time spent staring at Landecker doing his job (Can you imagine? Staring at a man doing his job?) from the glassed-off safety of that little WLS viewing room, wherein all DJs resembled captive zoo creatures with the most powerful microphones controlling the lives of us '70s chilluns; the ones who ran to Sears to get The Big 89 Surveys each week to see where the hits were charting as though life depended on it.*

Landecker (and to lesser degrees Sirott and J.J. Jeffrey) — these voices became actual men with the Best Jobs Ever! True, they were also guys clearly uncomfortable being stared at by punks like me, but here is why Landecker was my favorite. Whenever I came downtown to stare at him — he always, always, always stepped out to say hello, like he knew what his voice meant to us and, humble though he was, he did not want to disappoint. All I've ever done is remember that, and try to emulate it, even though I personally would never stand for being caged in a viewing room. Plus, who could look cooler than John anyway?

WHERE EVERYBODY KNOWS YOUR NAME

One night after I got off the air, we were heading up to Ann Arbor to celebrate my birthday. We had a VW Bug in those days, and the girls were still little enough to be able to sleep in the back. I know how bad this is going to sound, and believe me I'm not proud of it, but while they slept in the back, Judy and I were drinking wine and smoking a joint in the front seat… while I was driving.

Wouldn't you know it, I went a little too fast (c'mon, the speed limit was only 55), and the cops, the Michigan State Troopers no less, pulled us over. There was a mad scramble in the front seat. Judy hid the wine bottle under her dress, and I lit a cigarette to mask the smell of the joint. The trooper came up to the window, asked for my license and registration, and we sweated it out while he went back to his patrol car.

When he came back to the VW, he said: "Can I ask you a question?"

"Sure."

"Are you John Records Landecker from WLS?"

"Yes, I am," I answered.

The trooper looked back at his patrol car and screamed to his partner: "It's him!"

The partner came up to the car to meet me and shoot the shit for a few seconds. They asked where I was going, and I told them I was going home to Ann Arbor for my birthday. They could see from the license that I was telling the truth.

And while we were talking, I said, "Listen, I'm sorry I was speeding."

The trooper waved his hand at me and said: "That's OK!"

And they let me go.

JONATHON BRANDMEIER REMEMBERS

Johnny B on the power of WLS… *My pal Nudley and I used to pretend that we were Landecker and Sirott. He was Sirott, and I* was John Records. We would go 60 miles north of our hometown to this place called Long Lake Resort in Wapaca, Wisconsin. They had bands playing there, and chicks everywhere. We would get sort of dressed up and say that we were there scouting bands for WLS. People believed it. It worked every time. We either got free drinks, or got laid, or on a good night, both.

It worked so well, we took that act on the road. We were driving out to California to visit a buddy in Hollywood. I want to say we were maybe 19 or 20 at the oldest, and we were at this Holiday Inn in Denver. We only had enough money for one drink apiece (or Highballs, as we called 'em in those days). Anyway, there was a band playing, and we waited for them to break, and we went up and did our extreme bullshit, and I'm trying to talk like John Records: "Yeah, man, we're from WLS in Chicago, looking for some bands." And the guys said: "Really? You're from WLS? Get these guys some drinks."

It worked all over the country, man. That's how powerful WLS was in those days. And even if they knew what Landecker and Sirott looked like — I did sort of look like Landecker, and Nudley was blonde like Sirott. It's not like they could go on the internet in those days and match up the pictures. There was no way to check.

BILLBOARD PERSONALITY OF THE YEAR

In the mid '70s, *Billboard Magazine* had this big competition every year to name the air personality of the year. First you had to win the regional air personality of the year, and then that would qualify you for the national award. Well, one year I was nominated and won the regional award.

Now this was during a time when I was drinking *a lot* as will soon become evident. The night before the national awards dinner just happened to be the same night my pal Charlie Van Dyke was leaving WLS, and moving to Los Angeles for a new job. So, Charlie and I went out to Trader Vic's to celebrate. If you've never been to Trader Vic's, they specialize in those fruity drinks that get you smashed before you realize it.

That night was no exception.

Here's how smashed I got: I woke up in a first-class seat of an American Airlines jet, and had absolutely no idea where I was. When I looked out the window, I saw the Grand Canyon.

"What the hell?"

I had no idea how I got on this jet, (at least I had the good sense, even in my drunken blackout, to book first-class), but I wasn't with Charlie, and I wasn't with Judy. I was all alone. To make matters worse, I was supposed to work that night on WLS and hadn't asked permission to leave town.

To tell you the truth, I'm still not sure exactly what happened. The best I can figure is that I must have been convinced I was going to win that national *Billboard Magazine* award, which was being given out in LA, because that's where my flight was heading. When I landed, I got in touch with Charlie. He was shocked to hear from me too. This obviously wasn't a plan I had shared with him.

"What? You're here?"

And then I called the program director back in Chicago and told him where I was and what was happening. Let me tell you, that was not an easy call to make. They were not happy with me at WLS. I understand there was even a short conversation between the general manager and the program director about whether or not I should be fired.

Meanwhile, unbeknownst to me, the esteemed newsman Gil Gross and his wife had volunteered to babysit my kids. I found that out when Judy showed up in LA too. The two of us went to the *Billboard Magazine* Awards together.

Can you guess how I did?

Correct. I didn't win.

Ironically, a few years later (1977), I got a call from a reporter in Toronto during the weekend of the *Billboard Magazine* Awards.

"So, what's your reaction?" he asked.

"My reaction to what?"

"You've just been named *Billboard's* Air Personality of the Year!"

"WHAT?"

That's so typical of me. When I knew I had been nominated, I didn't win. But when I *did* win, I didn't even know I had been nominated.

FRED WINSTON *REMEMBERS*

Fred Winston is on the air before me every day now at WLS-FM. He and I have worked together several times, including that first stint at WLS in the 1970s. This is his take on that time all these years later... *I'm not sure if the talent made the facility legendary, or if the facility was so great that the talent became famous simply for being there. It's the old "which came first: the chicken or the egg" analogy.*

INFLUENCE PEDDLING

I've often wondered the same thing that Fred has. Over the years every WLS jock from that era has heard from radio personalities around the country that were inspired by what they heard on WLS. I can't tell you if we were the chicken or the egg, but we sure seemed to have an influence on the next generation of air personalities.

Rush Limbaugh used to be a rock jock, and was a huge fan of WLS, despite growing up in Missouri. He loved Larry Lujack; something he has said publicly many times, and even mentioned him in his memoirs. Rush patterned his entire delivery after Larry. Of course, all of us started out the same way, patterning ourselves after someone we admired, before we developed a style of our own. (To say the least, Rush has developed a style of his own.) Anyway, I met Rush a few years ago, and he told me that he once called me at home during his rock jock days to ask my advice about doing this format. I honestly don't remember the call. I know he was going by another name back then (Jeff Christie). According to Rush, I was eating a salad at the time. If he says so, it must be true, right?

Spike O'Dell hosted the #1 show in Chicago for many years at WGN. He wasn't from Chicago either, but grew up listening to WLS: *"When I was working in a factory on the banks of the Mississippi (The Quad Cities), I would listen to all of those WLS guys on The Big 89 and the guys at Super CFL. I remember thinking: 'Hey, these guys are having too much fun.' I wanted to do what they were doing. I loved 'em all. Fred Winston was great — he and Lyle Dean. Larry Lujack and Little Tommy with Animal Stories — that was tremendous. But to me, John Landecker was the best. I listened to him every night — and I still think he is the best rock jock that ever lived. The best of all time."*

Jonathon Brandmeier grew up in Fon Du Lac, Wisconsin… *"To me listening to John Landecker was appointment radio. I would look forward to six o'clock every night, just waiting for his show to begin. He didn't just talk. He had this rhythm in his voice. If Larry Lujack showed* us all that it was OK to be yourself on the air, John Records showed us not to forget the showbiz. Records was showbiz. He WORKED the music. He talked in rhythm with the music, on the beats; he became a part of the song. There was no better radio guy, pure Top 40 energy, no one better. Name me one guy that was better than John Records. No one was! In the whole country!

Let me give you an idea of the kind of impact he had on me. My father took my brothers and me fishing in Canada. Imagine, we were surrounded by this incredible scenery, breathtaking view, and here I was sitting in the boat with my crackling little transistor radio, waiting for six o'clock, so I could hear John Records Landecker booming on WLS. And I heard him too! In Thunder Bay, I heard him. I would have given anything to watch him in action.

To me, he was like Wolfman Jack was to those characters in American Graffiti. I imagined him in this tower somewhere, just mesmerizing us, just bringing it. Man, he was the best. I can still hear it in my head. All these years later I can still hear it. That's the kind of impact he had on me."

THE JOHN LANDECKER SOUND

Over the years a lot of people have asked me why it was that I sounded a little bit different than the other jocks on WLS. One of the great engineers I worked with, Alan Rosen, has an explanation for the radio-philes...

I started working with John his first night in his regular shift, and I discovered right away that there was something very different about him. As he was speaking on the air he looked at me and pointed to his headphones, indicating that something wasn't right. So, I tried to increase the level in John's headphones, and brought the music level down a little so he could hear himself better. After the first break he told me it still wasn't right, so I tried again, lowering the music level even more. I had John's mic going way into the red on the meter and the music level down around 40 percent so I didn't see how I could make him any louder.

I will never forget what John told me next. He said, "No no, I want the MUSIC louder and my mic brought down! I want to be INSIDE the record!!"

My mind started reeling. For one thing, No DJ had ever told me to bring his voice down before, and second, it DID sound amazing. When John did an introduction over the intro of a Chicago record, his voice was actually just a little lower than Peter Cetera's! It did put him inside the music and I think was a subliminal part of the Landecker show sound.

ENGINEERING A RECORD

WLS was a union station, so the engineers handled all of the controls, and that was an important job. I was lucky to have worked with a few really legendary engineers like Alan. There were also three old-timers that were great — Ralph Squires, John Husar (known to "Boogie Check" die-hards as J.J. Johnny) and Bob Ferguson (who once Xeroxed a picture of his butt), and some young, hungry and talented engineers like O.C. Gibson, Pam Murphy, Elaine Hinson, Ed Glab, Renee Tondelli and Marty Soehraman. These guys and gals were simply the best! (Ralph, John, Bob and Marty have all passed on).

In addition to being great engineers, they were all great with my kids. I brought my kids into the station quite a bit back in those days. I had to bring them to work with me or else I never would have seen them — when they had free time, I was working, and when I had free time, they were in school. We spent a lot of time together at WLS. The kids experienced all sorts of different things at the radio station, including a few things they definitely shouldn't have experienced.

For instance, WLS had a lot of contests requiring listeners to call in when they heard their names on the air. Of all the shows on WLS, I always had the most winners, which was a point of pride for me — it meant that I had the most loyal listeners. I found out many years later that there was a little more to it than that. It turns out that my daughter Amy, who was very young at the time, used to take the contest book with the names and phone numbers of the potential winners out of the studio, go into another room, and call the next person on the list. In her little kid voice, she'd say: "Hello, is this (insert name here)? It is? Oh. Tune in to WLS because they're about to call your name."

And all this time I thought I was so popular.

I don't even want to think about how many FCC rules and regulations this broke. Hopefully the statute of limitations ran out many decades ago.

YOU DON'T LIGHT UP MY LIFE

I always thought that our program director John Gehron had a tough job. On the one hand he was operating a Top 40 station in the purest sense of that genre. There were a limited number of hits on the playlist (that's what Top 40 means) and we had to repeat them over and over and over again, regardless of what kind of music it was. In the 1970s, the music was all over the map, so the hits could have been any type of song from hard rock to something like Debbie Boone's "You Light Up My Life."

There were a bunch of different ways to execute a format, but this is how WLS did it. We had four or five 95-minute stop watches in the studio and each one of them stood for a corresponding song (#1, #2, #3 or #4, etc.). When the light went off, you had to play the record that corresponded to that number next.

Now, if the song was a great rocker like "School's Out" by Alice Cooper or "Layla" by Eric Clapton, it wouldn't have bothered me as much. My problem was always with those wimpy namby-pamby syrupy pieces of crap like Debbie Boone's "You Light Up My Life."

I was doing nights! You gotta be rockin'! Well, one night, when Debbie Boone's song came up again, I had had about enough of this. The first thing I did was explain this whole stopwatch concept to the listeners. That was a big no-no. You don't explain things like that on the air. Secondly, I admitted that I couldn't stand "You Light Up My Life" by Debbie Boone, which was an even bigger no-no.

Then, just to be an asshole, I upped the ante.

"Here's what we're gonna do," I said. "For all you people that *have* to hear 'You Light Up My Life,' we're going to play it in installments. Right now we'll play you the first fifteen seconds of the song. In about a half an hour we'll play the next fifteen seconds."

By the time I was midway through this explanation, John Gehron, the program director, was in the studio. Now, with any other program director in any other situation, this would have been a fear-filled moment. But since he was who he was, and I was who I was, that's not how it went down.

"Look who's here!" I said. "It's our program director John Gehron. Let's put him on the air!"

He didn't like the bit — that was pretty obvious — but he didn't come in there to shut it down. He just came in to let me know that he knew I was doing it, and that he didn't approve. He more than likely didn't buy my semi-rational reason for doing it. I argued that there was at least *the possibility* that people were going to hang around for four hours just to see if I really was going to play the whole song that way. That's "time spent listening" baby; an important ratings measurement.

"OK, John," he sighed like he was speaking to a child. "This one time it's OK."

And I did play the whole song that way. The last fifteen seconds of my show that night was the last fifteen seconds of "You Light Up My Life."

Just an epilogue to this story, for the 20th anniversary of "You Light Up My Life" in 1997, I was reminiscing about this bit and it gave me an idea. Beginning in January 1997, we played 15 seconds of the song every *month*, and we didn't complete the song until December 1997. After we played the final fifteen seconds, we had Debbie Boone on the show to tell her the story. She got a big kick out of it.

> **JOHN GEHRON** *REMEMBERS*
>
> WLS Program director John Gehron... *I always felt like my job with John was similar to holding a helium balloon. I loved to see it fly, but if I let go of the string, it would have floated out of the atmosphere. He was wildly creative, and he had some unbelievably great ideas, but sometimes he needed someone to hold that string a little bit.*

THE WORST SONGS EVER

I did hate "You Light Up My Life," but it is definitely not the only lame song we had to play in the 1970s. I've given this a lot of thought, and I present for you now, the ten worst songs we played on WLS during that decade...

   10. "Heartbeat, It's a Lovebeat" by the DeFranco Family
   9. "(You're) Having My Baby" by Paul Anka
   8. "Muskrat Love" by the Captain and Tennille
   7. "I've Never Been to Me" by Charlene
   6. "One Tin Soldier" by Coven
   5. "Feelings" by Morris Albert
   4. "You Light Up My Life" by Debbie Boone
   3. "Seasons in the Sun" by Terry Jacks
   2. "The Night Chicago Died" by Paper Lace

And the number one worst song of the 1970s...

   1. "Billy Don't Be a Hero" by Bo Donaldson and the Heywoods

ELVIS & LARRY

I've got one more Larry Lujack story from that WLS era. I was at the station when the news came across the wire that Elvis had died (August 16, 1977). The first thing that crossed my mind was that nobody in the world would want to know this information more than Larry Lujack. (When someone calls you a Philadelphia fuck for not loving Elvis, you have a tendency to remember that sort of thing.)

So, I called him at home, and his wife answered.

"Judy," I said, "It's John Landecker. I've got something very important to tell Larry. Trust me; he's going to want to know about this."

"OK, hang on," she said.

A few seconds later Larry growled on the phone. "Yeah?"

"Larry, it's me, John Landecker. Elvis is dead."

"Who cares?" he growled again. "I'm taking a nap."

CHAPTER SEVEN
STAR TRIPPIN'

> The mid-to-late '70s brought us some of the biggest movie blockbusters of the decade, *Jaws* (1975), *Rocky* (1976) and *Star Wars* (1977), along with classic comedies by Mel Brooks (*Young Frankenstein* and *Blazing Saddles*). On television, ABC had a string of sitcom hits including *Happy Days*, *Laverne & Shirley*, and *Welcome Back Kotter*. Chicago sports teams were not good, but Walter Payton became one of the greatest football players in history. And in the world of music, gooey pop gave way to even more reviled genre, as disco became a worldwide craze.

To this day a lot of people associate me with the 1970s, but ironically, some important pop culture moments of the decade went by without my experiencing it.

You have to remember that I was doing nights in the pre-VCR days, so I couldn't watch prime time television. I was on the air opposite those shows. I didn't see a single episode of '70s hits like *Happy Days* or *Welcome Back Kotter* when they were on the air. For the most part, that wasn't a huge problem — I didn't really want to talk about my competition too much anyway. On the other hand, when stars from those shows were booked as guests on my show, I needed to find a way to get caught up in a hurry.

Bob Sirott, Al Rosen, and I pooled our money and went over to the Sony Store on Michigan Avenue to buy the first available video recording device. It was pricey and huge and clunky (in the ¾ inch format television stations used), and the tuner/timer only allowed one hour of recording time, but that was more than enough for my purposes. When Donnie Most (Ralph Malph) or Suzi Quatro (Pinky Tuscadero) were scheduled to appear, I could tape *Happy Days*. When John Travolta (Vinnie Barbarino) was coming on, I could tape *Welcome Back Kotter*. That was all I needed. It's a good thing I got it.

That John Travolta appearance became one of the most memorable of my career.

JOHN TRAVOLTA

Saturday Night Fever hadn't even come out yet, but thanks to *Welcome Back Kotter*, John Travolta was already on the verge of becoming a break out star. He had just released a record, and that's what he came to WLS to promote. I was the lucky one to get the interview, and it went very well. We got along great.

During that interview we agreed to meet the following day and do an appearance together at Woodfield Mall in Schaumburg Illinois. John's limo picked me up at my apartment, and I accompanied him to a few different stops along the way. The first stop was WGN Radio so he could be interviewed by Roy Leonard. After that we went to a hotel party room somewhere and met with a Travolta fan club of some kind. Then we drove out to Woodfield Mall in Schaumburg (suburban Chicago). As usual, I brought a tape recorder and recorded everything as it was happening, beginning in the back seat of a security vehicle. It was reality radio, if you will, before they called it that.

Now, Woodfield was expecting maybe two or three thousand kids to be there, which would have been great, but when we arrived, there were 30,000 girls in the middle of Woodfield Mall screaming at the top of their lungs! (I have never been to a Beatles concert, but I imagine it sounded just like this.) This huge crowd was screaming in an enclosed area, and the sound was echoing and reverberating and shaking the walls. It was positively deafening. I've never heard anything like it before or since.

I had tape rolling throughout the whole thing, and it's an amazing tape — you really get a feel for the mayhem. At one point you can hear a cop say, "My gun, my gun, my gun" because the force of the crowd literally forced his gun up and out of his holster. We finally got to where we were supposed to be, in the middle of this hysterical throng, and I got on the mic.

I told everyone they'd be on WLS between 8 and 9 that night, and then I said: "Give it up for Vinnie Barbarino!"

Total Bedlam. Shrill unbelievable screaming. I can't do it justice. I'm surprised the windows didn't shatter. Travolta got up there, and did his Vinnie Barbarino routine, the catch phrases from the show.

"What?"

"Where?"

"When?"

The crowd went insane for every word he said. Completely berserk.

(A full transcript of the bit as it aired on the radio is in the appendix.)

In the mayhem on the way out, Travolta and I got separated. I got knocked down and dragged out of there by two state cops. He got dragged out of there in a different direction. We were supposed to go to dinner that night, but that obviously never happened.

I played the tape on my show that night, and many other times over the years. I sent a copy of it to Travolta, and I believe it's stored along with some pictures and a few other things I sent in the archives of the Scientology headquarters in California. He sent me a nice note thanking me.

But that was far from the last time I saw or spoke with him. He later came back to promote *Saturday Night Fever* and the movie he was filming at the time, *Grease*. (If you listen to the raw tape of that interview, you can hear my daughter Tracy walking into the studio as we were taping it, and asking for me.)

A year or so after that, I was at home one night, and the phone rang. My wife answered it and handed it to me.

"John, it's John Travolta."

He was calling just to see how I was doing. This was during his heyday, the absolute peak of his celebrity. That's the kind of guy he was.

RADIO STAR WARS

When Star Wars came out, it was an ever bigger phenomenon. In fact, it was on the cover of Time Magazine the day we got a few of the movie's stars to appear on our station.

The WLS morning man was on vacation, so Bob Sirott was filling in for him that day. Bob had a phone interview scheduled with Carrie Fisher (Princess Leia). I was filling in for Bob on the afternoon show, and had Mark Hamill (Luke Skywalker) scheduled as an in-studio guest. Since we had access to two of the biggest stars from the movie, I came up with an idea for a bit, and wrote a script featuring all of us. Everyone agreed to participate.

I showed up at the station early in the morning and recorded Bob and Carrie Fisher reading their lines. Then I spent all day with the production guy, adding R2D2 sound effects, a Darth Vader voice (mine), music from the movie, and timing everything out. All of the pre-recorded segments were ready to go when I got on the air that day. The plan was to do the last part of the script, my interaction with Mark Hamill, live on the air. I really thought it would be easy to do. I don't know how many times I told the engineer the cue. All he had to do was hit a button at the right time, but when the time came, he messed it up.

We tried it again. He messed it up again.

It was messed up so many times I had to beg Mark Hamill to stay for an extra twenty minutes. We finally got it right and did a perfect take of the bit, and afterwards I edited it down even further, and it came out great. It was played on the air many times, and became a well-known bit. It really does feature the real actors from the movie, but if you hear the perfectly edited version, keep in mind that while we were actually doing the bit live on the air, it was a complete train wreck.

(The full transcript of that bit in the appendix.)

A PARASITE ON BOB SIROTT

Bob Sirott has always been a great interviewer, and when we both worked at WLS, there were several times he got interview opportunities with big stars. On those occasions, I inevitably became a parasite on Bob Sirott's body — hovering around to get an interview for my show too. One night Bob was taping an interview with Sylvester Stallone, with the idea of editing it, and playing it on the air the next day. Again, this was at the height of Sly's popularity — the film "Rocky" had made him one of the biggest stars in the country — so I asked Bob if I could get Sly live on the air with me after Sirott finished his interview. Bob graciously agreed.

My Stallone interview went pretty well, but I didn't really think it was extraordinary or special. The whole thing only lasted about seven minutes. So imagine my surprise a few weeks later, when a record label released it on an album. The A side had my entire interview with Sylvester Stallone. On the B-side, my interview questions were cut out, so anyone could pretend like they were interviewing Stallone. It came with a script. I have no idea why this was done. The interview wasn't that great — I'm sure Bob's interview was ten times better. No one ever asked me if they could use it, they just did.

The next time I latched onto Bob's show was the day he had Mel Brooks in the studio. You have to understand; to me Mel Brooks is the be all and end all. He is my comedy hero. I watched Bob's entire interview, just drooling at a chance to talk to him on my show too. When the interview ended, I made my move.

"Please, just stay another ten minutes," I begged.

"Sure," Mel responded. "What the heck."

And he did, and I loved every second of it. A few weeks later I even got a thank you letter in the mail from Mel Brooks. I still have that letter framed in my office, so I can tell you what it says, word for word.

Dated April 18, 1978 on 20th Century Fox letterhead, it says: *"Dear John, it was very fun to use up the first ten minutes of your show when we were in Chicago. You are a bearded pussycat. Please tender my best regards to nervous Jews and others at your site of broadcasting. All the best, Mel Brooks."*

STYX

I've known Dennis DeYoung, the leader of the band Styx, for many years. Dennis is a unique and complicated individual; very intelligent, a brilliant guy. The main reason we became friends was just a fluke. It was because I just happened to be the first disc jockey to play the Styx song "Lady" on the air on WLS.

Like most big AM stations at the time, WLS would not play songs on the air until they were hits. God forbid we put something on the air during any random fifteen minute listening span that wasn't a 100% proven hit, even if was recorded by a hugely popular local Chicago band like Chicago, Cheap Trick, REO Speedwagon, or Styx.

Styx was still on Wooden Nickel records, a local Chicago record label, and though they had a few regional hits like "Lorelei," WLS had never played any of their songs. Finally, when "Lady" came out, the powers that be decided it was time. Dennis was alerted to this, and was in his kitchen listening with his wife (the subject of the song); just waiting for the magical moment his hometown's biggest radio station would play his band's new song. I just happened to be the DJ on the air when it happened.

I said: "Styx, welcome to WLS!"

Dennis and his wife danced in the kitchen as the song played over our 50,000 watt clear-channel radio station that could be heard in thirty-seven states. This wasn't just a nice private moment for the couple. It was a career making moment for the band. They went on to become one of the largest acts in the world. That was the power of WLS at that time. We couldn't take a bad record and make it big, but we could take a good record and make it big. If that record hadn't gotten the exposure we gave it, it wouldn't have made it.

Dennis and I have seen each other many more times over the years — I've probably interviewed him on five different radio stations — and every time I do he is still appreciative of that first moment. He tells that story to this very day. He was on A&E recently and told the story. He told it on The Bonnie Hunt show. He told it on VH1's *Behind the Music*, and he even asked me to be on that show too. It's all very nice, because he really doesn't have to do that.

> **JIM SMITH** *REMEMBERS*
>
> Jim Smith was the music director at WLS who made the decision to play "Lady." This is how he remembers the story…
> *After we told Dennis DeYoung that WLS was going to play it, he asked how long we would play it, and I remember my exact answer: "Until it becomes a hit; and then it will go into regular rotation. Or until it has run its course in this category, and we'll replace it with something else." Dennis, of course, only heard the first part and has told the story innumerable times, then and since, that "Jim Smith says WLS is going to play 'Lady' until it becomes a hit!" Uh, not quite. Or was it? What happened next was beyond my expectations and possibly theirs too.*

MUSIC TO YOUR EARS

To give you an idea of the power of WLS' signal, I heard a rumor that the Allman Brothers listened to me in Georgia. I didn't really believe it until I got a call one night telling me the Allman Brothers were in town, and that Greg Allman was sending over a limo after my show so I could go hang out with him. I ended up drinking beer on stage behind the amps, and hung out with Greg and some chick (not Cher) at the Holiday Inn that night. (Nothing happened. We just hung out. Really. Honestly. I swear.)

Being on WLS also meant getting the very biggest interview opportunities, and no one was bigger than the Beatles. I did a pretty long telephone interview with George Harrison around the time he was going through the lawsuit about "My Sweet Lord." He had a new album out, and was coming to Chicago for a concert. Let me tell you, he was a *great* interview. He was friendly, courteous, ego-less, answered all of my questions without complaint — even about the lawsuit. He had a good time, and he was really funny. At the end of the interview I said to him, "Now you know George, I have to ask you the question that always gets asked. I don't want to ask, but I have to. George, will the Beatles ever get back together?"

"Never say never," he replied.

In addition to meeting, hanging out and interviewing musicians, we also often introduced them on the concert stage. One night I was asked to be the emcee at the International Amphitheater for a Shaun Cassidy concert. He was the big teen idol at the time, and the teenage girls were absolutely in love with him. When I got up on stage, I could have said absolutely anything and those girls in the audience would have screamed uncontrollably.

"My socks match!"

"WooooooooooooooooHoooooooooooooooo!"

I brought my daughters along to see the show. Tracy if I recall, chose to stay backstage, but Amy sat in the wings with me, on my lap. I had no idea this was going to happen, nobody told me, but when Shaun Cassidy sang his big hit "Da Doo Ron Ron," he sang it directly to Amy. (It wouldn't quite have the same impact today, but trust me; this was a huge deal in the 1970s.)

But while the Shaun Cassidy crowd loved us, the audience for the hipper bands thought AM radio sucked. They were into FM — you know, no static at all. Yet, we still somehow soldiered on broadcasting concerts from places like Alpine Valley, Wisconsin with bands like the Doobie Brothers, REO Speedwagon, and Kansas.

I learned a lesson early on at shows like that, and passed it on to the performers.

"Please do NOT thank WLS for providing the concert. If you do, they'll boo."

I took my own advice. I still introduced myself on stage as John Landecker from WLS, but I didn't wait a nano-second before I added "Give it up for the Doobie Brothers!"

Worked like a charm.

FINDING SPANGLES AND LEGITIMACY

For the occasion of my parents' twenty fifth wedding anniversary, I attended a show with my opera-loving college professor father. He decided he would take my mom and brother and me to a nightclub to see Peggy Lee. She was a pop star in the 1950s tradition; sort of a female big band crooner, Las Vegas-style. I was surprised my father even knew of her existence, let alone agreed to shell out quite a bit of money to attend her performance.

The nightclub in Detroit was called the Rooster Tail. It took its name from the plume of water that shot out of the racing boats on the Detroit River. It was gaudy, it was glitzy, it was showbiz; basically everything my parents were not. We got a great booth near the stage. Now remember, Dad was blind. He couldn't see what was happening, so while the orchestra was playing, my mother described what was going on to my father. The music was so loud my brother and I couldn't hear what she was saying, but as it turned out, she was describing Peggy Lee's glittering dress. I know this for a fact, because just as Peggy and the orchestra paused for a moment, my father's voice ripped through the silence declaring…

"SPANGLES?"

Whatever happened immediately thereafter has been erased from my memory, but I can assure you that from that day forward, anytime someone in our family mentioned "spangles" it was a showstopper — pun totally intended.

Despite that one night, and my popularity and success in Chicago, the disconnect with my father about popular culture and my career choice remained an issue for many years, until something dramatic happened to change it.

Scott Simon hosted a show on NPR called *All Things Considered*. One of those shows included a feature about radio, and part of that feature included me. It ran from coast to coast. Now you must realize, in university towns, National Public Radio is a very, very big deal, and at the University of Michigan, everyone my parents knew listened to Ann Arbor's NPR station, WUOM. They all heard me, and excitedly let my parents know.

I was suddenly, finally, very legitimate in my parents' eyes.

Thank you, NPR.

THEY'RE GONNA PUT ME IN THE MOVIES

In the '70s, one of my hobbies was making movies. I shot lots of home movies on Super 8mm film and taped soundtracks to play with them. They were good enough to show at parties for my friends from the radio station. We called these screenings "The Clique Film Festivals." Everyone who saw those films loved them, but that was probably because they were often the stars of the movies. I filmed quite a few of them at WLS.

My favorite home movie starred Wolfman Jack. Yes, the real Wolfman Jack.

Bob Sirott was on vacation, and Wolfman Jack was brought in to fill in for him. I probably drove him crazy running around and filming while he was on the air, although Wolfman and I also shared a common bond. As nighttime rockers we hated a lot of the lame music that AM radio played. The Wolfman had been on the air less than an hour when he decided that our playlist was crap.

"This is not what the Wolfman plays!"

Of course, after a few tunes of his own selection, the Wolfman was visited in the studio by our program director. I was filming from the control room through a glass window and captured that moment on film. Radio people always get a big kick out of watching that particular part… even the Wolfman had to put up with program directors. The Wolfman also gave me a great way to end the movie. He led a conga line out of the studio and into the hallway as the O'Jays sang "Love Train." (Epilogue: I was on the air after Wolfman that night, and noticed that he left an open pack of Kool cigarettes on the console. When I peeked inside the pack, it was filled with these funny looking cigarettes with twisted ends on them — certainly not Kools. I tried them later. I remember getting very hungry. And sort of horny too.)

After the good reception my home movies got, and the fun I had making them, I started thinking about taking this interest to the next level. It was always a fantasy of mine to become a filmmaker, so I enrolled at Columbia College in Chicago to take some film courses.

One class project involved making a 16 mm film with sound. I wrote a screenplay about a guy who was disabled playing high school football, but still sees himself playing the game and being a star years later. I thought it would be a better movie if I got some real football footage. At the time, Bob Sirott and I shared a secretary (in the professional sense), and she just happened to be married to the late Tim Weigel. Tim was arguably the best sportscaster Chicago has ever seen. He was more than just a great sportscaster, he was a great sport. He agreed to sneak me onto the sidelines of a Chicago Bears game to shoot some footage, as long as I came alone. So, I carried both the camera and the sound equipment on my back, and took all the light meter readings, and got the audio levels just right. I was really into it.

I was filming away on the sidelines when Walter Payton got the ball. He was heading right at me but was tackled about five yards from the sidelines. The thought of moving out of the way never entered my head. Anything for the shot! But when Walter hit the ground right by my feet, I believe I screamed… "HOLY SHIT!" That alerted the other press guys (network and local television reporters and cameramen, and newspaper reporters and photographers) to my presence on the field. They could tell I wasn't one of them.

"Who is that kid?" I heard. "What's he doing on the sidelines?!"

That experience turned out to be way cooler than the movie itself.

Another one of the highlights of my time at Columbia College was a film that sort of took on a life of its own. I enrolled in a film class taught by Jim Martin. He convinced me to participate in a 16 mm film called *Studio A: Profile of a Disc Jockey*. We got WLS' permission to let them come into the studio to film me in action. If you want to see it, the entire documentary is now on YouTube.

JIM MARTIN REMEMBERS

Jim Martin lives in Florida these days, but he remembers the making of that film very well… *I've always had an interest in* radio and after talking to John and listening to his show; I told him I thought his job would make a good documentary film. The idea was to bring the viewer into Studio "A" while John was on the air and let the viewer have a conversation with him. John and WLS agreed to let us do the documentary. It was a pleasure working with him and amazing to watch. He had no problem carrying on a conversation with us despite being constantly interrupted to go on the air and do his job. John would pick up the conversation as if it had never been broken.

After the film was edited, the Learning Corporation of America (LCA) offered us a deal. In the meantime the film won awards and ended up as one of the top ten documentaries at the American Film Festival. It was distributed by LCA for ten years to universities, colleges and schools with radio and television broadcasting programs. *Studio A – Profile of a Disc Jockey* also ran on the Nickelodeon cable TV channel.

EDDIE WEBB *REMEMBERS*

One of the people who saw *Profile of a Disc Jockey* on television is currently the nationally syndicated host of VH1 Classic Rock Nights, Eddie Webb... *I still remember it like it was yesterday. It was in January, and I was like 15 years old, living in Iowa, and WGN-TV aired this special show following John around the studio, asking him questions about the job — why he did it — what he loved about it. I was watching him in the WLS studio, doing his bit, doing his thing, and I was just MEZMERIZED. Since those days I've tried to listen to whatever Landecker stuff I could get my hands on; tapes, MP3s, you name it. He was tremendous — whatever he did made the music even better.*

> *I ended up having lunch with John a few years ago, and I was really nervous, more nervous than I was meeting any of the many rock stars I've met in the business.*

SIROTT LEAVES RADIO

While I was busy flirting with film, Bob Sirott was flirting with television. From the day I met him, Bob was determined to make the transition, and he wasn't afraid to pay his dues. I really admired his determination. He started going over to Channel 2 at noon to report on electronics for Lee Phillips, and would show up at the radio station for his afternoon show still wearing makeup. His duties continued to expand at the television station, and in 1979, Bob finally took the big leap and left WLS to pursue television full time.

He's never looked back. As of this writing, he's the co-anchor of the 9pm newscast (with Robin Robinson) on Fox-32 Chicago. I think he's really good on TV. He doesn't take himself seriously at all, and he is such a Chicago guy, he can immediately smell the real story when something happens in this town. Unfortunately, just a few years after Bob left WLS and a big local media story hit the headlines in Chicago, Bob sniffed out a real story about me.

CHAPTER EIGHT
THE BEGINNING OF THE END

The late '70s were the Jimmy Carter years in America. Three Mile Island made nuclear power really unpopular overnight. And we were struggling with an economy that was experiencing inflation. In the radio business, FM radio was starting to gain in popularity. The first two years of the 1980s brought us a year-long hostage drama, and the attempted assassinations of a new president, Ronald Reagan, and a new Pope, John Paul II. At the box office, George Lucas and Steven Spielberg ruled. They had the top hits in both 1980 (*The Empire Strikes Back*) and 1981 (*Raiders of the Lost Ark*). On television the nighttime soaps were king, and a record setting number of people watched the "Who Shot J.R." episode of *Dallas*. On the pop charts Pink Floyd told the children of the world they didn't need an education.

After Bob left, I was moved into his afternoon time slot. After doing radio for more than ten years, this was the first time in my career that I was ever given a drive-time shift. It was a little bit different than nights. For instance, during the night shift, big news stories rarely occurred. During the afternoon shift, they happened all the time. Probably the biggest story during my stint in the afternoon slot was the 1980 U.S. Olympic hockey team.

The 1980 Winter Olympics was on ABC. At the time, WLS was an ABC station, so we were privy to all the network feeds. There was usually no reason to use them for anything other than news and sports reports; we were still a music station. The jocks didn't mess with the feeds at all.

But on the day that the U.S. was taking on the Russians, the game took place in the afternoon, and the television network announced it would be played via tape delay during their prime time coverage. I suddenly realized that I could carry the last few minutes of the game on the air. I had the feed.

But who would do this on a music station?

I would.

I rolled tape on the last four minutes. When it was over, I went on the air and said, "Alright, we're going to play you the last few minutes of the USA-Russia hockey game. If you don't wanna know the score or who won, turn your radio off… BUT I WOULDN'T BE PLAYING IT IF WE LOST!"

KEVIN MATTHEWS REMEMBERS

Kevin Matthews grew up in Michigan and eventually became a big radio star in Chicago at WLUP, AM 1000… *When I was in college at Grand Valley State, I really started listening to Landecker. He was doing afternoons at the time. I can still vividly remember listening to John for the very first time. They had these WLS contest cards, and they would read a number, and instead of just telling people to get out their cards, John said: "go in your pants and whip it out." I thought — that is so cool! He was a rebel, and I loved the way he sounded on the air. He was really able to paint a picture. There was something about his cadence and pacing and style — and man, that guy had style — it was just so different than anything I'd ever heard.*

JOHN LENNON

Ironically, the biggest story of my time in the afternoon slot happened at night, and I wasn't on the air to talk about it. If you live long enough, certain events really stick in your mind. One of those, for me, was John Lennon's assassination. Culturally, obviously, it was a tragedy, but it was more than that to my generation. It burst the "will the Beatles get back together" bubble forever. George had just recently told me "never say never" about a Beatles reunion. Well, with John's death, you *could* say never. For Baby Boomers who had followed the Beatles since the beginning, this was highly significant — a certain part of our youth was now over.

I remember exactly what I was doing when I heard the news. I was watching Monday Night football and Howard Cosell broke the news to me and millions of others. That in itself is an indication of how much the Beatles had integrated themselves into the culture of the world. A rock musician being shot and killed ordinarily wouldn't have caused a news bulletin to interrupt regular broadcasting. But a Beatle, that was such big news, that the announcers themselves interrupted a *football* game. I know I'll never forget that moment, and I'm sure others around my age will also never forget where they were when they heard that news.

Who knew there would be Cirque de Soleil, and the Anthology, and a Beatles reissue every year for the next 30 years? At the time, it felt like it was all over. We didn't know that their music would literally live on forever. Nobody saw that longevity coming when we were kids.

AND THEN COMES DIVORCE

One thing that didn't live on forever was my marriage to Judy. After

12 years of marriage, and almost twenty years together, Judy and I got divorced.

It was really tough on the kids, no question. Amy told me she broke down and cried in school, and when the teacher asked her what was wrong, she said: "My parents are getting a divorce."

One of the other kids said: "Mine are divorced too."

And another one said "Mine too."

My generation has had its fair share of personal failings, but this is one of the biggest. For me personally, the divorce poured fuel onto the fire.

In no time at all, I was completely out of control.

SEX, DRUGS, AND ROCK AND ROLL

This was the era of sex, drugs, and rock and roll, and I did my best to be a part of it. All of my friends did drugs, and I found out pretty quickly that when drugs were involved, stupid things occurred. I bought this beautiful little sports car, an Alfa Romeo, and there were several times I could have been busted for drugs in that thing.

One night I was higher than a kite (on cocaine) and decided I wanted to see what that car could do, so I floored it on a Chicago side street. I must have been going 90 miles an hour, and out of the corner of my eye, I saw a cop car in an alley as I zoomed past. I knew it was all over, so I pulled over and waited for the cops to catch up to me. When they got to my car, I apologized.

"Sorry, officer," I said. "I just got the car, and well, I wanted to see how fast it could go."

The cop said: "Jesus, if you're going to do that, at least go out on the expressway!"

And that was that. He let me go. No repercussions.

Not too long after that, I was high as a kite again, and I decided that I had to go home and get some *more*. So, not even thinking about it, I pulled up to my townhouse and left the Alfa Romeo running. I went up to my place, and came back down to the car with a stash of coke on me. When I opened the car door, there was a cop sitting in the driver's seat. He scared the shit out of me.

"Is this your car?" he asked.

I assured him it was. He hollered over to his partner: "It's his ride!"

And he got out of the car and walked away. Once again, no repercussions.

I was even doing it while I was on the air. When the Rolling Stones were at Soldier Field, I was supposed to be doing phone reports during their performance. I had a gram of cocaine in my pocket in a small glass vial. For some reason I decided that this was a good time to climb up between the huge Soldier Field columns — what a dynamite place to take a hit of coke. Part of the ritual was tapping the bottom of the small glass container before opening it, but when I tapped it that night, the bottle broke into a million pieces, spilling my cocaine all over the Soldier Field concrete. It ruined my entire day. It didn't matter at all that I had tickets and backstage passes to the greatest band in rock and roll — dude, I just lost my stash.

Over the coming years my drug use expanded, and with the drugs, came the women. I had a relationship with one woman that involved getting really fucked up (by myself), calling her even if it was three in the morning, and then going over to her place.

Another girlfriend informed me that she and one of her girlfriends had "done a guy" together. I told her that I had never engaged in a threesome with two women before, so of course, she invited her friend over. Massive amounts of drugs were consumed and we got naked. In the movies and in men's fantasies, these are crazy, out of the world incredible experiences. Reality is a little different. Quite honestly, I didn't know what to do. I could have used an extra appendage. What was I supposed to do, go from girl to girl? Were they supposed to get together? How was this supposed to work? I don't know how it was for them, but for me it was a bit awkward. (But never being one to give up, the three of us did work on it for the rest of the weekend!)

I was pretty bad, no question about it, but as bad as I got during this time, I never did live up to the stereotype of the disc jockey in one way — my world did not include the groupie culture. Sure, there was that one girl in Philadelphia that would fuck any guy that worked in radio, and a female caller in Chicago that liked to call me up and tell me what she was doing to herself while I played "Why Can't We Be Friends" by War (or sometimes "The Cisco Kid"), but that was it.

PAULA

One winter night I went to work, and I decided that I was in the mood to party. So I called some friends that lived in Evanston to see what was going on. They said to come on out after my show, but they also asked me to do them a favor.

"Can you bring along Paula Mann?"

I was all over that. Paula lived on Lake Shore Drive and seemed really exotic to me. She was a model. She wore fur coats. Her father owned a company, and her mother was thirty years younger than her father. She had a lot of buzz happening; like something out of a magazine.

I picked her up in a Volkswagen Bug and drove out to Evanston and got completely hammered — I don't think she did, but I was completely trashed. I had taken mescaline or LSD or something similar. Under those conditions we started to hit it off. Maybe that's an ill-fated beginning right there — I don't recommend it.

We drove back to Chicago pretty late and everything was closed — but she said she knew a place we could get a bottle of champagne. We went to Gene & Georgetti's restaurant, which is one of the most famous steakhouses in a city known for their steakhouses. There was a big signed Frank Sinatra picture on the wall. Bob Dylan had signed a clock that they gave to Paula. I'm not going to say it was hip, but it was famous, and she had been going there her whole life. She knew the owners, and sure enough, they gave us a bottle of champagne.

We drove to the Adler Planetarium, which I think has the best view of the city. The Planetarium is right on the water, and if you're facing north you have this breathtaking view of the skyline. So we sat in my Volkswagen, in the dead of winter, with a bottle of champagne being chilled in a snow bank.

That was the beginning of our relationship.

Paula used to have to an expression — "Remind me to have a serious relationship sometime." She had this understanding with a boyfriend on the East Coast. They agreed that she could come back to Chicago in the summer and hook up with somebody, but only if she'd go back to him. The first time she did this to me, I was devastated. But I didn't stop going out with her. I was divorced, and had a few other relationships, a girlfriend here or there, but there was always this Paula hanging around, coming and going.

One night we went out to dinner with her mother, and we got really, really high on cocaine, and it was decided that we would fly to Las Vegas and get married — right then and there. Paula called her girlfriend in New York, and we called some friends in Chicago, and I was going to pay for this whole thing. The plan was to go to O'Hare and buy the tickets and just go to Las Vegas. Well, little did I know, her friend in New York called Paula's boyfriend in New York and told him what we were planning on doing. When we arrived at the airport, he was waiting for us there.

And Paula left with *him*.

NOT EXACTLY FATHER OF THE YEAR

One night I took my daughters to see the band Heart in concert, featuring the sisters Ann and Nancy Wilson. We not only got to see the show, we went back stage and met the band. I'll never forget that backstage setup. They brought all this furniture along with them so that their dressing room looked like a living room, complete with a couch and lamps and chairs.

We had a nice time talking to Ann. She was very friendly to me and my girls. Well, a few weeks later, Heart had another nearby concert, and I got a call from Heart's promoter.

"Would you like to come see the show in Milwaukee?" he asked. "Ann really enjoyed meeting you and would like to see you again."

For the record, I didn't go.

But it did offer a glimpse into something I would find out in even more vivid detail soon. A single father with two little girls is a chick magnet. That lesson became even more vivid when I took my girls on vacation.

By this time, I was definitely living a double life. I wanted to get fucked up all the time, but at the same time, I really wanted to be a good father too. Getting fucked up was no problem, but being a good father was a much bigger challenge. I was divorced, living alone, and going out with Paula when she was in town, but I needed to spend more time with my daughters.

I decided to take Tracy and Amy on a vacation to the Bahamas — just the three of us, not to some flashy resort, but an out of the way island with no night life or distractions — somewhere the three of us could spend quality time together, and I could simultaneously stay out trouble. My travel agent found us the perfect place. No phones. No bars. No trouble. In fact, there was only one dining hall for the entire island. Perfect!

After arriving and checking in, Tracy, Amy and I walked into the dining room for dinner. I spotted a potential problem immediately: two of the hottest women I had ever seen, wearing spiked heels, really tight t-shirts and spandex pants. I did my best to avoid them during dinner, but I heard some of the other guests talking, and found out that Playboy was doing a photo shoot on the island. These two women were Playboy models.

Cracks were beginning to show in my original vacation plan, but I was determined to be good. For the first couple of days I was successful. On the third day, I decided to call Paula using the only long distance phone on the island. When Tracy, Amy, and I got to the phone, guess who was ahead of us in line? The same two girls. This time they were wearing heels and bikinis. But still, I was good. The next evening Tracy, Amy and I were having dinner, and on the way out we decided to check out this little dance floor next to the dining room. An elderly Jewish couple from New York came over.

"Oh how cute you are," they said. "A father and his daughters on vacation together."

"Why thank you very much," I said.

"Listen," the woman said, "I've got two people you really have to meet."

That was when the guy who likes to get fucked up but still wants to be a good father was formally introduced to the two Playboy models. As it turns out, they were both from England and said they'd be there for the week. Oddly enough, the Playmates really hit it off with my daughters, so the five of us began sharing meals in the dining hall every day.

The brunette (Marilyn) and I had an instant chemistry. So, one night after the children went to bed, Marilyn and I went to bed. This was well before the AIDS crisis, and I wasn't a condom guy, so Marilyn used contraceptive foam. It was the first time I had run into that particular methodology, and it wasn't exactly my favorite. It was like taking a shave with a dick razor. I wanted to get there, but first I had to get through this soft creamy topping. The next night after dinner, the kids were in bed, and Marilyn and I were strolling in the Bahamian moonlight on the island golf course. Romance was in the air, as Marilyn and I reclined on the soft surface of one of the course's putting greens.

"Wait," she said, hopping up. "My skin! I have to hug a tree tomorrow."

Nothing like having to hug a tree the next day to take the heat out of a moment. I thought I had heard them all — "I have a headache," "I'm not in the mood," but never "I have to hug a tree in the morning." That was a first for me, and also the last opportunity Marilyn and I had together. We exchanged numbers, but I never heard from her again.

The guy that wanted to get fucked up and still be good father was ready to go back to Chicago. The next day we had to take a little plane to a different island, Grand Bahama Island, and from there, fly home. But when we got to the airport, we discovered that some unrest in Haiti (where our flight was coming from) was causing a delay. They told us we wouldn't be leaving for a few hours.

I made the acquaintance of a few other travelers going to Chicago, and someone decided that we should get a few beers. A few beers couldn't hurt, right? After a few beers, and a few more hours, our flight was officially cancelled. The airline agreed to pay for a taxi to take us to town, and put us up for the night in a hotel, but there were no taxis. There was only a white stretch limo parked outside the airport. Under the circumstances, it qualified as a taxi, so all of us piled in. My recent beer-buddy acquaintances, my daughters, and me. We were getting ready to leave when one of the other passengers made a rather bizarre announcement.

"I heard a small plane carrying marijuana to the US crashed in the jungle," he said. "I know where it is, and if we drive out there, I can get us some pot."

Well, who could say no to something like that? The limo drove out into the country in the pitch black darkness until the guy suddenly yelled "STOP!" He jumped out of the car, disappeared into the underbrush, and we waited in the spooky jungle darkness. Within a few minutes, he came back with a bag of marijuana.

"Alright!"

Was I setting a fine example for my children or what?

It was about 2am when we finally got back to town. We had dinner at a Pizza Hut before going to a hotel for the night. Thank God we got on a flight to Chicago the next day. Who knows what else could have happened in this place I was guaranteed to stay out of trouble.

JEFFERSON STARSHIP

Around this time, a momentous political event happened in Chicago. The city elected its first female mayor, Jane Byrne. By a strange twist of fate, Byrne became the Mayor of Chicago around the same time the song "Jane" by Jefferson Starship became a hit.

I had the idea to do a parody song about our mayor to the tune of that song. This is another story about the power of WLS. Because of who we were, and the number of listeners WLS had, someone actually managed to get Jefferson Starship to send me a mix of the song, recorded by the actual band, without any lead vocal on it.

I decided, in my grandiosity, that this wasn't big enough. Now that I'm looking back at this, I can't even begin to understand how in the world I pulled this off, but I did. I flew down to Dallas where Jefferson Starship was performing, and the record company flew in Jefferson Starship's producer Ron Nevison with the original tracks to the song. Even though I was all fucked up on coke and couldn't sing for shit, with the use of technical wizardry, Nevison somehow managed to put together a passable version of the song.

The hotel that night was wild. Just imagine, all of these people were staying there at the same time: Jefferson Starship, Molly Hatchet, Michelle Phillips from the Mamas and the Papas, and a former member of the Brady Bunch. It was quite the scene. The day after the recording, Paul Kantner, Nevison, Paula and I drove into Dallas. Kantner had some pot and lit up a joint in the car, but before passing it he warned me: "It's really strong stuff."

Paul was right.

He also said that Grace Slick told him that the shopping center we were going to reminded her of Oz. OK, Grace, if you say so.

My parody of "Jane" got a good reaction on the air, but it wasn't the only song I wrote about Jane Byrne. Around this time, I hung out with a band called The Kind. After I got off the air, I would go out and see these guys, get drunk, go up on stage, and sing "Gloria" with them. Eventually I got The Kind to back me on another parody song about Jane Byrne called "Cabrini Green" which was done to the AC/DC song "Dirty Deeds Done Dirt Cheap." It was about her controversial and bizarre decision to move into the Cabrini Green housing projects to prove that they really were safe. *(The lyrics of that parody can be found in the appendix.)*

THE END OF THE LINE AT WLS

I was doing 2:30-7pm every day. I was single, dating a model, and getting so blasted every night that the first thing I did every morning after waking up around noon was head over to the Burger King and get some grease in my system so I could do something that passed for a show. In addition to the changes going on in my life though, the entire radio landscape was changing. FM radio was becoming the "hip thing."

I remember going to ChicagoFest on Navy Pier. I was in the WLS van, and some kid across the way gave us the finger and screamed "AM SUCKS!" They had to restrain me from getting out of the van and going after that asshole. I wasn't taking it so well.

At high school assemblies I started hearing the phrase "Disco Sucks." Pretty soon I was hearing it at every school. So, I recorded the kids screaming it, and every time I played a disco song at night, I would play their "Disco Sucks!" chant over the record. I thought it was important to do that, because I knew how the kids felt, and I was supposed to be the hip jock.

That got me called into the general manager's office. Not because I was breaking or mocking our format, but because parents were complaining we used the word "suck" on the air. They thought this was some sort of an oral sex reference. I tried to explain to him that kids didn't use the word that way, that it was just an adjective that could refer to anything: "the hat sucks" or "the chair sucks" or anything at all.

They wouldn't believe me, and I was insistent.

"Are you telling me that if we don't say 'Disco Sucks' that it will hurt our ratings?" the general manager asked.

"Yes!" I answered.

A few months later Steve Dahl did Disco Demolition at Sox Park; an event that was front page news. It was a national story. It was huge. And I was totally pissed off. Not at Steve, this had nothing to do with Steve. I was mad at WLS management. In my opinion Steve Dahl is easily one of the most talented broadcasters in the history of radio; a groundbreaker, a chance taker, insanely creative, and innately hysterical. He has the ability to be talking about absolutely nothing and you still can't turn him off. At the time, he was considered a "shock jock."

On the other hand, I wasn't even allowed to say "suck" on the air. I was certain that there was no way a station like mine, the standard bearer of the youth of America, the official "anti-suck" station, would ever employ someone like Steve. As I learned from the movie *The Long Kiss Goodnight*, never make an assumption, because you make an ass out of "u" and "umption."

ABC had two radio properties in Chicago: WLS-AM, and downstairs on the fourth floor, WLS-FM. WLS-FM had tried various different formats over the years, but at that time was simply simulcasting the AM. I thought that was great. For years the kids had told me that AM radio sucked, but now there was a chance for me to be on FM as well as AM.

Not so fast! You can probably see where this was headed. ABC hired Steve Dahl to work 2:30-7pm on WLS-FM. In fact, the newspaper headline said: "Steve Dahl to do afternoons on WLS." It didn't say whether it was AM or FM and it didn't mention me. How did I feel about this? In my mind it sounded something like this… "John, you are a sucky AM disc jockey and the epitome of everything that is unhip in radio, and we just hired the coolest hippest mofo in radio to go up against you in an apparent rewriting of our company's moral code."

It wasn't about Steve. It was about a company that had spent years telling me things had to be done a certain way, suddenly doing a complete 180, with yours truly on the wrong end. I felt betrayed. I was hurt; extremely upset.

Bob Sirott was working as an entertainment reporter for the local CBS-TV affiliate when this story broke, and decided to file a story on Steve's hiring. Did he go to Steve? No. Did he go to WLS management? No. He came to me. He could smell there was a story brewing there, and he was right.

When he asked me how I felt about it I said: "I've been stabbed in the back."

As you can imagine, that did not go over very well, but what the hell was I supposed to say? "It's going to be great having Steve Dahl as part of the WLS family. He is a great talent and will undoubtedly kick my ass in the ratings."

Unbeknownst to everyone involved, I had been approached by a radio station in Canada to do mornings just before this happened.

In fact, I had already flown up to Toronto and checked out the station and the city. The offer from Canada was a good one. The money was the same as I was making at WLS, and the station was willing to pay for airfare from Chicago to Toronto twice a month so I could see my kids, and they were going to pay my kids' private school tuition. To say that I left to go to CFTR in Toronto because of Steve Dahl is not a correct statement. I had been talking to Bill Gable and Jim Sword at Rogers Broadcasting for months and was very excited about joining them. They ran a class operation all the way.

I took the offer, said goodbye to Chicago and left.

I love this picture of my mom and dad with my dad's first leader dog Mickey.
(From my personal collection)

Casual Day at U-High. (From my personal collection)

Fullback John Landecker of the U-High Cubs. This ran in the local paper. I'm sure number 74 told his friends he tackled me. I'm sure he didn't. (From my personal collection)

I was the music director of WERX in Wyoming, Michigan.
The station signed off at sunset. (From my personal collection)

College-age John Landecker for WILS Lansing, Michigan.
(From my personal collection)

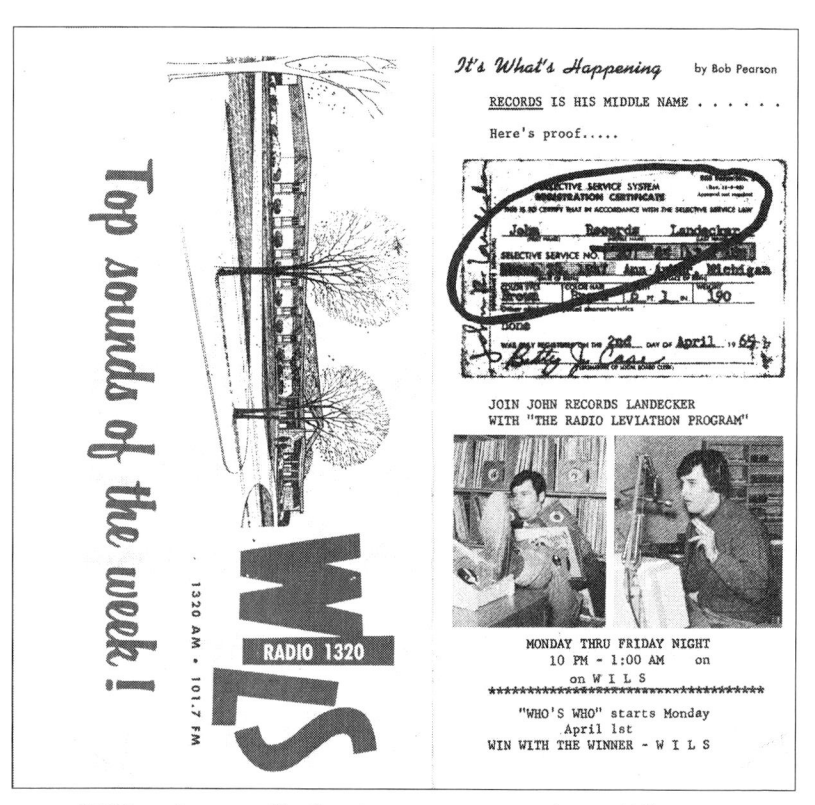

WILS music survey. The first time anyone promoted my middle name.
(From my personal collection)

RECORDS TRULY IS MY MIDDLE NAME

Rare photo inside the studios of WILS. (From my personal collection)

Ladies and Gentleman…Scott Walker. (From my personal collection)

A promotional piece by WIBG. (From my personal collection)

the WiBBAGE report

VOL. 1 — A Bi Monthly Publication of the Buckley Broadcasting Corporation — NO. 1

30,000 PEOPLE SEE "LEON" FREE

With almost hypnotic obedience, 30,000 young people made their way to a football field in the suburban town of Conshohocken on Monday, August 9th, to revel in the magnetic sounds of the rock world's newest Pied Piper.... Leon Russell. Bulging at the seams the whole field appeared to rock, as thousands of bodies began swaying to the soulful beat which roared from the mammoth speakers on stage. As Leon Russell and his Shelter People mounted the stage and began to play, the audience moved through the security barriers and tightly swarmed around the stage. To keep the crowd at a minimum, WIBG Radio kept the actual site under wraps, giving clues to listeners to help them find the location. And they did 30,000 people figured it out and arrived on the scene for an evening of free, peaceful entertainment.

This isn't just a survey. This is the very ambitious WIBBAGE report from WIBG in Philadelphia. It has extra meaning for me because it features Long John and Don Wade. (From my personal collection)

The Music Scene
by Sandy Mirzoeff & Long John Wade

the WIBBAGE report

WIBG - Philadelphia
effective 9-1-71
1. Uncle Albert - Paul & Linda McCartney
2. Go Away Little Girl - Donny Osmond
3. Maggie May/Reason To Believe - Rod Stewart
4. Ain't No Sunshine - Bill Withers
5. Signs - 5 Man Electrical Band
6. I Just Want To Celebrate - Rare Earth
7. Smiling Faces Sometimes - Undisputed Truth
8. Do You Know What I Mean - Lee Michaels
9. Spanish Harlem - Aretha Franklin
10. Take Me Home Country Road - John Denver

Hitbounds
Chirpy Chirpy Cheep Cheep - Mac & Katie Kissoon
Can't Go On Living - Nat Turner Rebellions
It's A Crying Shame - Gayle McCormick
Questions '67 & '68/I'm A Man - Chicago
I'm Still Waiting - Diana Ross

Hot Happenings
Mother Freedom - Bread
So Far Away - Carole King
Yo Yo - Donny Osmond

WDRC - Hartford, Conn.
effective 9-3-71
1. Go Away Little Girl - Donny Osmond
2. Uncle Albert - Paul & Linda McCartney
3. Maggie May - Rod Stewart
4. Signs - 5 Man Electrical Band
5. Whatcha See Is Whatcha Get - Dramatics
6. I Woke Up In Love This Morning - Partridge Family
7. The Night They Drove Old Dixie Down - Joan Baez
8. Ain't No Sunshine - Bill Withers
9. Take Me Home Country Road - John Denver
10. The Story In Your Eyes - Moody Blues

KOL - Seattle, Washington
effective 9-3-71
1. Go Away Little Girl - Donny Osmond
2. Sweet City Woman - Stampeders
3. Maggie May - Rod Stewart
4. Smiling Faces Sometimes - Undisputed Truth
5. Ain't No Sunshine - Bill Withers
6. Where Evil Grows - Poppy Family
7. Do You Know What I Mean - Lee Michaels
8. The Wedding Song - Paul Stookey
9. Colour My World - Chicago
10. I Hear Those Church Bells Ringing - Dusk

KFRC - San Francisco, Calif.
effective 9-6-71
1. Uncle Albert - Paul & Linda McCartney
2. Smiling Faces Sometimes - Undisputed Truth
3. Go Away Little Girl - Donny Osmond
4. Ain't No Sunshine - Bill Withers
5. The Night They Drove Old Dixie Down - Joan Baez
6. Saturday Morning Confusion - Bobby Russell
7. Maggie May - Rod Stewart
8. Sweet City Woman - Stampeders
9. If You Really Love Me - Stevie Wonder
10. Whatcha See Is Whatcha Get - Dramatics

CKLW - Detroit, Michigan
effective 9-6-71
1. Go Away Little Girl - Donny Osmond
2. Uncle Albert - Paul & Linda McCartney
3. The Love We Had - Dells
4. Maggie May - Rod Stewart
5. A Natural Man - Lou Rawls
6. Trapped In A Thing Called Love - Denise LaSalle
7. Stop, Look & Listen - Stylistics
8. Yo Yo - Osmonds
9. Spanish Harlem - Aretha Franklin
10. If You Really Love Me - Stevie Wonder

KHJ - Los Angeles, Calif.
effective 9-3-71
1. Liar - 3 Dog Nite
2. Smiling Faces Sometimes - Undisputed Truth
3. Spanish Harlem - Aretha Franklin
4. Riders On The Storm - Doors
5. Whatcha See Is Whatcha Get - Dramatics
6. Ain't No Sunshine - Bill Withers
7. If Not For You - Olivia Newton John
8. I Just Want To Celebrate - Rare Earth
9. Do You Know What I Mean - Lee Michaels
10. Mercy Mercy Me (The Ecology) - Marvin Gaye

WMAK - Nashville, Tennessee
effective - Wednesday - 9-1-71
1. Uncle Albert/Admiral Halsey - Paul & Linda McCartney
2. Go Away Little Girl - Donny Osmond
3. The Night They Drove Old Dixie Down - Joan Baez
4. Smiling Faces Sometimes - Undisputed Truth
5. Ain't No Sunshine - Bill Withers
6. Chirpy Chirpy Cheep Cheep - Mack & Katie Kissoon
7. Do You Know What I Mean - Lee Michaels
8. Liar - Three Dog Night
9. Maggie May - Rod Stewart
10. Sweet City Woman - Stampeders

GREAT BRITAIN - London
effective - Monday - 9-6-71
1. I'm Still Waiting - Diana Ross
2. Never Ending Song Of Love - New Seekers
3. What Are You Doing Sunday - Dawn
4. Get It On - T Rex
5. In My Own Way - Family
6. Let Your Yeah Be Yeah - Pioneers
7. Devil's Answer - Atomic Rooster
8. Soldier Blue - Buffy Sainte Marie
9. Co Co - Sweet
10. Bengla Desh - George Harrison

happenings

NEW JERSEY STATE FAIR
AT TRENTON

WIBG PRESENTS

FRI. SEPT. 17
TICKET INFORMATION AT ALL TICKETRON LOCATIONS

The RASCALS
EXTRA ADDED!
GRASS ROOTS
BROOKLYN BRIDGE ♫ WISHBONE ASH

WIBBAGE report from WIBG in Philadelphia, page 2.
(From my personal collection)

REFLECTIONS
by Janis Kerrigan

One of the coldest movies to hit the screen, Carnal Knowledge demonstrates men and women to be nothing more than organs, engaging in sexual gymnastics. With almost no plot to speak of, the film follows the sensual lives of two men from the beginning of their somewhat humorous conquests in college to their not so rewarding 40's. Although the subject matter is slightly tedious, the performers efforts make up for the shallow story line, proving the genius of Director Mike Nichols. Folk Singer Arthur Garfunkel's portrayal of a naive pre-med student, is surprisingly genuine. And Jack Nicholsons ability to mold lines into any form, has never been so compellingly evident as it is during his role of Jonathan, a smooth character, out for all he can get. As for the ladies, under Nichols expert guidance, Candice Bergen is able to show concentrated acting for the first time since "The Group." But the big shocker is Ann Margret, who sheds her tap shoes and giddy school girl image, emerging a seasoned actress. As a rather rumpled, over-used Bobbie, Ann displays exciting dramatic talents which were never apparent, making Carnal Knowledge a stepping stone for bigger and more meaningful roles to broaden her career.

* *

ONE OF THE TOP TEN LP ALBUMS OF THE WEEK IN USA

EVERY GOOD BOY DESERVES FAVOUR
Moody Blues (Threshold)

Many undergrounders taunt the group as being the most sensuous and versatile of them all. "Story In Your Eyes" and "One More Time To Live" are the excellent tracks along with others. Quite an experience.

OUTLOOK
by Bob Daleigh

The temper of young audiences continues to be as unpredictable as a Bhrama bull. Except for one bright spot, this has been a bummer of a summer for music festivals.

First, the ironically titled "Celebration of Life" in Louisiana turned out to be a celebration of death. Before that week long event, promoter Steve Kapelow told me how carefully it was all being handled and planned. "Top groups in the country, safety, security . . . . this is the way to run a festival". Well, the security force turned out to be a local cycle gang armed with chains; the music came from bands no one had ever heard of; and three people wound up dead.

The jazz weekend at Newport had all the organization the "Celebration" lacked . . . . its professionally handled and always well planned, but this year that didn't help. In the middle of a Dionne Warwick song, scores of hoods busted thru the fences and stormed the grounds threatening life and property. The rest of the acts had to be cancelled in the wake of this 'new barbarism.'

Tent city never got off the ground. It folded before opening. Andy Harabulya told me he had a beautiful park, a lake, showers, camping facilities and entertainment . . . . all for just $6. He expected to attract thousands of the kids travelling throughout the U.S. and Canada. Andy now faces criminal charges for fraud.

The one bright spot of the summer happened right here . . . . 30,000 people filled "A" Field in Conshohocken for the free Leon Russell gig; and you know what happened . . . . nothing; except that 30,000 had a ball. Proof that these things can come off . . . . but sadly, this is the exception and not the rule. How do we turn it around? Maybe if you don't want festivals to become totally obsolete, the majority should stand up and sound off for your rights. You can get hassled by freaks and well as by fuzz.

the WIBBAGE report

Faces
by Rick Menapace

Let's see now. This is our first issue. And they've asked me to write a few words about music. But writing a "few" words about music is only slightly harder than printing the entire Manhattan phone book on a pinhead.

But let's try. And let's start by saying that, at last, things are beginning to look up again.

They were pretty bad for awhile. I mean, I somehow couldn't reconcile myself to the fact that people like John Mayall were relegated to "bargain" bins in Woolworths, while tripe like Grand Funk Railroad were raking in money hand over proverbial fist.

But even now, while there seem to be some fairly decent and innovative, yet "emotional", groups releasing some excellent material, at long last. I can't help but wonder how many of them will wind up "2 for $2.98".

Let's put it a different way. If you don't find yourself walking into record stores and demanding things by John McLaughlin, Randy Newman, Jesse Winchester, Audience, Soft Machine, the Allman Brothers, Dr. John, New Riders of the Purple Sage (or Grateful Dead), Alice Coltrane, among a few longstanding others like the Who or the Airplane, then maybe there is something wrong with you . . . . or me . . . . or us . . . . or rock.

* * * * * * * * * * * *

ONE OF THE TOP TEN LP'S OF THE WEEK

TAPESTRY – Carole King (Ode)

What more is to be said for Carole and her LP "Tapestry." The masterpiece has been number one on the LP charts for over 3 months and she is approaching the 3 million mark shortly. Try "You've Got A Friend" and "Smackwater Jack" not to mention "It's Too Late" and "So Far Away" her latest two singles. Compare "Friend" with James Taylor's version. A must LP for any music lover.

WIBBAGE report from WIBG in Philadelphia, page 3.
(From my personal collection)

RECORDS TRULY IS MY MIDDLE NAME

THE WADE BOYS

LONG JOHN WADE — 3 TO 6 PM   DON WADE — 6 TO 9 AM

THE ONLY BROTHER ACT IN TOWN!

| Send me 17 issues of WIBBAGE REPORT and my FREE ALBUM first 100 subscribers | 17 issues for $2.00
3 DAYS BEFORE IT HITS THE RECORD SHOPS
WIBG, 117 Ridge Pike, Lafayette Hills, Pa. 19444
Name_____
Address_____
City_____ State_____ Zip_____ |

the **WIBBAGE** report

WIBG RADIO 99 PHILADELPHIA/117 RIDGE PIKE/LAFAYETTE HILL, PA. 19444/CODE 215/242-6300

WIBBAGE report from WIBG in Philadelphia, back cover.
(From my personal collection)

In the motorcycle photo, left to right: Ed Richards, Joe Niagra, Hy Lit, Joey Reynolds, Gary Mitchell, John Landecker. (From my personal collection)

RECORDS TRULY IS MY MIDDLE NAME

In thoughtful repose. One of my earliest WLS promo shots.
(From my personal collection)

WLS staff with J.J. Jeffrey, Dick Sainte, Bill Bailey, John Landecker, Chuck Knapp, Charlie Van Dyke, and Fred Winston. (From the John Gehron collection)

RECORDS TRULY IS MY MIDDLE NAME

John Records Landecker
6 P.M. to 10 P.M.

Anyway you look at him, the listening is great.

He's intelligent. Intriguing. Irreverent. Insane. (He sometimes thinks he's President Nixon.)

He's John Records Landecker, and Records truly is his middle name. (It was his mother's maiden name.) His carefree wit, his unique sense of humor, his music, and his recently recorded impressions of the President have made him the hottest personality in town. He not only topped all of his competition, he's won over one-third of the entire teen rock listening audience in Chicago. That's success, and nothing sells like success.

"Nothing should be taken too seriously," he says. "People should laugh at themselves." So he does. And with WLS' 50,000 watts of clear channel, he has the entire country laughing with him.

WLS MUSICRADIO 89
WLS MUSICRADIO 89
WLS MUSICRADIO 89
WLS MUSICRADIO 89
WLS MUSICRADIO 89

WLS Promo Piece. (From my personal collection)

WLS MUSICRADIO 89
45 RPM
2:45
Side 2
M7566B
Make A Date With Watergate
John Records Loudecker

"Make a Date with a Watergate" with my name misspelled.
(From my personal collection)

RECORDS TRULY IS MY MIDDLE NAME

John Travolta and I are standing in the midst of 30,000 screaming teenage girls at the Woodfield Mall. (From my personal collection)

Ralph Malph (Donnie Most) visiting with Bob Sirott and me in the WLS lobby during the heyday of *Happy Days*. (From my personal collection)

Bob Sirott set up this photo shoot so we could be like the Fonz in *Happy Days*. I have no idea who the girl is. (From my personal collection)

Bob Sirott and I on the WLS Shamrocks for Dystrophy float in the St. Patrick's Day parade. (From my personal collection)

Sure is bright in here. Belushi and Ackroyd in the WLS Studio. (From the John Gehron collection)

RECORDS TRULY IS MY MIDDLE NAME

WLS staff with Steve King, Bob Sirott, Yvonne Daniels, John Landecker, Fred Winston, and J.J. Jeffrey. (From my personal collection)

Larry Lujack and I in the WLS jock lounge. I'm on at 6pm. He's on at 5:30am. Why is he still here? Because he works very hard. (From the John Gehron collection)

You can't tell from the photo, but Stevie Nicks and I are at a party for Fleetwood Mac at the Playboy Mansion. I have no idea what she's pointing to.
(From my personal collection)

Bob Sirott and I with the Bay City Rollers at Comiskey Park.
S-A-T-U-R-D-A-Y Night! (From the John Gehron collection)

Rick Nielson from Cheap Trick pays a visit to the studio to borrow the phone. (From my personal collection)

In the broadcast booth with Harry Caray at Comiskey Park during a Chicago White Sox game. (From the John Gehron collection)

I did a promotion with Great America as the first person to ride the Tidal Wave. This is my daredevil outfit. (From the John Gehron collection)

JOHN LANDECKER
CFTR 680

CFTR promo shot. (From my personal collection)

RECORDS TRULY IS MY MIDDLE NAME

RIPLEY INTERNATIONAL LTD.
10 Price Street, Toronto, Ontario, Canada M4W 1Z4 Telephone (416) 962-6220

10th September, 1981.

Mr. John Records Landecker,
CFTR 680,
25 Adelaide Street East,
Toronto,
Ontario M5C 1H3.

Dear Mr. Landecker,

Thank you for your letter and the photo-copy of your birth certificate. After reading it, not only were we delighted to see your name really is John Records Landecker, but also that your mother's name being Marjory Victoria Records could qualify for a cartoon if chosen by our editorial staff.

As soon as we are informed that either of the suggestions have been accepted, we will notify you and send copies of the cartoon. In the meantime, we are enclosing a complimentary pass to any of the museums owned and operated by this company, as set out on the attached list. We are also enclosing a current pocketbook list, and should you be interested in purchasing any, please do not hesitate to contact us here at the above address.

Thank you for your enthusiasm, and keep up the good work with the early morning radio show!

Yours truly,
RIPLEY INTERNATIONAL LIMITED

Janet Florio (Mrs.)
Research and Exhibits.

jsf:Enc.

The letter sent to me by Ripley's. Believe it or not, I got in.
(From my personal collection)

> **American Broadcasting Companies, Inc. Memorandum**
>
> Department: WLS PROGRAMMING
> To: Jocks
> From: John Gehron
> Date: January 5, 1987
> Subject:
>
> These 7 dirty words have been outlawed by the Supreme Court in the George Carlin case:
>
> shit, piss, fuck, cunt, cocksucker, motherfucker, & tits.
>
> They should not appear over our air.
>
> cc: J. Trumper, file.
>
> JG/cm

(handwritten: LANDECKER / DON'T READ ON AIR!!!)

Maybe the greatest memo of all time. Although these are words you can't say on the air, John Gehron felt he needed to add "DON'T READ ON AIR!!!" (From my personal collection)

RECORDS TRULY IS MY MIDDLE NAME

To: All WLS/WYTZ staff
From: Tom Tradup
Date: 8/21/89
Subject: John Landecker

CAPITAL CITIES/ABC, INC.

On Friday, August 18th, John Landecker broadcast his program on WLS Radio for the last time.

Although John will not be part of our new talk format, his departure is no reflection on the superb work John performed during the music era of WLS. And any of you who caught John's final WLS broadcast on Friday heard a solid example of what a class guy he really is.

Since he will be in and out of the radio station during the next day or so, please take a moment to thank John and wish him well in his future endeavors.

Tony

CC: Kevin O'Grady

A nice memo about my departure to the staff of WLS by GM Tom Tradup.
(From my personal collection)

Backstage at a Paul Schafer show. He listened to WLS in Canada.
Was on my show once and talked over the intro of the Riviera's "California Sun".
(From my personal collection)

This is my 'I think I'll try television' photo. I auditioned to do weather in New York and Chicago and all I got was this photo. (From my personal collection)

The first WJMK morning show lineup. Richard Cantu, Lonnie Martin, John Landecker, Rick Kaempfer, Vicki Truax. (Photo by Paul Natkin)

Vince Argento and Rick Kaempfer dressed as the original Dancing Itos. Jay Leno, take note. (Photo by Bridget Kaempfer)

RECORDS TRULY IS MY MIDDLE NAME

All the excitement of Landecker & the Legends. (Photo by Dan Silverman)

One of our later morning show teams at WJMK. Rick Kaempfer, John Landecker, Leslie Keiling, Richard Cantu, and Vince Argento. (Photo by Paul Natkin)

The most recent picture of me, taken for WIMS in Michigan City, Indiana.
(Photo by Richard Warner)

The 2013 WLS staff. Left to right back row: Greg Brown, Brant Miller, Dick Biondi, Fred Winston, John Landecker. Front left: Jan Jeffries, Senior VP Programming/Cumulus Broadcasting (and program director WLS-FM 94.7). Front right: Tony Lossano (Landecker/Biondi producer). (Photo by Tony Lossano)

CHAPTER NINE
OH CANADA

> In the early 1980s, while America was adjusting to President Reagan, Pierre Trudeau was the prime minister of Canada, and his famous wife Margaret was in the headlines as much he was. The big story in the news was the discussion about how to patriate the Canadian Constitution. And England started a war against Argentina by invading the Falkland Islands. At the movies, Steven Spielberg's movie *E.T.* became an instant classic. The television show *M*A*S*H* aired its final episode, drawing a record setting audience. And on the pop charts, Michael Jackson's *Thriller* album was released and became one of the most important records in music history.

By agreeing to come to work in Canada, I had disturbed a whole hornet's nest without realizing it. For one thing, it's not as easy to move to Canada as you might think. There are immigration issues and employment issues, and if you're going to work in the Canadian media, there are additional issues that come into play. For instance, to hire an American, a radio company in Canada has to prove that there are no broadcasters in their entire country that can possibly match the qualifications of that American.

Of course there were many Canadian broadcasters that were just as qualified as I was, but somehow, CFTR was able to get me granted "Landed Immigrant" status. I had no idea how much this would anger some people. It was considered a very big deal that an

American was brought in to take one of those high profile Canadian radio jobs. Canada's leading newspaper *The Globe and Mail* wrote an editorial about it before I even went on the air.

And my entrance into the country wasn't quiet, either. The radio station did a major ad campaign blitz, and I don't think they realized they were reinforcing the whole "landed immigrant" issue with the slogan of that campaign. They called it: "Landecker has landed."

I felt the tension immediately.

Some of the on-air staff really resented me. I'm still not sure exactly why. They might have been friends of the person I replaced. They might have wanted the job themselves. But I'll never forget the first station party I went to after I was hired. I was literally shunned by everyone there.

CANADIAN RADIO RULES

I grew up listening to a Canadian station; CKLW in Windsor. But that had been a totally different era. CKLW was really an American station operating out of Canada, more of a Detroit station. By the time I arrived at CFTR, the Canadian version of the FCC had implemented a number of programming rules that had changed Canadian radio drastically.

They were very sensitive about having Canadian culture overrun by their neighbors to the south, so a "Canadian Content" rule was instated, ensuring that a certain percentage of the contemporary music played on the radio was performed by a Canadian artist, or written by a Canadian songwriter, or if there was a Canadian engineer that mixed the recording session, that would qualify too. Because of that rule, lots of songs were played on the air on a regular basis that otherwise never would have been played. Believe it or not,

I ended up really liking that rule. I didn't mind if we played a little more Burton Cummings or Anne Murray, because it was fair. Every other radio station had to do it too.

Canadian radio also had restrictions on the amount of money or prizes that could be given away, which was another rule I ended up liking. There was no way one Canadian station could buy their audience. That meant you had to rely on the quality of the programming as opposed to a contest or prize or stunt. You could do promotions, but there was a limit, and the limit was low enough to maintain a level playing field.

Another Canadian broadcasting rule mandated a certain amount of news and information programming during the day, even middays or overnights. Even on FM rock stations. They appreciated it was the responsibility of the radio station to serve the local community. I really liked that rule too. It made stations more accountable. It was already bothering me at that time that American stations were cutting news departments for budgetary reasons. Canadian stations simply couldn't.

Now don't get me wrong, the point of a radio station was still to make dollars and cents — it was a business after all — but striving for quality was something I felt should be commended and admired. WLS in the 1970s had been the same way, and they weren't even legally obligated to be.

EARLY REVIEWS

The station was a little disappointed with me at first. They thought they were getting this high-energy jock, and they felt that I was too laid back. I remember one reviewer in the Toronto Star, I believe, saying that I was "sleepy."

RECORDS TRULY IS MY MIDDLE NAME

It just made me more determined to succeed. CFTR had a great staff and once again I had a board op, Henry van den Hoogen. I worked really hard, and for a while even cut back on the drinking and the drugs (don't get me wrong, there were still some moments) but in the end the show did become successful.

There were a few bits that really stood out. I jumped right into Canadian politics and had a running segment about Canadian Prime Minister Pierre Trudeau. People really responded to it.

The *Ripley's Believe It Or Not!* people heard my show, and sent me a letter stating that if I could prove that it was really my middle name they would use it in a newspaper column. I proved it, and I was in *Ripley's Believe It Or Not!* (Their letter confirming my middle name is in the photo section.)

Two Canadians came up with a board game called Trivial Pursuit that took Canada by storm. I don't think I can properly describe just how popular that game was. The supply could not keep up with the demand. If you were walking down the street carrying the game, people would offer you cash for it on the spot. I recognized this, and contacted the manufacturers.

They gave me a few cases of the game, and I adapted it to be played on the air. "Trivial Pursuit, the Radio Game" was on every weekday morning. Winners took home copies of the game, plus stoves, refrigerators, televisions, all the stereotypical prizes you'd win on a game show. It was a huge sensation.

After a long hard slog, Landecker had finally landed.

GREG ECKLER *REMEMBERS*

Greg Eckler was a writer for *Mad Magazine,* and is now a comedy writer in Canada for the *Rick Mercer Report* on CBC.

He grew up in Toronto and listened to my show… *There was something so cool and sophisticated about "John Landecker" on CFTR. The name, the sound, the tone. Something about the CFTR transmission made everyone sound better than at any point in their career, and John's was the voice of god. At age 12 I tried to talk with his inflections and pauses, and still do sometimes. There were two big influences on my comedy growing up: David Letterman and John Landecker. And one wasn't more important than the other.*

In July of 1983, at a summer camp several hours north of Toronto, I pretended to be John Landecker every day at the tiny camp radio station. Then, just hours before "Visiting Day," I found out that John's daughter was at this camp! Without hesitation or shame, I decided to stalk. Not the girl, that didn't even occur to me. Her dad! Thing is, I had no idea what he looked like. So I did a lot of eavesdropping, wondering if THAT was him. No luck. But in the afternoon, while I was waterskiing, my mom found him. And in her unassuming way, forced him to sit on a bench for half an hour until I could be retrieved. I tried to be cool and surely fooled nobody, but John could not have been kinder. He answered every inane question with enthusiasm, gave me a CFTR t-shirt that I still have, and insisted on going on camp radio with me.

Another kid was on the air at the time, a 14-year-old kid named Adam. I interrupted Adam's show and said I was going to do my John Landecker impression, then handed the microphone to John and he rocked it. Then I handed it back to Adam and he hilariously said "Ten dollars to anyone who can tell us how Greg did that!" That 14-year-old, by the way, was Adam Chase, who

> went on to become the executive producer of the hit television show Friends.

SUED BY THE BEATLES

By far the biggest splash of publicity I got during my time in Canada occurred when I was sued by the Beatles. Without getting into a huge history lesson, the Canadian constitution was in England at the time. (Canada is a Commonwealth country — the Queen is on their currency.) Prime Minister Pierre Trudeau was in the process of getting it back, so I wrote a parody song about his quest called "Constitution," done to the Beatles song "Revolution." Naturally, it was played on the air. ATV Music, which owned the rights to the Beatles in Canada, sued me, claiming "copyright infringement."

I came to work one day and the story was everywhere. It was on the front page of all the Toronto newspapers, even the front page of the Canadian national newspaper *The Globe and Mail*. To their credit, CFTR backed me, and the case went all the way to the Supreme Court of the Province of Ontario. A reporter called me at home when the decision had been reached and asked me what I thought of the Supreme Court's ruling.

"What was it?" I asked.

"The court ruled in favor of ATV music," he said. "They said if people heard your version of the song it would irrevocably damage the meaning of the original."

My response? "Oh come on, it's not *that* good."

GREG ECKLER *REMEMBERS*

Greg remembers my departure from Canada well... *When I met John at the summer camp, he had also invited me to visit him at CFTR. But when I got home from camp a month later, he was on vacation. A week, then two, then three. Something was very wrong, I could feel it. Then I saw the Toronto Star headline that ended my childhood: "Landecker in Limbo." What a Bar Mitzvah killer that was.*

SOUTH OF THE BORDER

Paula and I decided to get married. We came back to Chicago for the weekend, actually, to tie the knot at the Conservatory in Lincoln Park in a very understated ceremony, followed by a small, small reception at Paula's mother's condo on Lake Shore Drive.

But shortly after we were married, my two-year contract was up in Toronto, and I had a big decision to make. Paula and I had really grown to like Toronto. My show was doing well, and I was really enjoying the radio station. They finally enjoyed me too. CFTR wanted me to stay. But my kids were back in Chicago.

I remember the one event that tipped the scales in favor of Chicago. My daughter Tracy was on a field trip in France with school, and one of her classmates stepped in front of a bus and was killed. I'm not sure why that triggered something — I guess it made me realize how tenuous life is — but it definitely triggered something.

So, when I got a job offer to return to Chicago, hosting afternoons at the Loop (WLUP), without really investigating what I was getting into, I took the job… and descended into a decade of darkness.

CHAPTER TEN
DESCENT INTO DARKNESS

> The mid-to-late '80s were the Reagan years in America. Ronald Reagan won his reelection with a landslide, told Gorbachev "tear down this wall," and became embroiled in a huge scandal, the Iran-Contra affair. George H.W. Bush was elected president, defeating Michael Dukakis. The Chicago Bears won the NFC in 1985 and Super Bowl XX in January of 1986. At the movies, *Back to the Future*, *Ferris Bueller's Day Off* and *Batman* were big hits. Television was ruled by Bill Cosby's show. On the pop charts, Bruce Springsteen, Phil Collins and Madonna were huge, while Live Aid was the biggest concert event since Woodstock. It was followed a few months later by the first Farm Aid benefit concert in Champaign-Urbana, Illinois.

From the late '60s to the early '80s including Toronto, I had a very successful run. The decade of 1982-1992, was exactly the opposite. It was like going from first to worst.

It was bad in nearly every way.

When I arrived back in Chicago, I was excited to be back near my kids, but I found out pretty quickly that going to the Loop (WLUP-FM Chicago) was a huge mistake. They thought they were getting someone that could do it all; run his own board, do his own production, produce his own show, etc. That person clearly wasn't me. I was used to doing a show with a whole group of professionals around me — people that were really good at what they did. They offered me interns instead.

I was used to an established station running on all cylinders; WIBG in Philadelphia, WLS in Chicago, and CFTR in Toronto were all powerhouses. The Loop used to be one before I got there, but by the time I arrived, they were a station in transition, between images. They did have Jonathan Brandmeier in the morning, and he was doing well, but he hadn't yet exploded like he would a few years later. The station was going through an identity crisis. They had been black t-shirts and rock and roll — now they sounded more like *The Big Chill* soundtrack.

But don't get the idea that I'm blaming the station, because I'm not. It wasn't their fault, it was mine. I should have investigated the situation better before I got there. They didn't get what they thought were getting and I didn't get what I thought I was getting.

It didn't last long.

I think my time at the Loop can be summed up symbolically by one particular incident that occurred during my time there. It hadn't happened to me before and hasn't happened since. I was discussing the salary of a well-known personality at another radio station — it wasn't anything that violated FCC rules or local morals or anything like that — but the program director of the Loop was so ticked off by this discussion that he came into the studio and turned my microphone off. He reached right in front of me and shut it down.

I shut it down myself not too long after that.

JAN JEFFRIES *REMEMBERS*

Jan Jeffries was the man that saved me from the Loop… *In early 1984, John and I made acquaintance. At the time I was on the air and programming Chicago CHR G106, and he was on the Loop. He said to me: "Why don't you hire me for mornings?"*

"You're under contract at The Loop," I said.

"I think I can get out of it and make them and me happier," he replied.

I drove to Skokie, a suburb of Chicago, to meet John at his agent's (Saul Foos) home. After some negotiating with his agent and The Loop, The Loop worked out an exit strategy for John. He joined me at G106 almost immediately. I remember going back to my high-rise at Buckingham Plaza after the meeting and looking out across the Chicago skyline, thinking "Oh my God, I just hired my favorite air talent in the business. Life is good!"

First day on the air at G106 sounded like the John Records Landecker we all know and love. Game on! Some people said John and I would butt heads because he was as strong willed as I am. Truth is, he was one of the most enjoyable air talents I have ever directed. Simply put, John needed and deserved to work with people who respected and loved him, bringing out the best of his talents on air.

G-106

G-106 was a Top 40 music station. It was relatively new in Chicago, and there were a number of stations on the air at the time playing the same contemporary music, so the competition for ratings was fierce.

It started out strong. I came in with high hopes, great fanfare, and even a television campaign. They gave me a fantastic board operator (the guy that runs the controls) named Ed Murphy. The program director Jan Jeffries and I got along very well. We really had a great time for a while there, but despite the fanfare, for whatever reason, it didn't quite fly. I think the bottom line is that there were just too many other stations offering the same thing we were offering.

Even though what we were doing was good, it wasn't so good that it would make anyone switch away from their favorite station like B-96, or Q-101 with Robert Murphy, or Johnny B at the Loop. So it really was a big uphill battle.

Plus, apart from G106's problems, I had my own problems at the time. I was drinking. I was doing drugs. I was in a less than great marriage. I wasn't happy, and I'm sure that was reflected in my work and in my attitude. I certainly contributed to whatever wasn't working. I did my own fair part to contribute, believe me.

WCKG

Jan Jeffries was wooed away from G-106, and moved down the dial to WLS-FM. After he left, on March 4, 1985, the station went from being the Top 40 station I signed up for, to an album rock station with new call letters: WCKG.

I had a contract, so I stayed on doing mornings, but that format was completely out of my element. We were playing things like "Manic Depression" by Hendrix at 7:00 in the morning. I had never been an album jock. At WCKG, I just never felt at home. But even through it was a struggle, and I didn't stay there too long, there were a few good memories at WCKG.

The first Farm Aid concert was one of them. I took a train down to Champaign, Illinois to cover it. This was a huge star-studded deal at the time — featuring Willie Nelson, Bob Dylan, John Mellencamp, Neil Young, and just about every other big star you can name. The media was all over the place. MTV was there — I remember seeing the MTV jock Martha Quinn.

But for me, the highlight was meeting Eleanor Mondale, the daughter of former Vice President Walter Mondale. She was covering

Farm Aid for a television station in Los Angeles. Eleanor and I hit it off right away. She was right next to me in the media tent. When she told me she was planning on coming to Chicago, I said; "My newsperson Brooke Belson is going on vacation. Why don't you fill in for Brooke and do the show with me?"

She agreed to do the show, and we had a ton of fun on the air together. It's safe to say that I had a huge crush on her. I found her to be breathtaking. She was smart, good looking, charismatic, plus there was something else, a wildly intangible quality about her. Nothing ever happened between the two of us, but I'm sure if the situation arose I wouldn't have hesitated. I wasn't the only one who felt that way. At that time, Keith Van Horne was an offensive tackle for the Chicago Bears. He was also a contributor to my WCKG morning show. He heard Eleanor on the air with me, and after she left town, asked me to introduce her to him if she ever came back. She did come back to town, and I did introduce them. The two of them eventually got married… and divorced. (After a long battle with cancer, Eleanor passed away in 2011.)

Another highlight of my time at WCKG was following the Bears as they headed to the Super Bowl during that incredible 1985 season. I had access to the players, and these guys were totally memorable characters — every single one of them. I went to dinner with them, and hung out with them at a bar on Wells Street called Alcock's (Keith Van Horne knew the owner). One night I was drinking with Van Horne, Jeff Fisher (who was a defensive back, and later became a head coach in the NFL), and some of the other Bears. We were just standing there, having a conversation.

A woman walked up to me and said "So, what position do you play?"

I didn't pretend I played, but I would be less than honest if I didn't admit I was flattered that she thought I could pass for a member of the team. As a former high school football player, that was a big thrill for me.

> **JAN JEFFRIES** REMEMBERS
>
> Jan was the man who rescued me once again, this time from WCKG… *In my second year at G-106, my deal was up for renewal when John Gehron called me and invited me to walk down North Michigan Avenue and take the reins of WLS-FM. I told him I could not talk with him because I was too busy packing! One of the first things I did was grease the skids to get Landecker back at WLS-AM. I personally purchased a brand new pair of his favorite headphones and a bottle of champagne and had them waiting in the control room as John walked in!*

RESTORING FORMER GLORY?

Returning to WLS was one of those things that sounded like a good idea on paper. But by then, music radio on AM was on life-support. To give you an idea how different it was from my first run at WLS, consider this. Back in the '70s, I was getting a 15 share of the audience. When I came back to WLS in the late '80s, I was getting a .5. That's right: zero point five.

Nobody was listening.

> **DON WADE** REMEMBERS
>
> My old friend from WIBG in Philadelphia, Don Wade also worked with me at WLS in the 1980s. He remembers that time… *In those days we were only playing about four records an*

hour because John Gehron, who was running the place — and really is a radio genius, recognized that the future of music on AM radio was pretty grim.

It was great working with John again. I've always considered him to be a great guy — always smiling and always positive. He was genuinely supportive of everyone else on the air. He would go out of his way to let you know when he heard things that he liked on the air. The other thing I've always admired about him is that he really works at his craft. He may come off like he's goofing off, but trust me, he really works at it. He takes it very seriously.

ROLL WITH THE CHANGES

During those last few years of being a music station, WLS made some interesting moves. At one point I was working at 7-11pm, and the show that followed me was "Sex Talk with Phyllis Levy." Phyllis was a therapist who had been on an FM station in town and done really well. It was a great show. Later it would be taken off the air because of FCC guidelines regarding sex talk. (I saw in a recent column by Chicago media columnist Robert Feder that she is happy and living in Hawaii.)

This was also around the time that Larry Lujack decided to retire from radio. I'm not going to speculate about why this happened, but I do have my copy of his farewell memo and a signed 8X10 photo that says "This is to certify that John Landecker knows me personally."

I was next in line to take over afternoons after he left. His show was chock-full of local Chicago area contributors, so I thought it would be a good fit. I was given the show, but I was also told that all those contributors would be gone, and I would have to do it alone.

Despite this little hiccup, there were a few highlights from those years.

Around this time we got new management and some new programs. One of them was Sally Jesse Raphael's syndicated talk show, which came on after me every night. That show had this ridiculously sappy opening theme; something about starting the day with a smile, blah blah blah. Well, one day I was driving around Chicago and saw a sign for the street Peshtigo Court. I had no idea that there was also a town in Wisconsin called Peshtigo (and neither did most Chicagoans at the time), and no idea that Peshtigo had a tie-in to Chicago — on the day of the great Chicago Fire, Peshtigo also suffered a horrible fire. There was just something about that word that clicked in my brain — and it sparked a new character. That night, during the last half hour of my show, I became Johnny Peshtigo, the nicest man in the world. The only reason I was doing it was to mock the entire Sally Jesse Raphael approach, but this caught on, and I started becoming Johnny Peshtigo during that last half hour every night. The WLS signal reached Peshtigo, Wisconsin, and they loved it. I was interviewed by a local Peshtigo newspaper, and a local Peshtigo store even had a Johnny Peshtigo special on meat.

Another unusual bit occurred at a remote broadcast during a county agricultural fair. I was having a blast broadcasting there — it reminded me of the fairs I attended with my grandparents in Indiana. But it also sparked a very strange idea. Steve Dale, who now does a really great syndicated pet show, was our entertainment reporter at the time, and he was at the Madonna concert at Soldier Field doing in phone-in reports. I thought it might be fun if I stuck the microphone in front of poultry (and I had already tested this off the air — poultry makes the noise that poultry makes — even with a microphone in their faces); while Madonna was singing live from Soldier Field. So, Steve held the phone up to the speaker while Madonna was singing, and I held the microphone up to the chickens, and I'm going to boldly say that was the only time in history that Madonna has ever performed with backup vocals provided by real chickens.

During this second go-around at WLS, the Supreme Court handed down their famous decision about the seven words you couldn't say on television or radio, inspired by the George Carlin routine. It was adopted as a broadcasting standard, and our program director John Gehron sent out a memo explaining this new rule (*that memo is in the photo section*). Notice what he felt compelled to write on my copy of the memo: "DO NOT READ THIS ON THE AIR!" It's a fine list of words, as you can see, but as I pointed out to the listeners on the air at the time, the word "asshole" was not on the list.

I was also a part of a show on WLS that was way ahead of its time. The Chicago Bears had won the Super Bowl and had a hit record ("The Super Bowl Shuffle"), but they didn't go away after that. The same group of wild and crazy guys stayed around for a few years, and WLS was all over it. Jim McMahon did a regular segment on Fred Winston's morning show (if you haven't heard the tape of a bombed Jim McMahon trying to talk to Fred and Fred trying to decipher his ramblings, you're really missing something). The backup QB Mike Tomczak did shows with me. I interviewed a different Chicago Bear every week at Jim McMahon's Lincoln Park restaurant (you haven't lived until you've seen Steve McMichael take on a bottle of Cuervo). Well, this constant Bears talk led to a show we called "The Sports Freaks."

The freaks were WLS sports director Les Grobstein, Scott Gelman who was with Jam Productions at the time, Al Katz —

a salesman for Empire Carpet, and yours truly as the host. Y'know, regular guys sittin' around talking sports. We were on every Wednesday night for an hour. It was a great time! Did it go anywhere? No. But turn on the radio today, and sports talk radio is one of the most popular formats in the country. When we did it, the format didn't even exist.

Like I said, way ahead of our time.

ERIC FERGUSON REMEMBERS

Eric Ferguson is the co-host of "The Eric and Kathy Show" on WTMX in Chicago. It's been the #1 morning show in Chicago for more than a decade… *My very first internship after college was with WLS in the late '80s. John was doing afternoons then and part of my internship was helping produce the show for him. Obviously, John is a perfectionist and a professional, and I didn't know anything about anything, so I'm sure I tested his patience.*

But here's the thing I really remember about him. I had always wanted to be on the air, and I had done a few shows here and there in college, and I had a tape of my show that I was playing for some of the people there. All of them said variations of "well, maybe you should think about trying something else." John is the only one that said: "You know, I hear something there. You should keep at it." And he was the one that I respected the most.

If John Records Landecker thought I had a chance, it gave me the boost of confidence I needed. If he had agreed with everyone else, I probably just would have walked away from the business.

DESCENDING INTO DARKNESS

While my ratings were descending, my personal life was too. By this time, I was really drinking heavily, and when I say heavily, that's not an exaggeration. One day I showed up for work with a full bottle of vodka. I was drinking openly in the studio, right out of the bottle.

I have to put that into context. I didn't just show up at work with a bottle of vodka because I was just beginning to party. Oh no, the drinking had started the night before, and gone all night. There was female companionship with me, and I had suddenly looked at the clock: "Look at the time! I have to go to work!"

While I was on the air that night, I said the word "Fuck."

It just slipped out. I've never said it on the air before or since, and my newsman and I both noticed it at the same time. We looked at each other like "uh oh."

Well, my boss heard it too. He not only let me finish the shift, he took me out to *a bar* after the show. No trouble. No consequences. No nothing.

At least not professionally. Personally it was a different story. Paula had figured out that I was fooling around again. It was obvious that the WLS thing wasn't going to last much longer, and there was a job possibility in St. Louis. I thought Paula was going to meet me at the station, and that we were going to go to St. Louis to see if we liked the area.

But when I got off the air, and walked out of the elevator in the lobby, somebody was there waiting for me, and it wasn't Paula.

"Are you John Landecker?" this guy said to me.

I smiled, and said: "Yeah."

"You're served," he replied. "She's divorcing you, buddy."

I opened the envelope, and there was a picture of Jack Nicholson from the Batman movie, and a note that read: "NOT THIS TIME, JOKER!"

Paula — always very dramatic.

PAULA'S LEGACY

My youngest daughter Amy is an actress now and she received great reviews for a role she played in the Coen brothers' movie *A Serious Man*. When reporters asked Amy where she came up with that character, a boozy flirty beauty, she said she had based the character on Paula.

Paula loved that.

My oldest daughter Tracy also paid tribute to Paula, along with the rest of us in the family. Among her many talents, Tracy is a fantastic writer, with an introspective and dark sense of humor. Tracy wrote a play called *Angst Giving* which was totally about our family. In the play, the mother and father were divorced. They had two daughters, and it was Thanksgiving. The father and his trophy wife were invited over to eat at the home of the girls' mother, who was a yoga instructor and a vegetarian.

The main course was lentil loaf.

Since these characters were obviously based on our family, the father in the play farted a lot.

THE END OF WLS

I was never officially told I was going to be fired, but on a Friday, one of the other air personalities at WLS asked me where I was going on vacation the following week.

I said "I'm not going on vacation next week."

He said "Well, I'm working for you on Monday."

I'm slow, but I'm not that slow.

So, I figured that was my going to be my last show. I can't remember exactly what I did on the air that day, except at the end of the show I said, "Who knows what the future will bring, but let me say goodbye to you, just in case," and then I played the Traveling Wilburys' song "The End of the Line" into the news.

When I walked out of the studio, the general manager was there with my severance check. Ironically I also got a bonus because my ratings went up enough to trigger the incentive clause in my contract. So, at least I had that going for me — a severance check with a little something extra. It turned out that I wasn't the only one to go. The station was completely changing formats, becoming the talk station it remains to this day.

CHAPTER ELEVEN
THE DARKEST DAYS

> The early '90s were the George H.W. Bush years in America. He talked about a thousand points of light. The first Gulf War united the country — and we watched it live on television. The Clarence Thomas confirmation hearings brought a whole new definition to the term "coke can." Germany was officially reunited a year after the Berlin Wall came down. And a man from Hope, Arkansas became the President of the United States. In the early 1990s McCauley Culkin was left *Home Alone,* and Dana Carvey, Jon Lovitz, and Mike Myers became big stars on *Saturday Night Live*. In Seattle, a new musical movement called Grunge Rock was gaining in popularity, and the Chicago Bulls won their first NBA championship.

After WLS, none of the stations in Chicago wanted me, but my agent got me another shot at doing a morning show, this time in Cleveland at Power 108. Cleveland wasn't a great time, but there were a few memorable moments.

I was buried alive there.

It was a radio stunt. I had no food, and no water, and was buried in a block of ice. This was done by a company that specialized in this particular stunt, and the point of it was to raise money for D.A.R.E. Drug Abuse Resistance Education (Irony alert, anybody?)

But they wouldn't let just anyone do this stunt. Before they approved me, they tested me to see if I was claustrophobic. They did this by taking me into a hotel room, putting me in the bathroom, and making me stand in the shower with the shower curtain closed and the lights turned off for a few minutes. The theory was that if it didn't freak me out, I'd be perfectly capable of being enclosed in a block of ice for 36 hours. That seemed like a bit of a stretch, but that's how they did it. Naturally, I passed the shower test, so I was approved for the stunt.

But this block of ice was no dark shower stall. I swear I've never felt claustrophobic in my life except for about fifteen seconds of absolute panic as they were closing the top of the block of ice on me. I was lying down and couldn't get up or kneel, and I knew I was going to be stuck in that position for 36 hours.

That's a long time.

And it really is a block of ice. It's insulated to a certain degree, so it's not *really* cold, but it ain't exactly warm either. There were also a few loopholes with the "no food or water" decree. For instance, certain items like Life Savers candy don't technically qualify as food, so I was allowed to have some of those, and while there was no water, there was something else to drink — although I can't remember exactly what it was.

Honestly, though, I wasn't really interested in eating and drinking too much, because if I had to go to the bathroom, well, that's why God invented baggies. My theory was, if you're not taking anything in, there won't be too much going out.

I think I only peed once, but needless to say, I was glad when it was over. It's the only "radio stunt" I've ever done, and that's the way it's gonna stay.

DRINKING IN OHIO

This is how bad my drinking got when I was in Cleveland. I started to map out the state liquor stores (in Ohio these are the only stores where you can buy liquor), so that I could go to all of them equally, so that no one state store would realize how much booze I was drinking. One night I bought a fifth of vodka, and the next morning when I pulled the bottle out of the kitchen cabinet, about 99.9% of it was gone. I remember thinking, "Whoa, anybody that drinks that much is going to kill himself."

I know it sounds crazy, but I still wasn't really thinking about me — it was about some other crazed Vodka drinker. And it wasn't just that I was getting drunk on nights when we hit the town and partied. That's not that big of a deal. It was when I found myself getting drunk even when I wasn't planning on it. That's when I really started to notice. When I got drunk unexpectedly, it was like wow, I'm drunk again?

"It's Tuesday. How did that happen?"

THE YOUNGER WOMAN

I met Laura Berliner in Cleveland during my short stint there. She was working as a producer at a television station (Channel 8) and called to say that they were going to do a feature on morning men, and wondered if she could come over and interview me? I went to this restaurant because I had a few hours to kill before she got there. Needless to say, I had a few drinks. Then I went back to the lobby of the radio station and saw this unbelievably attractive young woman sitting there. (She is 21 years younger than me).

I walked up to the receptionist and said, "I'm expecting this producer from Channel 8."

The receptionist said — "That's her right there."

"What?"

She was so hot I wasn't going to conduct the interview at the station. So, we went back to the restaurant where I had just been drinking, and we hung out for an hour or two. Over the next few weeks I kept running into her. First at a parade — I was on the float for the radio station — and I saw her there waving. Then I saw her again at a record release party. That led to a brief make out session in the front seat of my car, which then led to a few dates.

Before I knew it, we were a couple.

SIGNIFICANT MILESTONES

Sometimes sharing really difficult situations can bring a couple closer, and that's definitely what happened to us. We went through four hugely significant milestones together in our first year or two as a couple.

Laura was with me for what I call my last drunk. We were going to meet at a hotel in Cleveland, but she had to go back to her house in a nearby town called Beachwood. So, I stayed at the hotel and apparently emptied the mini bar and passed out. I was told this later; I have no memory of it. When Laura came back, she couldn't get into the room. She got the hotel to open the door, and I was passed out, sprawled on the floor. The next thing I remember was waking up in the morning and crying and telling her to leave me because I was the worst person on the Earth. But instead of leaving, she took me to a therapist. The therapist asked me if I had drinking problem, and I said "HELL YES!"

I haven't had a drink since.

The second significant milestone occurred when Laura and I also both lost our jobs at the same time. The end of my job was particularly ugly. My agent had negotiated a no-cut three year deal with Power 108, but I don't know how closely they looked at the details of that contract, because shortly after I started, they decided they didn't want me on the air anymore. Sorry boys, you signed a no-cut contract, you still have to pay me.

So this is how they decided to make me earn it. They said I had to come in to the radio station at 5:00 in the morning, and play the commercials and music for thirty minutes, but I wasn't allowed to say anything. Then, I was supposed to come back twelve hours later and do "production work." That wasn't going to happen. We came to a compromise that involved me coming in at 5:30, playing the music and commercials without saying anything, and then immediately afterwards doing whatever production work was required. The whole situation was ludicrous, so my agent finally negotiated a buyout deal, and I was free.

Our third significant milestone together involved Laura's health. Tests revealed she had a hole in her heart, and it had to be patched. The only way to do that was through open heart surgery. After the surgery I went over to her house almost every day, and helped care for her. The way I behaved during this crisis convinced Laura's family, especially her grandmother, that I was for real, despite our big age difference.

And finally, Laura and I shared one last milestone together, and this was the toughest one for me. Right before my parents' 50th wedding anniversary, my mom called to tell us she had cancer and the doctors had only given her a five percent chance to live.

LOSING MOM

Mom had her sense of humor until the bitter end. When she was diagnosed with cancer, it was pretty grim. I visited her all the time, and we'd watch TV or movies together (usually comedies to pick up her spirits.) One night we were watching Saturday Night Live, and if I can remember the skit correctly, there was a guy on a couch with an exposed brain, and a dog was chewing and yanking it. They had obviously put some peanut butter or something on this guy's head.

As this was happening, I panicked a little. "Oh No! Is my dying mother going to find it humorous that a man's brain is being eaten by a dog?"

Sure enough, mom lost it… but in a good way. She was laughing so hard, she was crying. My mother's condition improved sufficiently that she got out of the hospital and back home to celebrate their 50th anniversary. We went out to dinner and everybody had a great time, but right after that, things started to deteriorate quickly.

Mom died soon after that.

Even though the Cleveland job was a nightmare, there was one huge bright spot. Because I was out of work but still getting paid, I had the time to spend with my parents, helping my dad, and providing whatever comfort I could give my mother.

SAUL FOOS

Saul was my agent for nearly twenty years. Sometime in the 1970s when I was working at WLS, my contract was up, and the general manager told me that I should get an agent to negotiate my new deal. I know there are people working in radio today that are thinking "What? He told you to get an agent?"

You have no idea how rare the concept of a GM telling an employee to get an agent is — that just doesn't happen. Saul Foos became my agent. And Saul was a GREAT agent. When I was on top, he was there for me. When I was in the gutter, he was there for me, trying to convince me to stop drinking. At WLS, in Toronto, at all the different stations in Chicago in the '80s, to Cleveland in the '90s, Saul was the guy that put those deals together for me. I looked upon him as a really close friend, almost a father figure, like a big brother. I mean I really loved the guy — no reservations.

But yet, there was this other side to him. While my mother was in a room at University of Michigan Hospital in Ann Arbor suffering the effects of chemotherapy and cancer, I was in the basement of the hospital looking for the only Fed Ex mailbox so that I could send him a check for $30,000. He had called to say it was an emergency and that I must send the check right away. Think about that for a second — this guy I totally trusted called me in the midst of my dealing with my mother's cancer and told me I had to get this check to him right away, so I wouldn't miss the investment opportunity.

I honestly believed that Saul was one of the only people in the world that really truly had my best interests at heart. Even with the weird calls for money, I suspected nothing. I still have the first letter that Saul sent me about my investment.

It's on his law firm's stationary, dated April 20, 1992, and says: "Dear John, this letter will acknowledge that you have sent me $30,000 to trade certain commodities on your behalf. I will do this for a period of 90 days; however you may close this account at any time you desire by calling me. I will send you a check for your investment and any profit that the account has earned. You also understand that any profit earned is taxable income to you. I also personally guarantee that you will sustain no losses in this account. Very truly yours, Saul Foos."

I still have the second letter too. Again, on his company letterhead, dated August 13, 1992: "Dear John, this letter will acknowledge that you have added the sum of $14,000 to your trading account with me. That brings your total investment to $44,000. Your profit through August 12th, 1992 is $7812.00. I personally guarantee that you will sustain no losses in this account. Very truly yours, Saul Foos."

TRYING OUT TALK RADIO

I got a call from a woman named Turi Ryder while all of this stuff was going on in my life — during my very darkest time. Turi had been a disc jockey at WLS when I was there the second time — one of the rare female disc jockeys of that era. She had since made the transition to talk radio and was working at KSTP-Minneapolis, and thought I would also be a good candidate to try talk radio.

I left Ann Arbor after my mother died, and went directly to Minneapolis to fill in for Turi for three days — and I was never so happy to leave town. Here was this opportunity to go somewhere else and take my mind off this crap that was swirling around me at the time. I went to KSTP and did two or three days and had fun. It was a lot of work but it went pretty well. I thought, hmmm, maybe I can do this whole talk radio thing.

TURI RYDER *REMEMBERS*

Turi is now on every night on WGN in Chicago... *Landecker was THE radio personality of my youth. I wasn't a Top 40 music fan, but for entertainment between the records, Landecker was THE DJ. He was smart, funny, quick, and unpredictable. I was in love with his talent before I ever met him. Some of the kids* at my high school radio station had internships or flunky jobs at WLS, and the lore of Landecker grew. He was creative beyond anything we'd ever heard on the air, and every "Boogie Check" got recorded and replayed in school the next day. We talked about his show the way people discuss Mad Men. What was real? What was improvised? We cared about every detail.

Years later, John came "home" to WLS, where I held the overnight shift. He was charming, polite, and to watch him was like going to the Harvard of Top 40 radio. Once, when I had to emcee a high school comedy competition, John heard me whining about it. "Did you get any material?" he asked. "What kind of material could I possibly get at a contest like that?" John's answer to that question has been a guiding point in my work for years, "Kid," he said, "It's all material."

That's why when, years later, I had the chance to select a talent as vacation relief for my afternoon drive talk show at KSTP Minneapolis/St. Paul, I called John up and refused to take "no" for an answer. John's a great story teller. He listens, he's still smart and funny, he's got a wide variety of interests and life experience, and I love to work with him.

Not only that, he's such a pro, my blood pressure goes down the minute he walks into the studio. John's talent is timeless.

WLS, AGAIN

The KSTP experience went well enough that Saul Foos talked to Drew Hayes who was the program director of WLS-AM at the time. WLS had gone talk, and Saul convinced Drew to let me come in and do two weekend shows for WLS.

Now WLS was not exactly the same animal as KSTP. WLS was a far more political station than KSTP. Turi had put me in contact with a consultant who conducted talk radio questionnaires. I took his standardized test and passed with flying colors, with one exception. I wasn't considered opinionated enough. Not only did I resist foisting my opinions on people, I didn't like people who did. Even though I knew WLS wanted that, I also knew it was a great opportunity and I had to take a shot at it.

Well, a week before I came in to do it, I was stricken with the most incredible flu. I mean I hadn't been that sick in years. And in my typically over-the-top, overly dramatic, all-or-nothing point of view, I had to get to Chicago. I just had to. All or nothing, this was it, I couldn't blow it. So I went to a doctor and he loaded me up with I can't even tell you how many different anti-histamines, and I rolled into Chicago and WLS, and I… SUCKED.

Big time.

That's my impression of how I did, I'm sure that's the impression that WLS management had of my performance, and that was the last time there was any talk radio going on in my career for ten years!

WORKING FOR SAUL

After the Cleveland thing blew up, and the talk radio thing fizzled, Saul called me and asked me to come back to Chicago and work for him as an agent in his office. He had already hired a few of my former colleagues, and was offering me a very generous salary, so I figured what the heck? Why not? He gave me my own office, and I became an agent.

The first day I was back in Chicago working for Saul, I was listening to the news. They were reporting that an escalator repairman had been killed in an accident. The escalator repairman, Frank Jalovec, had the same name as the lead singer of The Kind, the band I had performed with before I moved to Toronto.

I thought, "That can't be him, can it?"

Well, the manager of The Kind got in touch me to tell me that, sure enough, it was the same Frank. When I went to the wake I found out that the band was no longer called The Kind, they were called The Legends, and they were performing oldies now. I chatted with the members of the band there, and they asked me to come out and sing some oldies with them.

At the time it didn't make sense to do that, but little did I know that just a few months later something would happen that would change the situation completely.

REALLY, I MEAN IT, I'M AN AGENT NOW

I called radio station general managers and program directors around the country and pitched the clients on Saul's roster. But something weird started happening almost immediately. Whenever I pitched one of Saul's clients, the radio guys would say to me: "What about you?"

The Oldies station in Chicago was particularly interested in me — and they absolutely refused to drop it. I finally pulled Saul aside and told him.

"Look," I said. "They keep asking for me, what should I do?"

"You have to make up your mind," Saul advised. "Are you an agent, or are you an on-air guy?"

Well, I thought about it, and after that decade of darkness I had just lived through, I decided I that I was done with being on the air. It was time to do something new. As far as I was concerned, it was time for a whole new beginning. It was time for a brand new career.

I was now an agent. But even though I had decided that I was going to be an agent, and I had told the oldies station that in no uncertain terms, they wouldn't give up. The GM was one of Saul's good buddies.

One day Saul came in to discuss it with me.

"I think you should try it," he said. That caught me totally off guard.

"But wait a minute," I said. "Just a few weeks ago, you said…"

"I know," he interrupted. "But I think you should try it."

So I went on the air on WJMK and did a tryout. It went OK, so Saul really started pushing for me to do it full time. When he told me how much they were willing to pay me, it was more than I ever made in my entire life — and that he wasn't even going to take a commission — I finally buckled.

"OK," I said. "But, I still want to keep my office. And I'll only do it with the understanding that if it doesn't work out, I can leave anytime and come back to work for you."

He agreed.

FOOS-FALL

Those first few weeks at WJMK were a little bumpy, because the show hadn't been fully staffed yet. But when I went back to Saul's office one day, there was somebody there I had never seen before, and the ride suddenly got bumpier than I ever could have imagined.

"What are you doing here?" the stranger asked.

"I work here," I replied.

"Not anymore you don't."

The Federal Marshalls had shut Saul down. It turned out that my trusted agent and friend had been running a Ponzi scheme — collecting money from people with the promise of big returns, but paying those returns with other people's money. He was ripping people off, including me. Saul was Bernie Madoff, before Bernie Madoff.

As you might imagine, this became a big story in Chicago. It was on all the television stations, and it was in all of the newspapers. I saved a lot of those stories.

The headlines tell the tale…

"The Scam That Rocked Radio (Agent charged in $7 million fraud)"

"Top Radio Agent is Charged (Some of city's leading personalities bilked in $7 million fraud.)"

"Foos Says Bad Deals Made Him Bilk Stars (Bilked investors likely out of luck, says U.S. Attorney James B. Burns)"

"Bankrupt Agent Comes Clean with Ex-Clients"

"Lawyer Charged in Running Scam Faces Disbarment"

"Agent of Agents Now A Fallen Star"

"Foos Absent at Bankruptcy Hearing"

SAUL'S LEGACY

That last article in my clipping file has a few gems, including the fact that Saul couldn't attend his own bankruptcy hearing because was suffering from "clinical depression."

When his attorney said that in court, an audible groan was heard in the gallery. According to the *Sun-Times*, somebody screamed: "Save us the bullshit!"

I decided to create a character for the morning show; an agent who always has the "next great deal" that never came through. The character's name was Saul Schmooze. I decided to play out the story that was all over the newspapers and television. This idea was noted in all the trade publications. It also made its way into my general manager's office.

He haaaaaated it.

Saul had ripped him off too. Needless to say, Saul Schmooze did not last too long.

It did however solicit a call from Saul himself. It was a very brief conversation. It sounded like he was on valium or something. Saul was always fast and quick-witted, but the person I talked to that day was slow and drawn out. That was the last time I ever spoke with him. I still feel sorry for Saul's family. His wife said she never knew, and I believe her. He had a son named Todd that was going to be an agent, and a daughter who had just gotten married. It had to be devastating for them. Saul did end up serving some time, and he never returned to the business. He passed away as I was writing this book in 2012.

I had long since forgiven him, if that's the right word, for what happened. I realized he had been trying to make amends when he got me the gig and refused to take a fee for the WJMK contract. He knew something was going to go down, and he wanted to help me while he could.

But while he did help me, he also left me in a very tough situation. Yes, I had a job at WJMK, but every time the general manager of the station looked at me, or listened to my show, all he could think about was that my contract had been negotiated by the guy who had stolen a ton of money from him.

A ton of money.

The honeymoon period at WJMK was over before it began.

CHAPTER TWELVE
OFFICIALLY AN OLDIE

> In the fall of 1993, President Bill Clinton had a huge Democratic majority in both the House of Representatives, and the Senate. The Keating 5 scandal was working its way through the Ethics committee. And the Brady Bill was signed into law, outlawing certain types of assault weapons. The top box office draw at the movies in 1993 was *Jurassic Park*. On television, *Seinfeld* and *The Simpsons* were the two newest hit sensations, and the sports world in Chicago suffered a dramatic blow when Michael Jordan announced that he was retiring from basketball after his third consecutive championship.

When I first started at WJMK (Oldies 104.3), I was very aware that a lot of my former WLS colleagues already had a shot at doing the mornings there, and hadn't received the support they needed to be successful. (Joel Sebastian, Tommy Edwards, and Fred Winston all worked there before me.) I had heard some horror stories.

I also knew that when the station told me they were prepared to give me an opportunity to build a personality morning show from the ground up, it was a potentially loaded phrase. My experience had been that when you're given the opportunity to start from the ground up, there's a tendency for some managers to supply you with people that have no previous experience doing anything with radio.

They say, "But you can mold them."

Well that's fine except for one small detail: WE'RE ON THE AIR! And we're on the air in the third largest market in the United States of America, and this is a morning show, and not a training bra. It never works. And it's happened to me multiple times. No one wants to hear it, but you know what it takes to put on a professional radio program? This is going to shock you. Are you ready? You need a team of professionals.

After stumbling along with well-intentioned but inexperienced people at the very beginning, the station, much to their credit, hired Rick Kaempfer as my executive producer and Vince Argento as my technical producer. Both of them were professionals, really good at what they did, and had been in the business for years.

When that happened, we had ourselves a show.

BUILDING FROM THE GROUND UP

Of course, it took the listeners a little while to understand what we were trying to do. We were doing a morning show that was about 50% content and 50% music on a station that had always been nearly 100% music. When you make a drastic change like that, especially when your target audience is older listeners, you have a very good chance of ticking off every listener.

That's what happened to us. The station was flooded with complaints.

It was a very tense time. For a while there it looked like we might not even make it through one ratings book. The listeners hated us. The general manager hated us. But we had a vision for what we wanted to do, and we stuck to it. We figured if they gave us some time, we would turn this thing around.

And as time went on, we did turn it around. Everybody on the morning show worked their asses off, and it paid dividends in a pretty short amount of time. By the end of that first year we had created a foothold in the market for a personality morning show on an oldies station. That was something that hadn't been done in Chicago before, and hasn't been done since. It meant even more to me this time around because the times had changed so much. This wasn't like the WLS days, when listeners really only had a few choices. In the 1990s there were dozens of choices in Chicago for personality morning shows, and we held our own for ten years.

TAKING THE SHOW ON THE ROAD

We loved taking the show on the road, and for a couple of years we were out on the road a couple of times a week. We were determined to win over the listeners, even if we had to personally go out and convince them one by one.

One of the ways we got listeners to invite us into their homes was creating a segment we called the "Elvis Wake up Call." We asked listeners to send in a letter to the morning show if they knew someone that was worthy of being awakened by Elvis. Not just telephonically, mind you. No sir, we brought Elvis to you (we found an Elvis impersonator who was willing to go along with this bit). Elvis would sneak into the pre-ordained bedroom of choice live on the air, start a karaoke tape, and SING! One of our producers would be there, putting a microphone to the sleeping person's mouth, and that person would be live on the air with Elvis.

We did this bit for quite awhile and it was extremely successful. There were a few that were really memorable. One time a mother sent us a letter saying we should go wake up her daughter who lived in Chicago's Lincoln Park neighborhood. But when we walked into her daughter's apartment around 5:45 in the morning, we found a bag of pot on the table.

I told her: "Don't forget, we were invited."

Nobody else was doing something like this on the radio. For once there was a radio station that was turning the tables. For once it was the parents' turn to get back at their kids! We had a lot of fun with those "Elvis Wake Up Calls," but they were usually only a half hour or so of show. We only sent one producer, an engineer, and Elvis.

But every Wednesday we took the in-home concept up a notch. We called it "The Cul-de-Sac of Life Radio Tour." The entire morning show staff would show up at a listener's home at 3:45am, and turn that home into our studio for a day. Why would anyone agree to something like that? Simple. If you invited us, and we picked you, you would receive a key that could possibly start a Ford Thunderbird.

It was just a fun bit at first. We'd rifle through a family's refrigerator, and mom and dad's underwear drawers, and have some wholesome fun. But as the year progressed, the listeners started producing the shows for us. They got bigger and bigger and bigger. Local celebrities showed up at their homes. High school marching bands came and performed for us. The mayor of the suburb inevitably showed up and declared it "John Landecker Day" in their town, and gave me the key to the city. It was a wild time, and we had tons of fun.

At one of these Cul-de-Sac shows, one of the kids that lived there was a Girl Scout. I spent a good portion of that show joking about wanting to be a Girl Scout too. Well, another listener heard that, and took it upon herself to make me an adult-sized Brownie outfit. That led to me doing the next Cul-de-Sac show wearing a

Brownie uniform. While I was broadcasting with this uniform on, something suddenly occurred to me.

"Wait a minute," I said. "What do Girl Scouts do? They sell cookies door to door. And here I am in a neighborhood. Let's go sell some cookies!"

I took a couple of real Girl Scouts with me and we knocked on doors. The people answering their doors were greeted by a full grown man wearing a Brownie Uniform.

The whole idea of going to listener's homes, putting on Brownie uniforms and going door to door was to promote the show. I always felt like being on the air was a little bit like a political campaign. We needed your vote, and this was one way to get it. In Philadelphia and earlier in Chicago I had used the high school assembly program. Obviously, our listeners weren't in high school anymore — but it was the same general concept.

RICK KAEMPFER REMEMBERS

Rick was my executive producer and right-hand man at WJMK, and he remembers what it was like in those early days… *On my first day at WJMK, John told me he wanted to create a big time larger-than-life personality morning show, so that's what we did. We had the biggest name celebrities on the show, we did huge live broadcasts, we toured all over the area with our band to hustle up some publicity, and we regularly got press coverage for our efforts. John even hired a great PR person named Janet Treuhaft, and paid for her out of his own pocket.*

The management of WJMK said they wanted that kind of a show too, but it was pretty obvious they never quite bought into the way we were doing it. That kind of unscripted spontaneity went against all of their instincts. I remember a meeting when one of the managers said to John: "Unless you're 100% sure it's going to be funny, don't say it." Try that sometime. Another time he wanted us to shorten the bits by eliminating the setup. He said: "Just do the punch lines." (Comedians love that story.)

We always knew that the only way we would be allowed to keep doing the show the way we thought it needed to be done was to get ratings — to show them that they needed to start thinking differently. We were highly motivated to make it work — each of us worked 10, 12, 14, 18 hours a day. There was no illusion of what awaited us if we were wrong.

KEEPING IT REAL

In some ways, my show on WJMK was totally different than anything I had done before. In the '70s, I had been a rock jock, making jokes, doing contests, talking to listeners, being up tempo, doing funny bits and imitations. But the culture had changed dramatically since that time. Personalities were suddenly sharing all sorts of private details about their lives.

That was certainly true of the morning show on WJMK.

Everything I considered relatable went on the air, including details about the personal lives of everyone on the show. When my technical producer Vince Argento proposed marriage, we made sure he was wired, and we played it on the air. I don't know what my producer Rick Kaempfer's wife Bridget thought about this, but when Rick and Bridget had a baby, Rick brought a digital audio tape recorder into the delivery room to capture it for all posterity — and to play it on the air. ALL THREE TIMES!

GREG BROWN *REMEMBERS*

Greg Brown works with me now at WLS-FM, but he also followed my morning show most of the time I was at WJMK. I made him a part of the show too… *John was always well prepped for his show, but it also seemed as if he liked to work in the moment. When we started doing our crosstalk each morning at about 9:45, I would come into the studio a few minutes early and say hello to Rick, Vince and John. John didn't always acknowledge me. At first I wasn't sure if he liked me or was angry with me or what? He would sit at his mic quietly, I would sit at my mic quietly… it felt a little awkward… but then as soon as we went on the air, "POW!" the electricity began! He was warm and kind and funny. I later figured out that he didn't want to spoil those first moments on the air together. You know the old adage, "save it for the air."*

CHAPTER THIRTEEN
STAR TRIPPIN' AGAIN

> In the mid-to-late '90s, Quentin Tarantino got a lot of attention with his movie *Pulp Fiction*, while other big movie draws were *Forrest Gump*, *Braveheart*, and of course, the biggest of all: *Titanic*.

We had lots of celebrities on our show at WJMK, but we had a rule — we would never just have a star come on our show just for the sake of having a star. We had to have a twist. We had to have a different take on it. It had to be more interesting than a standard interview. Some of these worked out great, and others didn't work out as well, but they were always, hopefully, memorable.

THINKING OUT OF THE BOX

One memorable incident was a practical joke we played on Mary Tyler Moore. It involved her former co-star on the Mary Tyler Moore show, Valerie Harper — who played Rhoda in that great sitcom. Valerie was in town doing a play, and we had her on the show and had an absolute blast with her. During that interview, we told her in passing that we were going to be interviewing Mary a few days later, and that's when we came up with this idea.

Since Mary was going to be doing our show via satellite from New York, it meant that she wouldn't be able to see us — only hear us. Valerie Harper came in that morning and pretended to be the co-host (Vicki), and her job was to irritate the normally unflappably nice Mary Tyler Moore. It came off even better than I imagined. Valerie asked Mary who her favorite co-star on the Mary Tyler Moore show was, and Mary began to say that she loved them all, but Valerie wouldn't let her go. She demanded an answer. Mary got a little huffy. When Mary finally said that her favorite co-star was Valerie, Valerie admitted who she was. Mary was completely taken in by that bit. She had no idea at all, and when it was revealed, she loved it.

Another time we heard that Martha Stewart was coming to Chicago to do an appearance at Marshall Field's downtown, but she couldn't make it to the studio, so the only way I could get an interview was to go to Marshall Field's and interview her there. Now, what Martha didn't know was that part of this interview was going to consist of me singing a song that we had written about her, and part of it was going to be filmed. Channel 2's weatherman Steve Baskerville was doing a Sunday morning talk show at the time, and he had invited me to appear as a guest that same week. I told him what we had planned to do to Martha, so he sent a camera crew along to record it as it happened.

It was Kamikaze-TV.

I walked up to Martha Stewart, put down a boom box, started the music, and began belting out the lyrics. Martha laughed. I mean really laughed. When they saw Martha laughing, her nervous PR people started laughing too. It turned out be a home run. We played it on the radio, and they showed it on TV, and Martha Stewart loved it.

I have one more out-of-the-box story about one of my favorite actresses — Marilu Henner. She is awesome. She is sexy. She is a good sport. We just knew she would go along with the bit we came up with, and she did. As soon as she sat down in the guest chair in our studio, I said, "OK, let's go, we're going to do this interview on Michigan Avenue" (our studio was on Michigan Avenue at the time).

Marilu and I went down to the street live on the air, and hailed a taxi. I conducted the interview of the *Taxi* star inside a taxi. It turned out to be absolutely killer. Not only was Marilu funny — the cabbie was funny too. In fact, that bit was so good we submitted it for an award, and because of it, The John Records Landecker Show was named the Best Morning Show in Chicago by the Achievement in Radio Awards that year.

RICK KAEMPFER *REMEMBERS*

Rick was the one that actually booked the celebrities on our show... *Marilu Henner was probably on our show a dozen times, and I remember one of those appearances more vividly than the others because it was so personally embarrassing. One year when Marilu came into town, John thought it would be funny to see if she did any nude scenes, and if so, he wanted to play the audio on the air to see if she could identify the significance of the scene.*

This was in the days before celebrity nudity internet sites or YouTube or Google. I had to go to the video store and rent all the R-rated movies she appeared in to see if there were any nude scenes. My last choice, "The Man Who Loved Women," contained her only nude scene. She was topless in a scene with Burt Reynolds for about five seconds. I dubbed off the audio and brought the clip into the show so John could play it on the air.

However, I hadn't considered that I would also be sitting right across from her when this audio clip was played. It took her only a split second to figure out what was going on, and she looked right at me.

"So, which one of you sickos watched the videotape to get this clip?" she asked. I'm told that she had a smile on her face, but I can't confirm that because there was no way I could look her in the eye. She guessed correctly anyway. "It was Rick, wasn't it?"

"He insisted," John replied helpfully. "He said he had to watch it a dozen times just to make sure he got it right."

Marilu thought that was funny, and I laughed too, but I must admit... that was an awkward moment.

REAQUAINTANCES

Very early on in my WJMK time we were doing a remote broadcast from Carson's department store in downtown Chicago. The remote was to promote the new line of throwback football jerseys, and three all-time NFL greats were on hand to sign autographs; Dick Butkus, Ray Nitschke, and the man who had nearly crashed into me on the sidelines while I was doing my college film project nearly twenty years earlier, Walter Payton.

We were excited about the possibilities of doing a show with these three guys, but discovered quickly that it was going to be a little different than we were told. The players made it quite clear to us that they didn't consider participating in a radio show part of their paid appearance. As far as they were concerned, they were there strictly to sign autographs.

Every time I put the microphone in front of them, I got nothing. Dick Butkus was particularly nasty about it. He looked like he was going to punch me. Ray Nitschke, who had previously been on our show and seemed to be a pretty cooperative guy under other circumstances, merely grunted, or gave one or two word answers to my questions.

Walter Payton treated the appearance of the microphone as an excuse to pinch me. It got a good laugh in the store, but it wasn't exactly spellbinding radio. In fact, we were beginning to think this was going to go down as one of our all-time worst broadcasts.

Luckily, just as we were about to throw in the towel, I noticed that while the Sam Cooke song "Bring it on Home" was playing on the radio, Walter Payton was singing along.

I grabbed the live microphone.

"Stop the music. Stop it for a second."

The board operator back at the station did as he was told. I continued.

"Good. Now start the Sam Cooke song again. This time we've got a special treat for you. This time Sam Cooke will be accompanied on lead vocals by Chicago Bears Hall of Famer Walter Payton."

The song started again, and sure enough, Walter Payton grabbed the microphone and really got into it, belting out Sam Cooke with all of his heart. He got a standing ovation in the store, but more importantly for us, his singing went out over the airwaves.

Being reacquainted with Walter was one thing, but it was topped by another re-acquaintance a few years later. I'll always treasure my interview with Mel Brooks in the 1970s, but during the WJMK years, I got the chance to interview him twice more. One time I had a chance to do a very lengthy interview with both Mel Brooks and Carl Reiner when they did *The 2000 Year Old Man in the Year 2000*. I must have talked to them for 40 minutes. The highlight for me was when I asked him a question about *Blazing Saddles*.

"You know the line about the Dr. Gillespie killings?" I asked.

"Yeah," Mel answered.

"That's a reference to Lionel Barrymore as Dr. Gillespie in the Dr. Kildare movies, right?"

He paused, and said: "You know what? Every once in a while I run into a kindred spirit. You're the only one that has ever asked me that question, and the answer is yes!"

To me, that was like John Lennon telling a Beatlemaniac that he was the only person in the world who ever understood a Beatles record. I was in heaven. Of course, just to show you never to take yourself too seriously, when I told that story on the air, I got calls from people who pointed out other jokes in that movie that I completely missed.

"John, what about the Laurel and Hardy handshake?"

"Yeah? What about it?"

"Laurel and *Hardy*!"

"Oooooh. Laurel and Hardy. Right."

My final time with Mel was when *The Producers* played in Chicago before it made its run on Broadway. Mel held a press conference, and I was one of the press members that attended. When it was my turn, I asked: "When was the first time you thought that Nazis were funny?"

"It was when I saw the shape of their helmets," he responded.

The next day in the *Sun-Times*, that was the headline. Then, a few weeks later when Matthew Broderick did his interview for *60 Minutes* just before it hit Broadway, he brought it up too. "You know," he said, "the first time Mel realized Nazis were funny was when he saw the shapes of their helmets."

Happy to contribute.

HARRY CARAY

Harry Caray, the famous play-by-play man we all knew and loved, also appeared on our morning show. Here's the background for the story: One of the TV stations in Chicago was promoting a Harry Caray special, featuring Bob Costas as the host. Costas was interviewed in the Chicago papers about the special before it aired, and said that Harry had told him a great story about Elvis, and that story alone was reason enough to tune into the special. But when the special aired, that story somehow ended up on the cutting room floor.

We were dying to hear it. It was made for us. Rick tracked down Harry at his home in the Ambassador East Hotel, and lined Harry up for a live interview on the following day's program.

But when he came on the air, it didn't quite go as planned.

John: Hey Harry, tell us the story about the time you met Elvis. I kept waiting for it on that special, but…

Harry: Aw that's too long of a story, and you know, it's early in the morning, and we both have other work to do.

John: Now wait a minute, Harry.

Harry: They can read it in my book. They can read it in *Vineline*. It's a great story. It's the truth. And this is one of those occasions where the truth sounds like fiction.

John: Well, this is an oldies station and we play a lot of Elvis, and when we read in the paper about your special with Bob Costas, he even said in the paper, in the *Tribune*, make sure you hear Harry Caray tell his story about Elvis. And then, I watched the TV show and the story wasn't on it. So, just to give you an idea how badly we wanted to hear that story, we got in touch with the production staff of the special, and asked them for the tape, and they said it was edited out, and now it's lost in some limbo somewhere. Then I realized, heck, Harry lives right here in town. Let's get you on the air and ask you about it directly.

Harry: John, listen, I've already been on with you longer I wanted to be, and it's early in the morning and I've got lots of things to do.

John: But Harry —

Harry: Another time, John. (Click.)

RICK KAEMPFER *REMEMBERS*

Rick remembers the bad interviews better than the good ones... *Not all of our interviews went well, as that Harry Caray story attests, but there was one interview that was even more memorably horrible. It was with the actress Joan Collins. We had prepared to surprise her with audio from an old Star Trek episode she had been on, and John had a whole bit prepared. Unfortunately, that interview was a satellite interview, and that led to a few problems.*

Joan Collins arrived for her morning interviews with freshly done hair, and she made it known to the producers in New York that she absolutely would not wear headphones. I could hear the negotiations over the satellite as we prepared for the interview. The producers told her that she wouldn't be able to hear the questions without her headphones, but she wouldn't budge from her demands. Instead of telling her she had no choice, they decided to rig up a tiny speaker so that she could hear the questions without mussing her hair.

> *Unluckily for us, we were the first interview.*
>
> *As soon as John asked her a question, we heard feedback. When she tried to answer the questions, we heard feedback. When we tried to play an audio clip, we heard feedback. It had been going on for about a minute, but it seemed like an hour. It was horrible radio.*
>
> *John finally said to her, "Listen, lady, you're gonna have to put on your headphones and turn off that speaker. This is ridiculous."*
>
> *When she wouldn't do it, John ended the interview.*
>
> *We went to a commercial break, and listened in on the satellite to hear what she was saying about the interview to the people in New York. The first thing we heard her say was:*
>
> *"Well, he was a rude little bastard, wasn't he?"*

FILM CRITIC

In the early '00s, I became a film critic, although that's a bit of a strong word for what I did. I would say I was more of a film reviewer. I started by doing reviews on the radio (with Daily Herald film critic Dann Gire), and then, thanks to Bob Sirott, it turned into a gig as the reviewer on television's *Chicago Tonight* on WTTW, Chicago's PBS station (Bob was the host of the show at the time).

The job of film critic sounds like a glamorous job, doesn't it? You get to watch three to five movies a day nearly every day of the week. What's not to love?

A lot.

Let me tell you. When those movies suck, it's torture! I think it was Richard Roeper, Roger Ebert's partner on television for years, who once said after a terrible movie we had just been forced to watch:

"Well, that's two hours of my life I won't get back."

That's the downside of being a reviewer. But the upside is pretty cool too. The Chicago Film Critics Association had incredible award dinners where we honored some of the biggest movie stars in the world; people like Tom Hanks and Paul Newman, and it gave me a chance to get some of these big stars on my show.

My favorite junket as a film critic was the press day for the film *Road to Perdition*, starring Tom Hanks. It was shot in and around Chicago and Illinois, so they had their big press day in Chicago. I had never been to one of these before — not at this level. They took over an entire hotel. All of the costumes were laid out so you could see the detail on the clothing. They had various conference rooms dedicated to interviews and questions, and then they started bringing a parade of people involved with the film; everyone from the director, to the cinematographer, to the producer, to Tom Hanks.

I was there as a film reviewer, but I was also there as the host of a morning show on an Oldies station, and Tom Hanks had done this great film about the music from that era called *That Thing You Do*. It really wasn't a big hit, but I loved it. Hanks had also starred in the movie *Castaway*, and Elvis songs had played a prominent role in that film. I always wanted to know if his love of music from that era was the reason those Elvis songs were in that movie.

Those questions had been festering in my brain for a few years, so I was determined to ask them. To ensure I could, I did something that I've never done before. There were a bunch of us in this room waiting for Tom Hanks, but I was the only actual morning host in the room. The rest of them were all producers and co-hosts of various other shows, but there was no other "name," if you will. So I played the "seniority card." I informed the others that I was going to take over the beginning of this interview session and ask these questions that I've wanted to ask him for years, and then I'd turn it over to everyone else. Nobody said a word.

Tom Hanks came in and sat down and I started grilling him about *That Thing You Do*, and he starting talking about it with some enthusiasm, because that movie was really his baby. He said: "Where were you when this movie came out?"

Then we talked about *Castaway* and I asked if the Elvis songs were in the movie because he was a big fan and he said: "No John, it's because Elvis was from Memphis, home of Fed Ex, you idiot!"

We talked about Oldies some more, and suddenly he realized that we weren't talking about *Road to Perdition*. He said: "Who is this guy?"

Everyone eventually got their turn and we talked about the new movie, and Tom Hanks was extremely nice. He took time to talk to everyone, and answered everyone's questions, and was very patient and understanding about all of it.

But I got the tape I wanted, and played it on the air the next morning.

LESLIE KEILING *REMEMBERS*

Leslie has a favorite memory from her time with the show…
John was in Peoria to speak at Larry Lujack's induction in the Illinois Broadcasters' Hall of Fame. Bill Murray was also on hand for the event. Realizing that getting back to Chicago in time for the next morning's show would be more than difficult, we arranged to do the show from a radio station across the street from our hotel.

> John invited Larry and Bill to stop by. And wouldn't you know it, bright and early the following morning Larry moseyed in and joined JRL on the air. It was the most animated I'd ever seen Ol' Uncle Lar, making for some really interesting radio. Unfortunately, Bill Murray was a no-show despite having given the impression that he too would join the fun. A good hour later, Bill did finally show up. Turns out the folks at the hotel were so solicitous that they had to arrange for a limo to pick up Mr. Murray and take him to his destination – across the street! Needless to say spending some broadcast time with John, Larry and Bill in a tiny studio in central Illinois was both surreal and hysterical.

ROGER EBERT

The king of the movie reviewers is Roger Ebert. In addition to being the best film critic on the planet, Roger is one of the smartest human beings I know.

Some people that become big stars get big heads. That wasn't the case with either Roger or Gene Siskel. Roger was totally welcoming to me when I became a critic, which wasn't the case with all of the critics. Remember, I was just this radio guy who was a big fan of movies, and happened to review them on my show — I wasn't really doing it as a job like the rest of them.

But Roger came up to me at one of my early screenings and made a big point of saying in front of everyone: "You finally have a worthwhile profession."

The highlight of my time as a film critic probably came when I was on a two-man panel discussion about film in Indiana with Roger Ebert — just the two of us. Not that we were on the same level in any way. This is a man who can dissect a film shot by shot, frame by frame. He has an encyclopedic knowledge of the history of film. He knows just about all there is to know... and suffice it to say, I don't know, and can't do, any of those things.

One of the people in the audience asked Roger what his favorite genre of film was, and he answered "Film Noir." I said, "I don't even know what that is!"

I have two more stories to give you an idea of how passionate Roger Ebert is about film. When the movie *Babe* came out, I loved it and I knew Roger loved it, but my wife at the time had no interest in seeing it. I asked him if he would come on my show to help me convince her that she *had* to see the movie. He did it with great enthusiasm. It's hard to say no when the greatest film critic in the world tells you that you have to see a movie.

Another time I invited Roger and his wife over to my house for a party (along with a bunch of other friends). I had just gotten this new plasma television, and asked Roger if he wanted to come in and see it. I put on the film *Wyatt Earp* which had just come out on DVD, because I love that opening scene — the way they use sound is unbelievable.

While we were watching that opening scene, with the sound cranked to ear splitting levels, Roger was doing a dissertation on why Val Kilmer should have been nominated for an Academy Award for that role, and Roger's wife Chaz walked into the room.

She looked at what we were doing, sighed, and said. "Oh great. Just like home."

RICK KAEMPFER *REMEMBERS*

Rick was also there for the Ebert movie dissertation that day...
My three kids, who were all little at the time, were also there.

> *They sat quietly and listened to Roger pontificating about the genre of Westerns, and the acting in some of those old Westerns, and before he was through, a small crowd had formed. All of us were spellbound. When we got in our car to leave later that day, my oldest son Tommy, who was about eight or nine, said to me, "Who was that friend of John's? Boy, he sure does love movies."*

GEORGE CARLIN

Usually when you're doing a morning show, and you do something spectacular on the air, it gets aired multiple times. You'll hear it on a "Best Of" show, or replay it in a different hour, or on the weekend, or when you're on vacation. But one of the funniest things that ever happened on our show at WJMK never again saw the light of day.

George Carlin, God rest his soul, came in to the studio and we hit it off immediately. He started riffing and ad-libbing, and doing this long ad-libbed bit about how much he loved it when there was tragedy, especially mass tragedy, and how he lived for watching smoke coming from the ashes of idiots that died doing stupid things, and went on and on, trumping himself over and over again.

It was hilarious. We were laughing so hard we had tears streaming down our faces. Everybody at the station came in to say how much they loved it, and how hilarious he was, that it was more like a performance than an interview, and even George Carlin called us from his office in LA and asked for a tape so that he could lift the bit and work it into his monologue. Our management loved it so much, they submitted the tape of that interview for an award because it was so memorably brilliant.

That tape was sent on September 8th, 2001.

Three days later, 9/11 happened.

All of the things that George Carlin was talking about in a satirical way as comedy happened in a real way as tragedy.

Needless to say, we didn't win the award, and the segment never aired again.

CHAPTER FOURTEEN
I'M WITH THE BAND

> The 1990s were a time of some very unusual news stories; a man got his penis cut off by his wife and became a national celebrity. Figure skaters went from lovely ice queens to knee-crushing thugs. And a football star's trial was the biggest story of the decade.

Shortly after I started up on WJMK, I was contacted again by my old friends in the band The Kind. They were now known as the Legends and wondered if I'd come out to sing a few songs with them. I ended up doing a lot more than that. The band performed the music on the parody songs I wrote and recorded, we released six different CDs for charity, and we did concerts all over Chicagoland as Landecker and the Legends.

BOBBITT

"The Bobbitt Song" was the first song that was hugely successful for us. It was to the tune of "If You Wanna Be Happy for the Rest of Your Life, Never Make a Pretty Woman Your Wife." Our version was "If you wanna be happy for the rest of your life, don't make Lorena Bobbitt your wife." *(The full lyrics of this song are in the appendix.)*

Lorena Bobbitt, you'll remember, cut off her husband's weenie, and then drove to the woods and threw it out the window. This was a huge story, and as long as you weren't John Wayne Bobbitt, it was funny as hell. Our song became so popular and got so many requests, that the station started playing it in other dayparts. It actually became the catalyst for getting the band together and putting together an actual honest to goodness stage show. We rehearsed, learned a bunch of songs, and started performing live.

Now, you can't just go out and stand on a stage like a dolt. You have to put on a show. If you can't have pyrotechnics and expensive lighting, which of course we couldn't afford, you have to give the people something special. For that first show we came up with a bit called "Pin the Penis on the Bobbitt." Now before you get all upset (what about the children?!), you should know that this was a 21 and older club, and people were drinking.

Pin the Penis followed the traditional Pin the Tail on the Donkey rules, except an anatomically correct John Wayne Bobbitt was the donkey. We blindfolded the participants, handed them the penis, spun them around, and they had to pin the penis in the correct spot (just like Bobbitt's surgeons had to do after they retrieved his actual penis in the woods near his house). Let me tell you, there were some very bizarre locations for where the penis ended up.

SHOE SHOPPING

When my co-host Vicki was pregnant, Rick and I decided to write a song for the Legends, a parody dedicated to her called "Pregnant Woman."

We were going to do an appearance at a club, and it was decided that the skit for "Pregnant Woman" would involve me dressing up as a pregnant woman; complete with a wig, pregnant belly, boobs and a dress. I decided that I also needed high heels. So, I marched down to the Magnificent Mile in Chicago to shop at one of those high-falutin' women's shoe stores.

I just blithely strolled in the door, not giving a second thought to how it looked, walked up to a sales guy and told him I was looking for a very large pair of high heels. He didn't even flinch. He showed me a few of their shoes, and I tried a bunch of them on, before settling on one pair. I bought the shoes and left.

It wasn't until two hours or so after I did this that it occurred to me what I had done.

"What in the hell was I thinking? What must this sales guy think? I just walked into this women's shoe store like it was Foot Locker and tried on high heeled shoes, and never once explained why I was doing this."

But then again, in today's society, who knows?

Maybe it wasn't that weird. Just another transvestite getting ready for work.

LAMBS FARM

I always felt that the primary purpose of the band Landecker and the Legends was to promote the morning show and the radio station. I never felt like it was the other way around. The band was a promotional vehicle just like a prize van or street machine, or whatever they call those things.

I noticed there were other oldies stations around the country that did charity concerts, and I thought it would be a very effective way to promote the station. The other stations had no trouble booking oldies acts because there were a ton of them out there touring every year. There still are.

But I felt we could even offer an extra wrinkle, because we also had our own band. We had already done a charity CD for an organization called Lambs Farm in Libertyville, north of Chicago. Lambs Farm is a non-profit organization serving people with developmental disabilities. As it turned out, Lambs Farm already had a stage and a large open area for fans, and it was the perfect place to do this.

The station went along with my idea, and we put on charity concerts for years. That first concert featured us opening up for the Flying Elvis' from the film *Honeymoon in Vegas*. We drew a giant crowd for that first one, and they kept coming every year after that — drawing crowds of anywhere from 30,000 to 40,000 people at a shot.

DAHMER

Most of the Landecker & the Legends songs were well received, but a few weren't. For instance, we did a song about Jeffrey Dahmer. It's not everyone that can say they did a song about Jeffrey Dahmer. It also happens to be the only song that management banned from the airwaves because it was in bad taste.

OK, in retrospect, maybe it was pushing the envelope a little bit. But Dahmer had been killed in a prison in Wisconsin by an inmate who thought he was God — and there was talk about saving Dahmer's brain to study what makes people crazy.

Now, doesn't that sound like material to you? It certainly did to us.

Our song was called "The Day That Dahmer Died" and it was done to the tune of the Paper Lace song "The Night Chicago Died." (Now THAT'S a song that should have been banned.) In the song we just basically told the story of his death. Now what is so bad about that?

At any rate, management banned the song, forbidding us to ever play it again. After reading the lyrics again when we were preparing this book, well, I hate to admit when I'm wrong, but maybe it was in slightly bad taste after all. *(The lyrics are in the appendix.)*

A GASEOUS DILEMMA

There was one other song we did that was controversial too, but I think it's one of the best songs we ever did. It's called "King of Farts," and it's done to the tune of Juice Newton's "Queen of Hearts." *(The lyrics are in the appendix.)*

Now you may not realize this, but some people actually didn't want to hear a song about farts, while others, namely the perpetually sophomoric like me, did want to hear it. Abe Lincoln said that you can't please all the people all the time. Well, Abe was wrong, especially here in the Land of Lincoln.

As it turns out, "King of Farts" and Debbie Boone's "You Light Up My Life" are pretty much exactly the same length, just by coincidence. And since WJMK was an FM station, we were broadcasting in stereo. That meant there was a right channel and a left channel.

I don't know where great ideas like this come from, perhaps it's just a bit of God-given inspiration, but this is what we did. On one single tape cartridge we put "You Light Up My Life" in one channel and "King of Farts" in the other. So, when the tape was being played on the air, both songs would play simultaneously. You, the listener, had control over your balance knob, and you could go to the left side (King of Farts) or the right side (You Light Up My Life). Or you could listen to part of one song, and switch it over, and switch it back, and switch it back and forth. I still think that was a truly unique solution to a truly unusual broadcasting dilemma.

Of course if you didn't have a balance knob, you might have been scarred for life.

THE DIAPER

Really, anything that was happening to me in those days was possible fodder for a song.

One day I got two insulting pieces of mail. The first was an invitation to join AARP, the American Association of Retired People. How dare you? My 85-year-old father belongs to that organization, not me. But that was just the beginning. The second letter said, "Hey John Landecker, you're entitled to a special offer from the scooter store." Great. Demographically I've just entered the age bracket most likely to need a scooter. Thanks for the reminder.

These two pieces of mail inspired another song, and introduced the strangest prop we ever used in concert. In protest of receiving that damn AARP card, we wrote a song called "Baby Boomers" to the tune of "Louie Louie." The song was all about our fear of getting old. One key to doing a stage show like this is that you have to have no qualms about embarrassing yourself in public. If you're uptight about that, do not, I repeat do not, come down this road. However, if you have no worries about embarrassing yourself, "CMON DOWN!"

When we played the song on the air, a listener made a man-sized diaper and bonnet, and got me a huge baby bottle and an oversized pacifier, and that's how I came out on stage to perform "Baby Boomers."

In a diaper.

It was a show stopper.

(*The lyrics to the song "Baby Boomers" can be found in the appendix.*)

THE DANCING ITOS

Another Landecker & the Legends incident remains unresolved as far as I'm concerned. It happened during the O.J. Simpson Trial.

Landecker and the Legends were scheduled to appear on the bill with the Buckinghams and a few other oldies acts at the Star Plaza Theater in Merrillville, Indiana — no small potatoes, my friends. That's a big theater that holds about 3,500 people. At the same time we were working on parody songs about the O.J. Trial, and I came up with the idea of doing a song about O.J. to the Village People song "YMCA" and calling it "Why DNA?" My producer Rick and I came up with the lyrics to the song.

When we were tossing around ideas for how to present this song on stage, I suggested that we get a couple of people to dress up like the judge in the trial, Lance Ito. We could get them to wear fake beards, and judge's gowns, and have them dance to the song on stage. I suggested we call them, "The Dancing Itos."

And we did it, and it was a huge hit!

So, weeks went by, and the trial was still going on, and the song was getting lots of airplay on the station and people were loving it, so I said to myself, "Why don't we send this to Jay Leno at the Tonight Show?" It seemed that Letterman was leaving the O.J. trial alone for some reason. So, we packed up the song, and overnighted it to Jay Leno.

Later that week, my phone started ringing. My brother was calling from California. He was screaming with excitement.

"They're doing your song!" he said. "They're doing your song!"

Well, as it turned out, the Tonight Show with Jay Leno also performed a parody of "YMCA" about O.J. Simpson. The lyrics weren't the same as ours, but the concept was the same. And the icing on the cake was that the Dancing Friggin' Ito's were on stage while the song was being performed. They even called them "The Dancing Itos."

Our listeners were pissed! They called and faxed the Tonight Show in significant numbers expressing their dissatisfaction. I sent Jay a letter about it. I still have that letter in my computer.

April 11, 1995
Jay Leno
NBC-TV
Dear Jay,

Early last week, I overnighted a package to you that contained a parody of The Village People's "YMCA" called "Why DNA?" I've been playing this parody for a while now, and it is by far the most requested song on our station. I also enclosed a lyric sheet and a letter.

In the letter, I explained that I had been using the Dancing Itos on stage since January. Although I didn't ask for it, I fantasized that you would mention my program, play the song, the nation would love it, my ratings would go up and my contract would be renewed!!

Cut to last Thursday night. I'm watching NBC prime time, and Bingo! A Tonight Show promo hits the air. It's some sort of Ito/Village People/O.J.L.A. thing! I can't believe it!!

When I got on the air Friday morning at 5:30 am, the first call came in... "John, did you see Jay Leno last night?"

241

For the next 4½ hours, it was pretty much non-stop on the fax machine and the telephone. Did The Tonight Show take our idea? Why didn't Jay mention you? And on and on. I said on the air, in my opinion, you might not have even seen the package that I sent. Maybe some writer grabbed it and used it, or maybe it was just a coincidence.

At any rate, I'm still a desperate radio personality pleading for plugs. Can I get a) a mention, b) an appearance, c) an interview d) all of the above, or should I just go f**k myself?

Say, did I ever tell you I really like motorcycles?

> *Love and kisses, Your pen pal,*
> *John Records Landecker*
> *Oldies 104.3 WJMK*

JAY CALLS

Sure enough, Jay Leno got enough angry calls and letters that he called into our show. I interviewed him on the air. He insisted that they don't take unsolicited material, and if he was going to rip somebody off, he wouldn't rip off somebody of my stature, blah blah blah.

I was Conan O'Brien's opening act!

I'm only kidding, of course. I have no knowledge of how the creative process worked on The Tonight Show to come up with that concept, but I find it to be almost inexplicably coincidental that the song concept was used, *and* the Dancing Ito concept was used (because that was a really weird concept), the exact same week we sent it to him. *(The transcript of a portion of Jay Leno's call to the show is in the appendix of this book.)*

VIVA VIAGRA

One of the parody songs that Landecker and the Legends did during this era at WJMK — another concept that Rick Kaempfer my producer and I came up with — was a song about Viagra. This was right when Viagra came out and it was the only erectile dysfunction medicine on the market.

"Oh my God, it's a pill that will give you a boner! Let's do a song about it!"

And we did. In 1998 we did a song called "Viva Viagra" to the tune of Elvis' "Viva Las Vegas," and we did it live many, many times, all over the Chicago area. We did it for years. We even recorded it and released it on our fifth CD.

Well, lo and behold, I was watching television years later and on came this commercial for Viagra, and guess what? They had a jingle to the tune of "Viva Las Vegas," and it was called "Viva Viagra."

So, I called a copyright attorney.

"Did you copyright that?" he asked.

And of course, no, we didn't.

So he said, "Well, that's too bad. You might have been able to make some money."

It just goes to show you that you never really know where your ideas are going to end up. In the future, if I ever come up with another concept for a tune, and I go so far as to record it and release it, I'm definitely going to copyright it.

By the way, the lyrics printed in this book *(in the appendix)* are now officially published by me. Capice, Mr. Viagra?

THE BOYS IN THE BAND

Working with Landecker and the Legends is definitely one of my favorite memories of those WJMK days. I have to say, we put together quite an entertaining show. And we had a long multi-year run doing concerts in and around Chicago, everywhere from county fairs and festivals, to the Star Plaza Theater in Merrillville, to the Rosemont Theater in Rosemont, to doing shows with the Animals, and opening shows for the Monkees, and releasing CDs at Christmas time to benefit charities. We eventually released six different CDs and raised thousands of dollars for Lambs Farm in Libertyville.

Just getting up on stage with the band was so much fun. I loved it! There was one summer I believe we did 25 concerts in three months, which is basically every weekend, and often multiple shows during those weekends. One time we even did two shows in one day in two separate venues.

There were a few different lineups of the Legends over the years, but the core always remained the same. Mark Gardner (guitar), Tim Kennedy (lead guitar), Steve Jacula (bass), Steve Vasoli (keyboards), and Jay Slowik (drums). Steve Jacula also produced all of the Landecker and the Legends CDs at his Old Plank Studios. Unfortunately, he had to leave the band for health reasons, and Steve passed away during the summer of 2010. He is missed. As we were working on this book in March of 2011, our keyboardist Steve Vasoli passed away too. He was only 54. Sad, sad, sad. Both of the Steves were great guys.

The other key members of the band were Dan Gardner (our awesome soundman), Jeff Knutsen (our stage announcer and roadie), Jim Knott (a former intern and roadie), Bridget Kaempfer (our back stage coordinator — who, by the way, is qualified to be the next president of the United States — she's amazingly efficient and can do absolutely anything, including running these Landecker and the

Legends shows), Rick Kaempfer, Vince Argento, and Tom Sochowski (our producers and bit performers), and the other musicians that played with us along the way, including Pete Kapp, Ryan Veitch, Craig Meyer, our horn players Randy Kulik, Ryan Miller, Craig Roselieb, our accordion player Tim Sleep, our child prodigy Dylan Gardner (now a recording star in his own right), and each and every family member of the band.

That band became like a family to all of us as we toured around the Chicago area. I can't thank them all enough for their hard work and patience dealing with that radio guy who always had "just one more idea for the show."

THE END OF THE TOUR

After touring with Landecker and the Legends for seven consecutive summers, it eventually became a bit too much for us all. I was doing a morning radio show every weekday, and that was challenging enough. Then I had knee problems, and that further caused us to slow down. And then finally, when I moved out to Indiana, and the band was still located in Naperville, it just became too difficult to rehearse.

The summer of 2000 was our last summer doing a full-time tour.

The songs live on though, and you just never know where they'll turn up. Bob Sirott was in Miami over Christmas break in 2012 and sent me a photo of one of our CDs in a music store in Florida.

CHAPTER FIFTEEN
AN OLDIE, BUT NOT A GOODIE

The late '90s to early '00s gave us the most controversial election in American history, when the Supreme Court elected George W. Bush. We also experienced the worst attack on American soil, and the beginning of two wars to avenge that attack; one in Afghanistan and one in Iraq. The late '90s to early '00s saw the end of the Michael Jordan era in Chicago, and the classic Steve Bartman moment at Wrigley Field. It was the era of the blockbuster adventure movie with *Spiderman*, *Star Wars Phantom Menace*, and *Lord of the Rings* all drawing huge crowds. Reality television also exploded thanks to the mega-hit *Survivor*. Meanwhile, the most popular musical group in America became a pariah overnight after their lead singer said a few words she probably shouldn't have said at a performance in England.

Laura became my wife during my decade long run at WJMK. We didn't have any kids together, but we did have dogs. In my first two marriages the idea of owning a dog never occurred to me. When my kids were younger we had a bird, a couple of guinea pigs, and a cat, but no dogs.

That all changed during my marriage to my third wife Laura (boy, do I love the sound of that.) Laura started taking yoga, and the instructor was a dog zealot. Laura became somewhat of a follower, and it wasn't long before I was informed it was our civic duty to offer a home to an abandoned canine. That's when Zeke, an

Australian cattle dog, became a part of our family. I know, I said it, a part of a family. Ready for this? I was Daddy, Laura was Mommy. We were those people. Zeke even got a little publicity. The *Chicago Tribune Magazine* did a feature on Chicago celebrities and their dogs, and Zeke's picture was on the same page as one of Oprah's dogs.

Now, when you're a dog zealot, one is never enough. Laura met a Chicago police officer who rescued pit bulls from the projects, and those that he could rehabilitate were placed in private homes. You guessed it. I was told we needed to adopt a pit bull. This is where I drew the line. These dogs are killing machines and have no place in a civilized household. Laura started to work on me. If someone doesn't take this pit bull, she will be put down. Why don't we take Zeke over to the pit bull halfway house and see if two of them get along? So I walked into the pit bull halfway house and sat on the couch. They let the pit bull into the room and she immediately came up to me and lay down under my legs.

Now we had two dogs; Zeke the Australian cattle dog and Stella the pit bull.

OUTGROWING THE NEIGHBORHOOD

At the time we lived in Lincoln Park; a densely populated upscale neighborhood on Chicago's north side. Dogs were to be kept on leashes there at all times, and Zeke was an Australian cattle dog, which is a high-strung extremely intelligent working breed. He needed room to run and there wasn't any. Stella was a pit bull, and quite frankly the neighborhood looked down on her. She loved all people, but except for Zeke, dogs were not her friends. Every time we took the dogs for a walk it was a huge stressful undertaking.

So we decided to look for a weekend place out of the city somewhere where the dogs had some room to run and be themselves. We found a great place; a three bedroom house built in 1947 on ten acres just a few miles on the Indiana side of the Michigan-Indiana border.

Our nearest neighbor was on the other side of the field, and they rescued horses. At that time, there wasn't a fence around the barn. Zeke took one look at those horses and instinct took over. It was amazing really. He just ran over, did his thing, and herded those horses into a small barn. He did it a couple of times, and I thought to myself, "I'm going to have to buy a fence."

One afternoon Zeke took off after the horses again, only this time Stella thought she would join in. Stella had no horse herding skills. The next thing I saw was Stella flying head over heels like a football, having just been kicked by a horse. I went chasing after Stella. She had gotten up and was ready for round two. Zeke, the two horses and Stella ended up in the small barn before I could reach them. It was here that I did something that no rational human would do. I decided to go in there and rescue my dogs.

There was only one entrance to the stall, and when I went in, both dogs were barking with their teeth bared, backed up against the wall. The horses had this crazed look in their eyes and were in a state of panic. That's the last thing I remember. In retrospect, my theory is that a horse charged me in an attempt to gain his freedom, and in so doing, knocked me unconscious. It's only a theory though because the next thing I remembered was laying on my back in the dirt, staring up at the sky. I propped myself up to survey the surroundings. The two horses were up against a fence, eating grass. Zeke was a few yards away from them, keeping an eye on the horses. And Stella, was slowly limping towards me, finally ready to call it a day.

Needless to say, we got a fence.

ANOTHER CHANGE

By now, I've made it pretty clear that this decade long stretch at WJMK was a little bumpy. During one of our typical "what will we do with the morning show?" periods, someone decided without asking me that I needed a new female co-host. I found out by mistake at a radio function when someone said to me: "What do you think about your new co-host?"

What?

The station had entered into negotiations with Catherine Johns. I had worked with Catherine at WLS. She was a first rate news person at that time, and had since gone on to become a great talk show host. Although no one asked me, in this case, I thought it was a great idea. But here is where this great idea got sidetracked: They wanted Catherine to not only be my co-host, they wanted her to do traffic. Traffic in morning drive radio is its own domain. It requires training and the ability to interpret computer shorthand as you broadcast the information. Catherine had never done traffic in her life. Instead of tapping into her many strengths, we led with a weakness. The amount of time and energy expended to deal with this was ridiculous. Every day after the show I would say the same thing: "Get somebody else to do the traffic! Let Catherine just co-host!" For some reason that was not going to happen.

I think this is a pretty good example of the sorts of things that go on behind the scenes at radio morning shows trying to make it in a big market like Chicago.

CATHERINE JOHNS REMEMBERS

Catherine remembers her time on the show... *You might remember, in the late '90s... there was a lot of buzz about the ancient Chinese practice of Feng Shui. It literally means "wind water" and it's all about organizing your space to promote happiness and harmony. Design my way to happiness and harmony? I was completely fascinated!*

And of course John made merciless fun of my interest in something that seemed like airy fairy nonsense to him and the boys. But I figured out how to turn him around. Feng shui principles, I explained, can be used to increase prosperity and fame. Fame, you say? No one was more interested in increased prosperity and fame than John Landecker. Now he was up for it!

We actually had a Feng Shui consultant come in and rearrange our office. We changed the angles of the desks and put a plant in our fame area. Hung a waterfall picture in the career corner, and I believe it was a money tree in the prosperity zone. A mirror figured in somewhere. And there we were: ready to be showered with prosperity and fame. It wasn't long after our Feng Shui makeover that John signed a new contract – and its terms were not what he would have hoped for. And it wasn't long after that that I got blown out altogether. Apparently John was right: this Feng Shui prosperity and fame business wasn't quite what it was cracked up to be!

SEPTEMBER 11th

The most unique broadcast that I have ever been a part of, has nothing to do with planning, promotion, prizes, and listeners. It was the morning of September 11th, 2001.

I'm sure that every morning show in the country has their own story of what they did when the planes hit the twin towers in New York. This is mine.

We were doing our regular show. Our producer Rick was on the phone with Butch Patrick, who had played Eddie Munster on *The Munsters*. He was going to be a mystery guest — listeners were to call in and try to figure out who he was. When Rick got in touch with Butch, the news had just broken that a plane had flown into the World Trade Center.

"Are you watching this?" Butch asked Rick.

"Yeah," Rick replied. "I don't think we're going to do this mystery guest bit."

"No, you better not," Butch replied.

Brant Miller was our weatherman and had a broadcast line hookup to his home. He was also the meteorologist for NBC-Channel 5 in Chicago, and had access to all of the NBC News information. Richard Cantu was our news man, and he's a real journalist, and was connected to the CBS Radio network.

Needless to say, after the news had come across that the first plane had hit, we turned on the television in the studio, and we were all watching it, and the microphones were open, when the second plane hit the tower.

I'll never forget what Brant Miller said: "We're under attack."

Well what do you do in a situation like that? Our decision was to go all news right on the spot. There weren't many details early on, so there was a lot of repetition, as to the content, but we didn't play any music. I thought it would really be ridiculous to play "Hang on Sloopy" and then do more content about being under attack.

We did play commercials, but not because the clients had paid for them to air — because we needed that time to regroup and find out as much information as we could so we could better inform our audience what was going on. News stations didn't play commercials, but they were set up to handle this much better than we were. They had a full staff on hand. We just had the four or five of us in the studio.

But I'm really proud of what we were able to deliver. Brant was able to tap into what NBC was getting. Richard was able to tap into what CBS was getting. And I sort of quarterbacked and anchored the whole thing; repeating the facts as we knew them, and encouraging people not to jump to conclusions about who did this, because we didn't know anything for sure.

I found out later that listeners stuck with us during that morning show, and didn't tune into the news station, and that the radio station itself toyed with the idea of keeping us on the air until noon. The adrenaline, the being in the moment, and the feeling you have in that situation takes on a whole different sensation — one that I hope I never have again frankly.

It was certainly one of the most memorable mornings I've ever spent on the air.

LESLIE KEILING REMEMBERS

Leslie Keiling was one of the co-hosts of the show during the WJMK run, including the day of 9/11. This is how she recalled that time… *I wouldn't trade the time we spent together on the morning show at WJMK for anything in the world. Being with everyone on that show on the morning of 9/11/2001 is etched in my head and heart. I now have a glimmer of understanding about sharing a foxhole.*

ON THE ROAD AGAIN

Eventually we revisited our concept of taking the show on the road, something that had been one of the keys to our early success, and super-sized it. We went out of the country, usually to some warm climate during the winter, and we took a whole bunch of listeners with us. Apple Vacations came to us with this great promotion idea. I believe the first location was Jamaica. It was an absolutely great promotion — we went all over the place. We went to the Dominican Republic, Mexico, St. Lucia, you name it.

On this first trip, I had just had my knee scoped for a torn meniscus cartilage, and I had to do the entire thing with crutches. And actually, it wasn't so bad. It sure was easier getting around an 85 degree all-inclusive resort in Jamaica than it would have been getting around snowy, windswept Chicago.

It was on this first trip that I had a revelation about the listeners of our show. The stereotype of an oldies station listener had been force-fed to us from the moment our show went on the air. We were told that these were upstanding all-American family people who only wanted clean, family entertainment. And that's what I honestly thought. At their homes, that's what they were like.

But when they got to Jamaica, they got drunk off their asses and took their clothes off! That was an eye opener. It's one thing to say something to a survey taker, but it's a whole different thing when you can get out of town and let your hair down. They got crazy in Jamaica. At one point, in the middle of the afternoon, they were sliding into the pool — ass backwards — completely naked.

They got crazy in the Dominican Republic too. At one point all the men dressed up in women's swimsuits and showed up for the broadcast that way. They got crazy in Mexico. I'm betting our listeners set some sort of tequila consumption record at the hotel that week. I mean, after all, it was "all inclusive."

RICK KAEMPFER REMEMBERS

Rick was such a worry wart. He worried about every little thing that could or would go wrong in a broadcast, and one day all of his worries came true... *One of the problems we encountered at WJMK was of a technical nature. There were months at a time when we couldn't do the show we wanted to do because of technical limitations. They had to build a new studio for us twice, once at our original location, and once when the entire station moved to a new location.*

The second time it took several months to build the new studios, and while they did so, they took bits and pieces out of the old studio until we were working with just enough equipment to keep us on the air. Needless to say, this limited what we could do on the show.

So, with great fanfare, we finally moved into our new studios in 2003, and we wanted to celebrate our first day in the studio by having celebrity guests to help us christen it. After months of doing a bare-bones show, we were excited to be doing a full-fledged morning show again. I booked comic actor Martin Short to call in.

But the first thing we discovered when we showed up that first morning was that they had forgotten to set up the phone lines for listener calls (listener phone calls were a crucial ingredient of the show). After seeing that everything else also wasn't working right, I decided to double check the hotline.

It was dead too.

We had no way of broadcasting anything through the phone lines, and Martin Short — who we had been promoting all morning — was about to call.

And call he did — right on time. I asked Martin if he would mind calling twenty minutes later, hoping we could resolve our issues in that time, but he told me he had another interview scheduled — if we wanted to talk to him, it was now or never.

"Give him my cell number," John said.

When the commercial ended, John conducted the entire interview on his cell phone. He asked the questions into a combination of the microphone and the cellular phone, so Short and the listeners could hear, then he held the cellular phone up to the microphone for Short's answers.

I don't remember what they talked about in the interview except for the first few seconds, when John explained the situation to him. Short thought it was a bit because the concept of a major radio station in Chicago holding a cell phone to the microphone was so ridiculous.

"Are you serious?" Martin finally asked.

"Totally serious."

"Who owns you guys?" Martin asked.

"CBS, the second biggest radio company in America."

"And you guys are in Chicago?" he asked.

"Yup. Third biggest media market in America."

"And I thought I had seen it all," he replied.

It was actually a pretty funny interview, considering. I gained even more respect for John Landecker that day. He took a potential disaster and turned it into a memorable radio moment.

I bet Martin Short remembers that very bizarre interview to this day."

SOBRIETY

One thing that I realized about being sober was that I was now available to handle responsibilities, and many of those responsibilities arose during horrible situations, whether you liked it or not.

My father took a fall, and I came home to take care of him. I stayed with him for a couple of weeks and did my radio show out of Detroit back into Chicago. I remember one moment distinctly from that stay with him. I've mentioned that my father was blind. Well, he also had leader dogs. In case you don't know, leader dogs are working dogs. Nobody else gets to feed them, or groom them, or play with them. You can hang out with them, but they can't play. They're working.

Part of Dad's regular routine with his leader dog was taking him out multiple times a day to go to the bathroom in this area behind the garage. Well one time when I was home with him, my father said to me: "Will you take the dog out?"

Now, I was floored, because no one was allowed to do any of these official functions with the dog. But I was also a little pissed off, because quite frankly, my father was being grumpy and had been grumpy for days, and it was cold and raining outside. So, I put on my raincoat, walked the dog behind the garage, and stood in the rain with my arm sticking out, holding the dog's leash. And the friggin' dog just stood there. We just stared at each other in the rain.

And that's when it dawned on me, that this is why I was sober. So I could come back to Ann Arbor to help my father. So I could stand out in the rain, and watch his dog take a shit.

ASHES TO ASHES

Kathy and Judy, who were WGN radio hosts at the time (around 2003), had managed to convince Mayor Daley to declare a "Take Your Parents to Work Day," their spin on "Take Your Kids to Work Day." I was still doing the morning show on WJMK, and when I read about Kathy and Judy's idea in the paper, I got an idea of my own.

My father had recently died, and had been cremated, and for some odd reason, I still had the box that once contained his ashes sitting in my office. (His actual ashes were buried.) The outside of this box was stamped with the words: "Contains the ashes of Werner Landecker."

Even though this box didn't contain my father's ashes anymore, it occurred to me that this could be a funny practical joke for "Take Your Parents to Work Day." You see, my producer Rick, and my co-host Leslie Keiling and her husband Tim had driven all the way to Ann Arbor when my father passed away to attend the reception after the funeral, which just impressed the hell out of me. And they, along with my technical producer Vince, knew there was nothing in the box. It was the perfect setup.

It worked better than I ever could have imagined. I put the box on the console and said I had brought my father into the studio for "Take Your Parents to Work Day."

"Well, hello, Werner," Leslie said. She thought that was the bit. Ha ha, Werner's box of ashes is here. But then live on the air, I opened up the box, and looked perplexed.

"Wait a second," I said, "there's still a little bit in here."

"Oh no," Leslie said.

And I blew into it, and this cloud of what appeared to be ashes, plumed into the air. Everybody FREAKED!

The part of Werner Landecker was played by Sweet & Low.

THE DIXIE CHICKS

I've always been into political satire, ever since the 1970s when I was doing Nixon, and doing parody records about the politicians, but I never really got into the politics of it — only the humor. I never really got into serious political issues.

Never.

But there was one incident that happened toward the end of my ten year run at WJMK that was significant to me, because for the first time in my career, I felt motivated to do something about free speech.

Here's what happened. In the aftermath of 9/11, I decided to play the Star Spangled Banner at the beginning of every morning show. However, I didn't want your normal radio station standard Star Spangled Banner, and I couldn't find one done by an oldies artist, because quite frankly, all of them sucked. But then, lo and behold, the Dixie Chicks did the Star Spangled Banner at the Super Bowl. It was perfect; beautiful three part harmony. Awesome! We had our regular sign-on song.

We played it every morning and it sounded fantastic. But then there was an incident with the Dixie Chicks. If you don't remember, they were doing a concert in London and they said they were ashamed that George Bush was from their home state of Texas. Country music stations across the country banned them for this comment — they were burning their records — and right-wing talk radio stations were criticizing and vilifying the Dixie Chicks 24 hours a day.

And here we were playing their version of the National Anthem every morning at 5:30. But we never said on the air: "Here are the Dixie Chicks." We never identified them on the air as the Dixie Chicks. Not once. Not ever. And I saw no reason to take this song

RECORDS TRULY IS MY MIDDLE NAME

off the air. We had been doing it for months. It's the Star Spangled Banner! Why stop? Nobody had complained about it to me, and I talked to the listeners on the phone every single day.

Apparently, unbeknownst to me, there were a few complaints to the program director. I never found out how many, but I'll never forget how I found out there were any at all. This program director was new to the station and was having a meeting with us, revamping our show (yet again). There was nothing new about this; program directors, general managers, and consultants had come and gone and revamped our show a million times. He started the meeting by asking us what we did on the show.

"Well," I said, "We come out of the first record and play the Star Spangled Banner."

"What version of the Star Spangled Banner?" he asked.

"The Dixie Chicks," I said.

"Aha!" he said. "That's where the complaints came from. You can't play the Star Spangled Banner by the Dixie Chicks."

Now this wasn't about lewd comments, dirty jokes, bodily functions, or any of the usual complaints I had gotten in my career. This was something completely different. This was about being ordered to desist playing the Star Spangled Banner. The National friggin Anthem.

"I don't know if I can do that," I said.

Wellllll, a bomb went off in that room. I mean, it was a nuclear blast.

This program director lost it more than any other program director I've had in my life, and listen — I've been around. I've never seen or heard a more out of control, vindictive program director ever, and I've had more program directors than I can count. He was out of his mind. He was turning red. The veins were popping out in his neck. He was screaming at me!

"If you play it again," he screamed. "You're fired."

I began to get out of the chair, and he added: "And if you get out of that chair, you're fired!"

Even in the midst of this heated confrontation, I knew what was going on here. If I left that room at that moment, I would have been walking away from a potential severance package. So, I crossed my arms in front of me and said "I'm not leaving this chair."

I don't even want to get into what happened the rest of that day. It was tumultuous. It involved agents. It involved screaming on the phone. It was bad. By the time it was over, I decided that it just wasn't worth it. That kind of stance wasn't really the kind of thing I did on my show. But I must admit, that next morning when we came in to do the show, my producer Rick and I talked about it again, and we did seriously consider playing it again, because it just didn't feel right to stop. Plus, we knew that this new management team didn't like us, and more than likely wouldn't be renewing us in a few months anyway, so, wouldn't this be an honorable way to go out?

At the last second we decided not to do it. We played a different, lamer version of the song. And sure enough, a few months later the station opted not to renew our contracts.

The next time the Dixie Chicks came into town for a concert, I went backstage and met them, and told them the story, and they all autographed their famous *Entertainment Weekly* cover for me.

I still have it on my wall in my home office.

THE WRITING ON THE WALL

Radio station management can be diabolical if they want to make your life miserable. There was another incident that had never happened to me before. Every morning show is going to get some complaints. Every previous radio station I ever worked for realized this, and went to bat for me. I mean, listeners can complain about the way you do the weather. They'll complain about just about anything. It's ridiculous. Normally, management only warns the talent if there is something really important.

But this GM told me that I was to personally call every single complainer and apologize. Are you shitting me? The idea of the morning host personally calling every single person who has a complaint is nothing more than management harassment, and showed a total lack of class and professionalism on their part.

It pleasures me to no end that this station has never regained the ratings that were there on my last day.

AWARD WINNING SHOW

We were on the air for ten years at WJMK, and I'm proud of the quality of our work during that time. We weren't the only ones that thought it was a good show. The John Landecker Show was named the best morning show in Chicago by the Achievement in Radio Awards (1996), and was nominated three other times.

We were also named the Best Oldies Morning Show in the country two years in a row by one of the most respected trade publications in our business, Radio & Records (2002 and 2003).

Just to show you not to take yourself too seriously, just a few months after they named us the best show in the country in 2003, our contract was not renewed.

RICK KAEMPFER *REMEMBERS*

Rick managed to find a bright spot about this situation... *John had told me about his station in Cleveland, and the way his bosses there tried to humiliate him into quitting. Then, at the tail end of our long run at WJMK, we had another little taste of that as the bosses tried to make the show into something we couldn't stomach doing every day, hoping that we would quit. The combination of those two stories had a profound effect on me. It inspired me to write a novel called $everance (ENC Press, 2007). The hero of that story was a morning radio host working for a company that wanted him to quit, while the host tried to do whatever he could to inspire the management to fire him, so he could collect his severance.*

CHAPTER SIXTEEN
TALKING THE TALK

> In the mid-to-late '00s, George W. Bush was reelected president and doubled down on the war in Iraq. A young state legislator came out of nowhere in Illinois to be elected Illinois' Senator, and then, President of the United States. But most importantly, the housing bubble burst, Wall Street collapsed, unemployment zoomed, and America was launched into the worst financial crisis in the Baby Boomer's lifetime. Chicago celebrated a couple of sports championships in the latter half of the decade, the White Sox won the World Series in 2005, and the Blackhawks won the Stanley Cup in 2010. At the box office, sequels ruled the day; *Revenge of the Sith*, *Spiderman 2*, and *Harry Potter and the Goblet of Fire*. On television *The Sopranos* ended its run, and *The Daily Show* became a cultural phenomenon.

I don't know if it's a coincidence, but as I look back over my life and career, the things that I go for, or apply for, I don't get. Usually somebody calls me out of the clear blue sky or somebody else has an idea, and that's what gets the ball rolling.

When we were let go by WJMK, I really didn't know what I was going to do at that point. I've heard people say things like "I'm going to take some time off and reassess my options," but I hadn't really considered that. At the time I had accumulated a little bit of money — money I had saved, my IRAs, money my father had left me — not a ton by any stretch of the imagination, but enough that right then and there I wasn't in panic city. (Now if I knew *then* what I know *now*, I may have been legitimately in panic city, but I wasn't then.)

MARY JUNE ROSE REMEMBERS

Mary June Rose was the program director of WGN in Chicago...
One day I was listening to John on WJMK on my way to work, looking for a little Motown – a break from my usual WGN talk-fare. He was going on and on about [Sun-Times columnist Robert] Feder's column regarding Felicia Middlebrooks. I couldn't believe my ears. First of all, this was an oldies station, and I KNEW they wanted him to "shut up and play the hits." He wasn't doing that. What on earth was he doing? Digging his grave? Second, he was having an opinion! WHAT? WHY? Was he crazy?

The first thing I thought was, "I am so glad I'm not his PD today. We'd have to have a 'come to Jesus' meeting about breaking format." The second thing I thought was, "he should be doing talk radio."

Not very many months after that, John was out of his oldies job, looking for some work. I called him and said I'd meet with him, even though I knew he really didn't have experience in our format. We hit it off right away. I explained that he would have to unlearn much of what he'd been taught over the years. Talk. About what? What do you care about. Talk about that. And I told him about that day I'd been listening, and if he hadn't broken format, he probably wouldn't be sitting in my office. Funny how things turn out.

WGN RADIO

I don't know if I can describe this properly, but WGN radio was the gold standard of radio in the United States at that time. WGN was a giant money-making juggernaut owned by the *Chicago Tribune*. Starting out at a station like that is like graduating from Star Fleet Academy, and being asked to work with Captain Kirk on the Starship Enterprise.

It was that big to me. It was huge.

Now, the only experience I've had doing talk was the KSTP thing which went OK, and the WLS thing, which had been a debacle, so I had no idea how it was going to go. But I went in there and everyone was so friendly and helpful. I was going on everyone's show — having the time of my life. I hit it off with Mary June. She was very supportive, and gave me some very constructive criticism. I began hosting the occasional show on the weekend, and doing some vacation relief during the week. But I really didn't know what I was doing.

I had a track record as a music personality. I had never done anything like this. I didn't feel like I was in too far over my head, but I also didn't exactly work my way up, and I was very aware of that. The way it usually works in radio is, you go to a small market, and you do the menial jobs, and pay your dues, and work your way up the ladder. That wasn't going to happen in talk radio for me.

I went immediately to the top station in Chicago after only doing five full talk shows, twelve years earlier. And nobody had given me any input about what I had done right or wrong. It was hard work but I felt I was making headway. The listeners of WGN seemed to like me. There were plenty of times when it was evident that I was pretty green and pretty raw and I had a steep learning curve, but I was still

John Records Landecker on the air in Chicago. The listeners of WGN knew me, and weren't half as critical as everyone else was. I really thought that this was the place to be.

And it was for awhile.

MARY JUNE ROSE REMEMBERS

"The first time he filled in on a weekend shift, the calls were predictable: "Landecker! What are you doing at WGN? Where have you been? It's great to hear you," etc. etc.

I told him after the show that once all the "hey, I grew up listening to you" and "it's great to hear you again" calls were out of the way, he'd actually have to work – and work very hard. No records to fall back on (even if it truly is his middle name).

"You may be a legend," I told him, referring to his Landecker and the Legends days, "but NOT in this format."

He laughed 'til he cried. Or maybe he cried 'til he laughed. For the next few months, I would remind him of that, as he had to start his career over in many ways. He took it well. Turns out, you CAN teach an old dog new tricks after all.

IN TRANSITION

I was still doing movie reviews for Bob Sirott on Channel 11, and that wasn't paying a lot of money, but I had some money in the bank, and it looked like my career was going in a certain direction. I was happy with that. I really enjoyed working at WGN, and I thought it was going pretty well.

And then one day it just ended. Boom. Done. Just as quickly and unexpectedly as it began. The general manager of the station and Mary June Rose both left WGN, and in came another general manager and another program director, and without any explanation whatsoever I suddenly noticed that my phone wasn't ringing.

I was given no concrete reason why. I can sit in my own paranoid mind and come up with a bunch of scenarios, and walk around screaming at the walls that this was totally unfair — "Just tell me what is wrong. Just tell me that I suck."

But it would all just be guessing, because no one ever bothered to call me.

WIBC

John Quick was Operations Manager/Program director of WIBC in Indianapolis (the station I listened to when I was in the back seat as a kid driving to see my grandfather). He was driving through town and heard me on WGN.

I just happened to be talking to my Uncle Hugh in Franklin, Indiana that day, who was a farmer. Max Armstrong, one of the farm reporters at WGN, had been in Indianapolis at some farm convention as a keynote speaker, and I had him on, along with my Uncle Hugh. You gotta hear Uncle Hugh to understand why he's such a memorable character — he's very dry, and very direct. It was an entertaining segment, and John Quick really liked it. When he got back to Indianapolis, he called Mary June Rose at WGN, and asked about my availability. She put me in touch with him.

John invited me down to Indianapolis to do a few shows at WIBC — which was a complete gas! I mean, WIBC was the WGN of Indianapolis. They had a great staff, they had great people there, and I had an absolute ball doing shows on that station.

Over the course of the next six or eight months I went down there three separate times. But once again, the economy changed, the situation changed, cutbacks were instituted, and suddenly John Quick was no longer at WIBC.

That phone stopped ringing too.

AND THEN COMES DIVORCE (AGAIN)

During this time period, my marriage with Laura started to unravel. I could get into the reasons, but it's really not that hard to figure out. When your wife is one year younger than your oldest daughter, and one year older than your youngest daughter — well, let your imagination run wild.

I think I'm just going to leave it at that.

We were married slightly over ten years, although the tenth anniversary came while we were separated. For some reason we were able to handle the big, traumatic problems together, but our everyday life deteriorated over time. We went to marriage counseling two different times, and nothing got better. There came a time when we discussed going back for a third time.

"You know what?" I said. "This is ridiculous. We'll go back, and the same crap will be discussed, and nothing will happen. The only thing that we haven't tried is separating. Who knows, maybe that will work?"

It didn't.

We got divorced.

KIPPER MCGEE *REMEMBERS*

Kipper McGee was the program director of WLS at that time… Having been heavily influenced by WLS and their battles with cross-river rival Super 'CFL, I had been a John Landecker fan since his arrival at the station in the early '70s.

> *After being named Program Director of WLS, one of my first moves was to reach out to the legendary talent who I felt might have the chops for talk radio. John was one of the first calls. Several years earlier, when I was in St. Louis, programming KTRS, I had met John at the birthday party of a mutual friend, and bounced the idea of his considering talk. At the time, he was still ensconced playing oldies at Chicago's WJMK-FM; I made the point that his performances had always been topical, and the leap from "Boogie Check" to taking callers would be more of a baby step for him.*
>
> *Fast forward to my arrival at WLS.*
>
> *John was interested in a return to "The Big 89" and before you could say "Americana Panorama," he was on our roster, hosting regular weekend shows, and filling in as needed, always to great response.*

WLS... AGAIN

By this time I had a smattering of experience doing talk radio on WGN, but there was one huge asterisk about applying that experience to WLS. WGN was mass appeal, apolitical, non-confrontational, information, entertainment, news-talk radio. WLS, on the other hand, was a right-wing conservative Petri dish, with syndicated and local personalities who were unabashedly bashing anything that had to do with Democrats and the Left. This was the home of Rush Limbaugh and Sean Hannity. How was I going to fit in there?

I figured, you know what I'm going to do? I'm just going to keep my mouth shut about politics and see if I can bring something else to the station. They were loaded with people who did confrontational political talk, so I came in and pretty much started doing the same thing I had done on WGN. I filled in for vacationing shows, and I eventually got a weekend show of my own. Unfortunately, the way I got that show wasn't exactly ideal. There had been some cutbacks, somebody was fired, and I was given the slot on an interim basis until someone could be hired. Well, whoever was supposed to be hired never arrived, so I just stayed there; very early on Saturday mornings.

I did get some constructive input from Kipper McGee, and the impression I was given was that I was doing better, and they were pleased with my progress. In fact, he even went out of his way once to show me the ratings that I was getting on Saturday morning and they were pretty good. I was shocked that I was doing that well on a talk station.

But it was a weird shift. I did two or three hours of a talk show, then I would sit in as a second fiddle on a car show, then I'd be off for a couple of hours, and then I'd come back and anchor an infomercial for an hour. This infomercial was run by a guy named Joe Aldeguer and it paid good money, but infomercials only talk about one thing, and that's whatever the guy is selling. In this case it was everything from mortgages to VOIP to a resort in the Dominican.

Some would say that would be a real come down for an air personality to be employed as the host of an infomercial, and I suppose on some level it was, but it also paid money, and I wasn't too proud to say no to something like that. I even managed to have a good time doing it.

In the fall of 2005 I was filling in for Don & Roma on WLS, when the Chicago White Sox won the World Series. It was the first World Series title in Chicago since 1917. I called my old producer Rick Kaempfer to help me write a parody of the poem "Casey at the

Bat," and I read it on the air the morning after we won. Listeners got a big kick out of it, and WLS even posted the poem on their website. (It's in the appendix of this book.)

This situation at WLS went well for a while, but then, unfortunately, Kipper left the radio station. The GM that hired me left the radio station too, and a new regime came in. The new regime, especially the program director, was not a fan of the John Landecker talk show.

You guessed it: the phone stopped ringing.

JIM BOHANNAN REMEMBERS

Jim Bohanann is a nationally syndicated talk show host based in Washington... *I admire the many ways John pioneered things: "Boogie Check" was really a precursor to Alan Colmes' "radio graffiti." With songs like "YDNA" he was out-weirding Weird Al.*

John can do the scripted to perfection, and still handle the off-the-cuff with hilarious spontaneity. He's a lot like a shortstop, able to handle the line drive, the pop up, the high hopper and the slow dribbler (that last one being my specialty, according to several women I've known). Let's just say he's a guy who epitomizes the era when talent and creativity, not bombast and boorishness, reigned supreme. Radio will never flush John from its ranks of all-time greats.

CHAPTER SEVENTEEN
CLOSURE

> The late '00s and early '10s are the Obama years. A time of worldwide financial peril, and a time of hope and change. It's also a time that Baby Boomers are beginning to reach retirement age, and worry about things that they never in a million years thought they would need to worry about.

My entire life I grew up knowing that my father was Jewish, but I wasn't considered Jewish because my mother was Protestant, and in the Jewish religion, your mother determines your religion. So, I didn't go to synagogue, and we didn't celebrate Jewish holidays, but it was always there — we always knew Dad was Jewish, and we knew a few of the stories from the days of living in Germany at the time of Hitler and the Nazis.

After my father died, my brother and I discovered that he had been receiving an annual stipend from the government of Germany, and had been for quite awhile. We had to inform the German government that he was no longer alive and that they should stop their payments, which we did. A few years after that, out of nowhere, my brother and I both received a letter written in German. It included some sort of a form, but we didn't know what it meant because neither of us spoke German. This led to a very strange moment in my life.

I had the form in front of me on the desk, written in German. I called the German Consulate and talked to them about the Jews in World War II and payments. Everybody at the Consulate spoke with really thick German accent. As I was talking to them, this feeling came over me that's very hard to describe.

Suddenly I felt a connection to my father; about being Jewish, about the Nazis. As I looked down at the form again, I saw there was a serial number next to my name, and the emblem of the German government on the letterhead. It brought up emotions that I had never experienced before. I know this sounds bizarre, but it almost felt like I was back in Germany, and was understanding my father's experience for the first time.

After the phone call, I decided to do two things. I got my serial number tattooed on the inside of my left forearm (as many Jews were forced to do in concentration camps), and I bought a gun. I had never thought about getting a tattoo in my entire life. I had never thought about getting a gun. But in this moment of whatever you want to call it, let's call it extreme anger for lack of a better term, it was my way of saying to myself that if I were ever faced with a situation in which it was kill or be killed, I was going to kill. If I can paraphrase Aerosmith: "Half-Jew Got a Gun."

We eventually hired a translator that told us that the letter from the German government was a notice telling us we were qualified to receive a death benefit. The form was asking us for our banking information so that they could send it to us. Apparently the German government has paid out more than $25 billion since the end of World War II.

A very, very small part of that went to my brother and me.

THE SOUL MATE

So I've told you about my first love (Judy), my trophy wife (Paula), the younger woman (Laura), and now we have, definitely the LAST, but not the least; the soul mate.

I know, I'll pause right now while everyone goes "awww."

I met a wonderful woman named Nika (who also had been married three times) through mutual friends, and in the beginning, all we did was talk. I was feeling pretty down, sort of numb from the collapse of my marriage to Laura. That was the first time I ever got divorced sober, and for me it was absolutely brutal. BRUTAL! I was wiped out, devastated, an emotional wreck — it hit me hard and took an emotional toll on me, even though I knew it was the right thing to do.

So Nika and I started talking about it. That's all it was at first. But after it blossomed into more, Nika moved in with me. We started discussing marriage, but we decided to go get the marriage license first, figuring we could think about it some more after we got the license.

Now, when you've already been married three times, you've pretty much exhausted the grandiosity of the wedding event. Not the importance, just the glitter and the show. One day both of us were working out at a health club, and we were all sweaty — dressed in our work out clothes, and we decided, why not just go pick up the marriage license that day? So we drove down to city hall and were filling out the forms with the clerk.

The clerk asked me: "So when's the wedding date?"

These unexpected words popped out of my mouth: "How about right now?"

They put the call out to the courtrooms, and wouldn't you know it, there was a judge available. So, just like that, the two of us got married.

Each of us has gone through three prior marriages, and we're not kids. We've each already had a full life, so there really is a connection there that is unique. For lack of a better explanation, I call us soul mates. I've heard that phrase from everybody and their brother — "Are we soul mates, honey, are we?" Let me tell you, if you have to ask if you're a soul mate, you're not. And I don't have to ask that question.

WHAT ABOUT MY KIDS?
I want to devote part of this book to my children. My contribution to Tracy's and Amy's lives has been uneven at best. My drugs and alcohol did heavy damage to my family and my relationship to my children. I put my children in many inappropriate situations. I exposed them to parts of life that are not for kids. I ignored my responsibility as a parent when I needed to use drugs or get alcohol. I don't think it serves any purpose to list each of these transgressions. Suffice it to say that any family with a parent using drugs or alcohol is going to have problems.

I can only try to be a better person today. I have an eight year old granddaughter who has never seen me drunk, and I love her to death. Whatever parental DNA I've got left will be passed on to her when needed.

Both Tracy and Amy live in Los Angeles. Tracy is the author of *Are you there God, it's me Mary: The Shangri-Las and the Punk Rock Love Song*. It's through Warner Brothers Music and Rhino Records on "Single Notes" online. The Shangri-Las were one of my all-time favorite girl groups of the '60s. They were tough. They were sexy. They sang the greatest songs: "Walking in the Sand" and "The Leader of the Pack." They had great lyrics. *"Is he tall? Well, I've got to look up. Yeah? Well I hear he's bad. Mmm, he's good bad, but he's not evil."*

Well, Tracy has taken the analysis of the Shangri-Las to another level. It's fantastic! So well written, with insight I could never have imagined (Carl Jung!) What's great about all this as far as I'm concerned is that I'm more than likely the person who introduced the Shangri-Las to her. She writes about our house playing all sorts of music from Frank Zappa to Bette Midler. She writes about a jukebox that was in her room that lit up in different colors. As a parent who carries loads of guilt about the way I behaved, it's nice to see something positive came out of her childhood.

My youngest daughter is an actress in Hollywood. She's done a boatload of commercials, television, and movies. She worked for it. When she was still living in Chicago, she started doing commercial voiceover work while she was working at Starbucks. (You will find that in Chicago, most of the people working at Starbucks are in the theater.) She did well enough to drop Starbucks and support herself by acting and doing commercials exclusively. After a short period of time, she decided to move to New York and did very well there. And after a short period of time, she decided to move to Los Angeles.

I'm not going to list all of her achievements, but there is one story that was incredible for me as a parent. Amy was cast as Mrs. Samsky in the Coen Brothers movie *A Serious Man*. Now this was a great movie — it was nominated for numerous Oscars. From the time the movie wrapped until the evening of the Oscars, more often than not every time the movie was discussed in the media, a clip with Amy was shown. She appeared in the print ads. The evening of the Academy Awards I was watching with my wife in Indiana and Amy was driving around L.A. going to Oscar parties. I was talking to her on the phone when the category of best screen play came up. Tina Fey was the presenter and said: "The Coen Brothers, *A Serious Man*."

A scene with Amy came on and I was screaming into the phone: "It's you! It's you! It's you!" I was out of my mind! Can you imagine watching your daughter on the Oscars? Luckily I had it on the DVR, so I could actually take it all in when I calmed down.

Tracy will continue as a writer. It may be a screenplay, it may be a book, or it may be about rock and roll. Whatever it is, I'm looking forward to it. Amy is an extremely talented actress. Right now, she's working on a few things that *I'm not allowed to talk about*. I'm not kidding. One time I actually told someone something she was working on that I wasn't supposed to tell, and I got into a shitload of trouble. So trust me, she's working on some stuff that I'm not allowed to talk about.

What I can say is that I love my kids.

AS LONG AS YOU HAVE YOUR HEALTH

I was diagnosed with a lazy bladder a few years ago, which means that I have to take a catheter and stick it up my weenie whenever I want to urinate. After a while it becomes like brushing your teeth. OK, maybe not like brushing your teeth. Let's just say it's part of the routine.

Well, one day not too long ago, I stuck that catheter in, and nothing came out. Not a good thing. So I went to St. Anthony's Hospital in Michigan City, Indiana and I was lying there on a table telling everyone what was happening to me. There was a nurse, a doctor, and an administrator taking my insurance information.

"What's your name?" the administrator asked.

"John Landecker," I replied.

"John *Records* Landecker?" the doctor asked.

"*Boogie Check*?" the administrator asked.

That just cracked me up.

Those kids that called up and farted, and burped, and said "FUCK" on the air on WLS in the 1970s are now the pillars of American society. They are the doctors, nurses, and administrators of today.

And right now they're going to stick this catheter back up my dick.

ANOTHER DOOR OPENS

My radio life began at WOIA/WOIB Ann Arbor in Saline, Michigan in a small building under the transmitter on a country road. It was one of the best times I've ever had in my life. I thought it would be cosmically appropriate to end my career the same way, so I attempted to make contact with two local stations: WEFM in Michigan City, and the Eagle in La Porte. The guy who ran WEFM told mutual acquaintances that he wouldn't know what to do with me. I actually met with the program director of the Eagle, and I was sitting in the reception area reading a book about radio.

I was in the book.

But nothing came of that meeting.

A while later, a local Michigan City radio station WIMS that had been off the air, was sold to new management and signed back on as a talk station. I knew the owner Ric Federighi from his days

RECORDS TRULY IS MY MIDDLE NAME

operating a traffic service for Chicago radio stations. I met with Ric a couple of times and finally after convincing him that I would not be offended by his bare bones studio, and that I would work for minimum wage, I went on the air at AM 1420 WIMS, the talk of the south shore… in a small building under the transmitter on a country road… just like the station where I got my start.

My good friend Joey Reynolds says that we're compelled to be on the radio, and I think that's true. And since I'm compelled, and since that's what I do, I figured why not have a good time doing it instead of a bad time? There is an option after all. I'm only human and there's a lot in this world that can influence your thinking down a negative path, and there are people I've worked with that can take your thinking down a negative path.

But none of those people worked at WIMS. Ric is an extremely positive person — always upbeat — so it was fun to be there. I teamed with a wonderful person named Paula Griffin and did small town talk radio for a while. There are only 33,000 people in the entire city. It was small, but there also wasn't any pressure at all. We just went with the flow. Remember the story of young John sitting in his closet with a tape recorder and a sound effects record pretending to do play-by-play? At WIMS, I got to do it for real. I did an entire season of Michigan City football, both home and away. I might have been a jinx though; they only won one game and got blown out most of the time. Try to find the highlight in games like that, Mr. Play-by-Play. I did basketball play-by-play for the Marquette Blazers too. Some of their games were nail-biters. Very exciting!

But the best thing about working there was meeting some of the fine folks in Michigan City. Take it from me, if you ever find yourself in Michigan City, take the family over to Captain Ed's on Route 20, a couple of blocks east of Franklin Street. It's a one-of-a-kind store. You can thank me later.

More than likely I would still be at WIMS were it not for a series of coincidences coming together in a job offer.

THE LAST CHAPTER

This really is the last chapter. Not my last chapter, but the book's last chapter. I didn't know how I was going to end this book. As it turns out, in the process of creating it, the ending sort of wrote itself. A connection made in the '70s was made again in 2009.

When I was at WLS and was #1, a company in Dallas that made radio station jingles wanted to put together a demo of their product, and contacted WLS about building the presentation around my on-air persona. They also contacted other radio people around the country to participate. They wrote a script, came to Chicago, and I just said my lines and went home. The jingle folks were obviously big fans and had written a bit that really was what my show was all about. In the demo there was a section where I took phone calls. Remember, I was reading a script — I wasn't actually on the phone. The jingle company then went around the country and recorded the other various radio people portraying the callers. One of them was a man named Jan Jeffries, who I had not yet met.

Jump ahead to the mid '80s, my decade of darkness, my job at the Loop was down the drain and I was hired by Cox Radio G106. The program director was Jan Jeffries. He later got me back into WLS. Jan left to go on to bigger and better things. I stayed at WLS, but I did fly down to Atlanta for his surprise birthday party.

Jump to May 28, 2007. WLS decided to break its talk format for WLS Rewind, a Memorial Day recreation of the '70s format for one day. I came in and did 6-10pm. Among the many e-mails I got was one from Jan Jeffries. I gave him a shout out on the air.

At that time WLS was owned by Disney. It had a format on the FM that had changed continually over the years. While I was doing fill-in talk shows on the AM, the FM was changed to the "True Oldies Channel," a 24/7 syndication format run by the programmer out of New York. My agent Elliot Ephram and I made an appointment to talk to their general manager. He informed us that they wanted absolutely nothing to do with the WLS heritage or the WLS heritage personalities in Chicago.

Okay.

One weekend I was on WLS doing a talk show, and I thought I'd go downstairs to the FM and just see what this True Oldies Channel was like. I looked in the studio and it was being run by a machine. There wasn't a human being to be found. After a while they decided to add a live morning show, and soon rumors started circulating that they might want to do a live afternoon show. That's when I went to the new general manager at WLS and said, "Look, why don't I continue to do the fill-in weekends on the AM, and do afternoons on the True Oldies Channel."

I ended up signing a two-year contract to do afternoons, 3-7pm.

As I said, the radio station was being run at arm's length by program directors in New York. During that time I also began to host a once-a-week syndicated show called "Into the '70s" that started playing around the country. I worked at both the AM & FM. There was actually one time when I filled in on the morning show on the AM, and then came back in the afternoon to do my own show on the FM.

Nine months into my contract, I was told that I would not be renewed. My ratings were fine. What was the problem? I'm not going to try to explain a move I can't understand. Just let me say that I don't think it had to do with anyone that was actually working here in Chicago. I believe it all came from New York.

Eventually the True Oldies Channel decided to use the WLS call letters on the air. (Remember that whole WLS heritage they wanted absolutely nothing to do with?) After a couple of years, rumors circulated about Citadel (which had bought WLS from Disney just a few years earlier) being sold to Cumulus broadcasting. The executive vice president of Cumulus broadcasting was Jan Jeffries.

I called Jan and laid out the whole nasty 94.7 story to him, and told him that if Cumulus bought Citadel — I wanted back on! The purchase process took more than a year to complete. While it was going on, Jan decided two things. He decided to move back to Chicago, and he decided that along with being the executive vice president of programming, he would also be the program director of WLS-FM.

After months of e-mails, I finally met Jan for dinner in Chicago. Jan wanted to bring me in for a weekend to see if what we wanted to have happen could really happen, but it wasn't a done deal. Somehow the media picked up on this and had me employed doing weekends and vacation relief before I even uttered a word! As you can guess, I walked into the station that weekend and never left. I think I went on mid-December 2011, and had my own show by January of 2012.

This is the third time I'm working with Jan (including that demo tape), and counting that brief stint on the AM as the weekend talk show host, it is the fourth time I've come to work at WLS. There's gotta be something to that, don't you think?

It feels fantastic. Unbelievably cool. Just way beyond anything I could conceive of. It's like somebody built a radio station for me to work on. And Jan and I get along unbelievably well. This is his concept, and he's the driving force behind it, and I'm there to have a good time and be the icing on his cake from the WLS music era.

Ever since I left nights at WLS in the '70s, everything has been a challenge. I did different shifts. Afternoons. Mornings. Talk radio. I sought out those challenges, but in all of those situations I never would describe it as being in a comfort zone. I'm glad I did 'em, but this is a party. To quote Foreigner: "It feels like the first time." (PDs and on-air talent: take notice how I cleverly included a music tie-in.)

Any more about this job would be ass-kissing, so let's get to the facts. It's no longer the 1970s, and radio ratings are not done the same way. Everyone wondered: Can you still do it today? Without getting into the minutiae, let me put it this way: After about two months of doing the show, Jan brought in the ratings for the week of March 11. It was for the 35-64 year old age group. It was for my shift.

The WLS call letters were at the top.

I'm John Landecker, and *Records Truly is My Middle Name*.

APPENDIX
HITS & BITS

Over my forty plus years of doing radio I've done hundreds of parody songs. I've picked out a few of my favorites, along with an explanation of the news stories that inspired them, and printed the lyrics over the next few pages. I've also included the transcripts of a few of my most memorable bits — all of which have been previously described in the pages of this book. If you ever want to hear these hits and bits, most of them are available on CD.

MOM AND DAD EXPLAIN MY MIDDLE NAME

No one ever believed me when I said that "Records Truly is My Middle Name," so I got my mother and father on the air one time at WLS to prove it…

John: What is your name?

Mother: Marjorie Records Landecker.

John: Now, that's true, right?

Mother: That's true.

John: Many years ago I came waltzing into the world, right?

Mother: You certainly did.

John: Now why would you name me the way you did? Why would you do that?

Mother: Because that's my maiden name. I named you Records.

John: Was that a tradition at the time or what?

Mother: There have been John Records for many generations.

John: And no one ever believes that Records is my middle name. They think it's a joke.

Mother: It's no joke. Records truly is your middle name.

John: Let's call my father.

(Phone rings)

Father: Hello?

John: Dad?

Father: How are you?

John: There's someone else here that wants to say hello.

Mother: Hello.

Father: Well, hello.

John: I'm putting this on the air to prove that Records truly is my middle name.

RECORDS TRULY IS MY MIDDLE NAME

Father: Well, it's a matter of record!

John: What is your version of why I got my middle name?

Father: The fact of the matter is that is your mother's maiden name.

John: That's right. As I've had to explain to *many* people, *many* times.

Father: I'm glad I was able to make a contribution to the situation.

John: You always did love this rock and roll music, didn't you, Dad?

Father: There's nothing closer to my heart.

Mother & John: (Laugh)

ON THE AIR IN ANN ARBOR, 1966

The earliest recording of me on the radio still in existence is a request call I did on WOIA in Ann Arbor. It was recorded, of course, by Art Vuolo. In fact, Art was the caller.

SFX: Phone ring from "Our Man Flint"
John: Hello, the live-line is on the air. Are you there?
Caller: I'm here. This is good old Art Vuolo calling in from Jackson.
John: Jackson?
Caller: Yup. You're coming in like a local here.
John: That's great, Art. And where do you go to school?
Caller: The greatest community college in Southern Michigan.
John: That'll be $150 for thirty seconds.
Caller: Hey listen, why don't you play a record for me?
John: Sure, which one?
Caller: For all my teachers that aren't giving me good marks like they should be, can you please play, 'cause I love it so much, "The Work Song?"

MAKE A DATE WITH A WATERGATE

The song that was actually made into a bona fide record (with my misspelled name). It's to the tune of Lou Reed's "Walk on the Wild Side"...

(In Nixon's voice) Good Evening, My Fellow Americans.
At our convention, Miami, FLA
A campaign, across the USA,
Let me make this perfectly clear, let me stick this in your ear,
They said "Hey babe, make a date with a Watergate."
My fellow Americans I said, "Hey honey, make a date with a Watergate."
And Martha Mitchell says, Do de doo doo doo de doo…
(Backup girls sing)
Reelection committees never ever give it away,
Everybody has to pay and pay.
Let me make this perfectly clear, it can't be denied,
My fellow Americans, I've got nothing to hide,
Ain't it great?
I said, "Hey Spiro, make a date with a Watergate."
I said, "Hey Joe, make a date with a Watergate."
Martha Mitchell? She say Do de doo doo doo…
(Backup girls sing)
My personal lawyer, counsel John Dean,
He came from out on the island, my fellow Americans,
Standing at the telephony,
Ain't exactly an island, A bugger here, a bugger there,
Washington's the place where, they said…
Hey babe, make a date with a Watergate,

Let me make this perfectly clear my fellow Americans,
I said "Hey Sugar, make a date with a Watergate."
I said "Hey Spiro. Hey all you people. Make a date with a Watergate."
And the public (clears throat)
The public says Doo de dooo dooo dooo…

© Lyrics by John Records Landecker. Used by permission.

ANIMAL STORIES

Of course, this is not my bit. It's Larry Lujack and Tommy Edwards' bit. This is the time they made fun of me. (Thanks to Larry and Tommy for letting me publish this.)

Larry: Get your greasy little face up next to the radio because it's time for America's favorite radio program, Animal Stories. And now here in person is the Animal Stories news team anchormen, I, your charming and delightful Ol' Uncle Lar, and him,
Tommy: Hi.
Larry: In person, little Tommy. How you doin' little Tommy?
Tommy: I'm fine, Uncle Lar.
Larry: We were sent a picture. I guess in Cedar Rapids they had one of those donkey basketball games.
Tommy: Oh yeah, I'd like that.
Larry: All of the players ride donkeys around, and look at the floor. The donkeys left… uh…
Tommy: (Laughs)
Larry: Uh… unsightly…
Tommy: Droppings.
Larry: All over the basketball court.
Tommy: Uh, well that makes it kind of slippery.
Larry: That's one thing our WLS basketball team does not do. We do *not* leave droppings on the floor. However, Landecker plays like a donkey dropping.

© Larry Lujack and Tommy Edwards. Used by permission.

THE B.S. LOVE COUNSELOR

This is also not my bit, it's Bob Sirott's. While my career was exploding in a good way, my marriage with Judy was exploding in a bad way. This little moment on the radio probably illustrates the situation pretty well. Bob Sirott used to do a bit called "BS Love Counselor," and on this one particular occasion I was the subject of it. Thanks to Bob for letting me republish it here…

Bob: WLS, How is your love life?
Caller: My love life is terrible. I have a crush on John Landecker, but I know he's married.
Bob: Mrs. Landecker probably would object to that. Let's call her.
(SFX: Phone rings)
Judy: Hello?
Bob: Hello, is this Judy Landecker, the wife of John Landecker?
Judy: Yes it is.
Bob: There is someone on the loveline here that says she is in love with John, who is your husband.
Judy: All I can really say is… I don't really care.

TRAVOLTA AT WOODFIELD MALL

This is the transcript of my famous visit to Woodfield Mall with John Travolta in 1976. The audio of this is available on CD.

Landecker: We are currently going through a whole security number.

Security Guard: It's like we're guarding the president.

Travolta: Am I returning in the same car?

Security Guard: You're returning in the same car.

Travolta: So I can leave everything here?

Security Guard: Don't worry about anything. Just worry about you.

Landecker: OK, we follow you, right?

Security Guard: Just follow us.

Landecker: What do you think John?

Travolta: Who's the guy in the '50s that had all the cop shows?

Landecker: Broderick Crawford?

Travolta: No, no. The one that produced them and everything.

Landecker: OH! Dragnet, Jack Webb.

Travolta: Yeah, yeah. That's him. That's this guy.

Landecker: Just the facts, ma'am.

Security Guard: OK, we gotta surround him. Two guys in back of him.

Landecker: This is really it.

Travolta: This is really it. Good luck to you, John.

Landecker: *(laughs)* Good luck to you, John.

Security guard #1: Your teacher's not here to correct you.

Security guard #2: OK, uniform guys first. Two guys in back, one guy on each side of him.

Landecker: Here we go, into the mall.

(Jostling noises)

Landecker: We're heading into the mall with Vinnie Babarino, and we'll see what happens.

Girl: Can we have your autograph? C'mon, please John, please?

Landecker: We're heading into the main portion of the mall. We're surrounded by police.

(Crowd starts screaming)

Security Guard: My gun, my gun, my gun.

(More jostling noises)

Landecker: As you can hear, the crowd has made eye contact.

(Crazy crowd screaming. Girls at the top of their lungs)

Landecker: It's a little extreme, baby.

(Crazy crowd screaming.)

Landecker: Vinnie Babarino at the Woodfield Mall on WLS. I don't know if you can hear me, but it's all going down. I don't know what it is we're going to do here, but stare at each other.

(Crazy crowd screaming for several seconds)

Landecker on stage: All of you will be on the air tonight between 8 and 9 on WLS. Give it up for Vinnie Babarino!

RADIO STAR WARS

This is the full transcript of Radio Star Wars from 1977. The newsman in the bit was Jack Swanson, who was later named the best program director in America at KGO-San Francisco. I played the part of Darth Vader. The remastered version of this, which we redid twenty years later for the rerelease of Star Wars, can be found on CD.

John: Mark Hamill is our guest this afternoon.

Newsman: John, John, I hate interrupt…

John: What are you doing here, I'm trying to interview Mark Hamill

Newsman: Look, I'm sorry to interrupt, but this is important.

(Star Wars music in and under)

John: Judging by the music, it's very important.

Newsman: Yes, listen. There's a guy on the phone here. He's says he's Darth Vader.

Mark Hamill: Hey! Wait a minute. He's the villain from Star Wars. Stay away! He's evil.

Newsman: Oh God, it's terrible.

John: Relax, relax. What line is he on?

Newsman: Pick up Line 2.

John: Think it's alright if I talk to him, Mark?

Mark Hamill: Well, I don't know. He is the most evil force in the universe, but he is deathly afraid of ducks. John, please be careful.

John: OK. Hello?

(Sfx: Helicopter sound effects, heavy breathing)

Darth Vader: Hello, this is Darth Vader. Is this John Landecker on WLS?

John: Yes it is. Yes.

Darth Vader: Are you there with Luke Skywalker?

Mark Hamill: Oh yeah, I'm here, Darth.

Darth Vader: Listen to my demands. I have kidnapped Bob Sirott and the Princess Leia.

Bob Sirott: Help, John, Help!

Carrie Fisher: Luke, save us!

Darth Vader: I have stolen the WGN Traffic helicopter. Bob and the Princess are inside. We are flying over the Dan Ryan. If I am not given full control of WLS, Bob and the Princess will be dropped into the rush hour traffic below me. They will die!

John: Great googly moogly, what to do?

Mark Hamill: John, I think my experience as Luke Skywalker can really be of some help here.

John: How's that?

Mark Hamill: Well, I've got the Millennium Falcon, the starship from the movie. It's parked right outside the station. I've got my droid R2D2. I'd be willing to give it a shot.

John: You don't mean?

Mark Hamill: That's right, John. RESCUE!

(Star Wars music swells)

Darth Vader: Rescue is futile! Turn over the station to me now or Bob and the Princess are dead meat.

Bob: John, don't do it.

Carrie Fisher: Oh Luke, be careful.

John: Wow, this starship is bigger than it looked in the movie.

Mark Hamill: Well, strap in, and be careful now while I program R2D2 for our flight. R2, set a course for the WGN traffic helicopter over the Dan Ryan and take off.

(R2D2 sound effects)

(Dramatic music kicks in, the battle is underway)

Darth Vader: You have thirty seconds.

John: Luke, shoot him down!

Mark Hamill: I can't, John. My ray guns are too powerful. They're designed for other galaxies. If I fire, all of Chicago will be destroyed.

John: Wait. Didn't you say that Darth Vader had a deathly fear of ducks?

Mark Hamill: Yeah.

John: Well, I think I've got the answer. We've got an open radio channel directly into the copter.

Mark Hamill: Right.

John: I've got a cassette of the song "Disco Duck" right here.

Mark Hamill: And you want to blast that song right into the copter? Great! Give the song to R2D2 and he'll program the song directly into the copter's communication system.

John: OK. R2D2, take it!

(R2D2 sound effects)

John: Fire!

(The song "Disco Ducks" begins)

Darth Vader: Oh no, not that duck record! NOOOOO!

(Explosion)

Bob Sirott: John, John, can you hear me? Darth Vader's body exploded. I've got control of the copter. We're all right.

Carrie Fisher: Oh John, THANK YOU!

(Star Wars theme kicks in)

CABRINI GREEN

These are the lyrics to the song I wrote for Mayor Jane Byrne when she made the unusual decision to move into the Cabrini Green housing project in Chicago in the early '80s. It's to the tune of the AC/DC song "Dirty Deeds Done Dirt Cheap." We eventually remade and released this song on CD.

Having trouble where to make your bed? I heard it in the news,
Janie found a place to rest her head, here's what you got to do,
Ignore the slide, forget the crime, 'cause we're takin' quite a turn,
1-1-6-0 Sedgewick, You can look up, Janie Byrne
Cabrini Green
(Rent's Dirt Cheap)
Cabrini Green
(Rent's Dirt Cheap)
Cabrini Green
(Rent's Dirt Cheap)
Cabrini Green where the mayor sleeps, Cabrini Green where the mayor sleeps.

© Lyrics by Landecker/Kaempfer. Used by permission.

MARY TYLER MOORE

This is the transcript of the satellite interview I did with Mary Tyler Moore. Valerie Harper was in the studio with me, pretending to be my co-host Vicki Truax. Mary had no idea that she was being set up by Valerie...

John: Would you please welcome to Oldies 104.3, Mary Tyler Moore. Good morning, Mary.

Mary: Good morning John.

John: Let's turn it over to Vicki. Vicki, I know you have some questions for Mary Tyler Moore.

Valerie: Yes, I do. Mary hello.

Mary: Hi Vicki, How are you?

Valerie: I'm so thrilled and excited because you're one of my favorite, favorite actresses in the whole world.

Mary: Thank you. That's nice. Thanks a lot.

Valerie: And I read your book in hardcover and it's fantastic. I have a question for you if I may. Everyone should read the book, but I want to ask you a question that has long bothered me. Of the wonderful supporting cast, who was your favorite of those actors?

Mary: I couldn't possibly choose a favorite. It's like saying of your six brothers or sisters, which one is your favorite?

Valerie: But there is a favorite, let's face it, Mary. I love all the people at the station here, but I have a favorite. So that's a little disingenuous of you, don't you think, to say that?

Mary: No, I've NEVER been disingenuous. (snippily) Don't start a fight with me, Vicki. I loved them all for their different aspects. Don't tell me I had favorites.

Valerie: Fine. Then of the women, which was your favorite?

Mary: Oh, well, of the women, certainly Valerie…

Valerie: OH GOOD! OH GOD! You dirty dog, when did you get it?

Mary: Get what?

John: She didn't get it. She doesn't get it.

Mary: Is this you?

John: She was just doing it on her own.

Mary: Valerie! Oh geez! (happily) What a wonderful surprise this is! Valerie!

MARTHA STEWART

This is the song I performed live on television directly to Martha Stewart's face. It was to the tune of Roy Orbison's "Pretty Woman," and though Martha said "it's a little racy, isn't it?" she laughed out loud as I sang it. Rick Kaempfer wrote the lyrics to this with me, and it can also still be found on CD.

Martha Stewart, I see you on TV,
Martha Stewart, with all your potpourri,
Martha Stewart.
You have given me the incentive, to be domestically inventive
Martha Stewart, let me be your fella,
Together, we'll fight salmonella,
Martha Stewart.
What you do is art, you have stolen my artichoke heart.
Martha Stewart is on the phone,
So we can talk about pinecones,
And all the things that those pinecones can be, for you and me,
Martha.
Martha Stewart, you're really built,
Martha won't you share my quilt,
Camouflage and kitchen ware,
Flannel shirt under your hair,
Cause I need you. I need you bad.
You're guacamole's, the best I've had. Had. Had. Had.
Martha Stewart, now you're sanding stairs
Martha Stewart, now you're poaching pears,
Martha Stewart.
What's that you're bringing to me? To me.

Why, it looks like grapes and brie.

Or is it some new ratatouille,

Oh won't you hold my zucchini? Yes, she'll hold the zucchini.

Oh, oh, Martha Stewart.

© Lyrics by Landecker/Kaempfer. Used by permission.

THE BOBBITT SONG

This is the parody song we performed about John Wayne Bobbitt and his wife, Lorena. If you don't remember the news story, she got angry at her husband one night, chopped off his penis while he was sleeping, and threw it in the woods. Rick Kaempfer wrote the lyrics of this song with me, and it's to the tune of "If You Wanna Be Happy" by Jimmy Soul. It is still available on CD.

If you wanna make Lorena Bobbitt your wife,
You better hide the butcher knife,
John Wayne Bobbitt found out that's true,
When she woke him cutting off his wazoo,
Lorena said John wasn't treating her well,
So he wound up in a prison cell,
When he got acquitted Lorena scoffed,
"That's the last time he gets off!"
It's a story we all have heard,
And the controversy that it stirred,
The story of their marital strife,
That ended gruesomely with a knife,
She just sliced off his manhood,
And then she tossed it in the woods,
They say the ground there did get greener,
Fertilized by a sliced off wiener,
If you wanna make Lorena Bobbitt your wife,
You better hide the butcher knife,
John Wayne Bobbitt found out that's true,
When she woke him cutting off his wazoo,
We know how it will end of course,

The Bobbitts will wind up divorced,
Their problems simply cannot be patched,
And John is once again unattached
If you wanna make Lorena Bobbitt your wife,
You better hide the butcher knife,
John Wayne Bobbitt found out that's true,
When she woke him cutting off his wazoo,
Lorena said John wasn't treating her well,
So he wound up in a prison cell,
When he got acquitted Lorena scoffed,
"That's the last time he gets off!"
If you wanna make Lorena Bobbitt your wife,
You better limit your marital strife,
She really knows how to wield that blade,
Every night you're gonna go to sleep afraid

© Lyrics by Landecker/Kaempfer. Used by permission.

THE DAHMER SONG

This is the song that was banned by WJMK management after we played it. It aired exactly once, the day after Dahmer died. In retrospect, it was probably a good call by station management to ban it. At the time we couldn't resist the weirdness of this story. Dahmer was killed in a prison in Wisconsin by a man who thought he was God, and scientists were begging for his brain so that they could study what makes somebody that crazy. Rick Kaempfer wrote the words with me. It's to the tune of "The Night Chicago Died" by Paper Lace, and it's still available on CD.

Dahmer was a con, in a prison in Wisconsin,
Slept on a hard bunk bed, wonder what he was fed?
Jeff was kneeling on the floor, near the prison hobby room,
In November 94, he was scrubbing the bathroom,
And then an angry cheesehead,
Beat him up til he was dead,
The clean bathroom became stained,
By Jeffrey's Dahmer's brain,
The day that Dahmer Died,
Another racial prison homicide,
Brother what a day it really was, deader than doornail yes he is,
Save his brain.

© Lyrics by Landecker/Kaempfer. Used by permission.

KING OF FARTS

This is the song that we only played for the half of the audience that appreciated sophomoric humor, by putting it on the same cartridge as "You Light Up My Life." "The King of Farts" was in the left channel, "You Light Up My Life" was in the right channel, and the listeners got to choose which channel to listen to by simply using the balance knobs on their radios. Rick Kaempfer wrote the lyrics with me. It's done to the tune of Juice Newton's "Queen of Hearts" and is still available on CD.

Fartin, saying hey who cut the cheese?
You know it's a universal male ability,
Baked beans, they're the favorite of this old coot,
They're the magical fruit and boy do they make you toot,
They're calling me the King of Farts,
I've been makin' fartin' an art,
Just watch how my sonic boom,
Clears out every room,
Yes, I'm the King of Farts,
Shootin' out my sulfur darts,
You know I'd never take a pass,
At a chance to pass some gas,
Coffee, gets me started right every day,
Within a few minutes my digestive system has it's say,
Cabbage, a big heapin' plate of sauerkraut,
I love to eat it and wait for my bowels to shout! Yeah.
They're calling me the King of Farts,
I've been makin' fartin' an art,
Just watch how my sonic boom,

RECORDS TRULY IS MY MIDDLE NAME

Clears out every room,
Yes, I'm the King of Farts,
I'm famous in these parts,
You know it's a long lost art,
To fart without leaving your trademark.
Went camping, I discovered my favorite trick,
Lightin' a poofter at the end of a big old match stick,
Gigglin', you know that when I felt it,
And everybody knows that he who smelt it, dealt it.

© Lyrics by Landecker/Kaempfer. Used by permission.

BABY BOOMER

This is a song that Rick Kaempfer and I wrote the year I turned 50. I performed it in concert for many years dressed only in a diaper (baby boomer, get it?) It appeared on our third album, "Landecker & The Legends: Baby Boomer." On the cover of the CD, I'm wearing the infamous diaper.

I'm a Baby Boomer, oh yeah, and I'm getting old.
(wah, wah, wah, wah)
I'm a Baby Boomer, oh baby, I'm getting old
I'm a Baby Boomer, and it ain't fair,
That I'm growing love handles and I'm losing my hair,
I'm saving rubber bands and other worthless stuff,
And when I try to read my arms aren't long enough
Cause I'm a Baby Boomer,
There's no denying that I'm getting old
(wah wah wah wah)
I'm a Baby Boomer,
There's no denying we're all getting old.
Mylanta, My Tums, My Tagamet HB,
My Pepto Bismol, and My Pepcid AC,
Well it really don't matter where my food chain begins,
'Cause I'm never gonna get no acid indigestion.

© Lyrics by Landecker/Kaempfer. Used by permission.

WHY DNA?

This is the song we did to the tune of the Village People's song "YMCA." Every time we performed it on stage, and we did so many, many times, the Dancing Itos (usually my producers Rick and Vince wearing Ito beards and robes) would come on stage and dance along. These are the slightly revised lyrics Rick and I wrote after the trial ended...

O.J., did you murder your wife?
O.J., did you use a big knife?
O.J., you'll hear that all of your life,
Now that you have been acquitted
Ito, you're the judge with the beard,
Ito, the judge the media feared,
Ito, we're so glad that you cleared,
Having cameras in the courtroom,
But now the Juice is saying, Why DNA?
Oh yes the Juice is saying Why DNA?
Big ol' droplets of blood, found at the scene of the crime,
Don't mean that they're mine.
Broncos, it's a product from ford
Broncos, they go fast when they're floored,
Broncos, but when AC's on board,
You were going slow on the highway,
Kato, oh when you testify,
Kato, all the women they sigh,
Kato, oh how hard will you try,
To turn this into a career,
(Chorus)

Fuhrman, you're the cop on the case,
Fuhrman, was it a matter of race?
Fuhrman, can we set you a place,
Down at Farrakhan's new restaurant,
Marcia, oh your short hair was neat,
Marcia, and your clothes so discreet,
Marcia, still wakes up in her sleep,
Screaming — "Wait don't try those gloves on!"

© Lyrics by Landecker/Kaempfer. Used by permission.

JAY LENO INTERVIEW

I have to give Jay Leno his props, he did call into the show to defend himself live on the air. This is a partial transcript of that telephone call.

Jay: You know we're not allowed to open packages, right? We don't.

John: No, I don't know that. I don't know that you're not allowed to open it.

Jay: First of all, we had recorded it three or four days prior to it airing. We have to do that. Just to get the studio singers in there. Second of all, if you're going to rip somebody off, you rip off somebody who is mailing jokes to you from a 7/11 somewhere, you don't rip off somebody that has his own radio show. It would be easier for me to call you up, and say "Hello, John, here's a pile of money, let me do your bit," than it would be to steal it from someone as well-known as you, knowing that you and your listeners would go ballistic if we took it.

VIVA VIAGRA

These are the lyrics to the song that Rick Kaempfer and I wrote several years before Viagra started using similar lyrics in their commercials. It's to the Elvis Presley tune "Viva Las Vegas" and is still available on CD.

Now that I'm older, find I need some help, yes I need some help down there,
When I read about this pill I was really glad, 'cause I've got so much love to share,
I winked at my wife and I said it's time,
Showed her that little blue pill of mine,
Put my hands on my hips and said "RISE AND SHINE"
Viva Viagra. Viva Viagra.
Now I admit, that I was a bit, a bit embarrassed at first,
But I realized what I really prized, the alternative was worse,
Now when I get my prescription no one's gonna make fun,
I'm a middle aged man on the run,
Pharmacist winks 'cause I'm getting' some,
Viva Viagra. Viva Viagra.
Viva Viagra, now she don't need to nag ya, if your little rascal's gonna jump up and say HI
Viva Viagra, it's a pricey pill, that you're wifey will, want you to run right out to the store and buy
Now when I pull out my little pill, my wife just rolls her eyes,
She says put that away, and just for today, go hang out with the guys,
Well, I'm back to being her sexual pest,
I'm going out so the little woman can rest,
I still think that these pills are the best!

RECORDS TRULY IS MY MIDDLE NAME

Viva Viagra, Viva Viagra,
Viva, Viva, Viagra

© Lyrics by Landecker/Kaempfer. Used by permission.

PIERZINSKI AT THE BAT

This is the poem I read on the air the day after the Chicago White Sox won the World Series. It was written by my former producer Rick Kaempfer, a huge sacrifice for the lifelong Cubs fan…

The outlook wasn't brilliant for the White Sox nine that day,
The Angels led one game to none, game two was slipping away,
And then when A.J. got strike two, and missed strike three the same,
A pall-like silence fell upon all the Sox fans at the game,
The Angels catcher tossed Pierzinski's ball out to the mound,
But A.J. turned and ran to first, with outrage all around,
The umpire calmly stood his ground, achieving instant fame,
And A.J. somehow found a brand new way to win a game,
The White Sox never lost again, and shining stars were born,
Each time Joe Crede came to bat the other team would mourn,
And he and Juan Uribe were magicians with their gloves,
And Paul Konerko was the home run hero we all love,
When Ozzie came out to the mound, he motioned round and fat,
And Bobby Jenks showed the Astros why he wanted that,
And little Scott Podsednik hit the home run in Game 2,
And the White Sox starting pitching was like a dream come true,
In Game 3's fourteenth inning the Astros fans were glum,
Beaten by a former Astro named Geoff Blum,
And Jermaine Dye had a shining moment in game four,
When he knocked in the winning run, the White Sox shut the door.
And though each game was close and tight, the White Sox never feared,
Ever since A.J.'s run to first, they knew this was their year,
And now the catcher catches the ball, and now he lets it go,

And now the air is shattered by the A.J. we all owe,
Oh, somewhere in this country, some fans are screaming foul,
But White Sox fans say let them scream, let them cry and growl,
Cause White Sox fans are laughing, and White Sox fans can shout,
The south side is rejoicing,
Pierzinski has struck out.

© Landecker/Kaempfer. Used by permission.

ABOUT THE AUTHORS

John Records Landecker has had a legendary radio career spanning more than four decades in places like Ann Arbor, Flint, Lansing, Philadelphia, Chicago, Toronto, and even Michigan City, Indiana. Want to know more about him? Read this book. It's his memoir.

Rick Kaempfer was the executive producer of John Landecker's show on WJMK radio in the '90s and '00s, and prior to that the Steve & Garry show at WLUP in the '80s. He has since written *The Radio Producer's Handbook* (with John Swanson, Allworth Press 2004), a satirical novel about the broadcasting business called *$everance* (ENC Press, 2007), and another novel with Brendan Sullivan called *The Living Wills* (Eckhartz Press, 2011). All of his previous books are still available through amazon.com, encpress.com, or eckhartzpress.com. In addition, Rick writes a weekly column about parenting for nwi.com, a monthly media column for the *Illinois Entertainer*, and is a contributing editor to *Shore Magazine*. He lives in suburban Chicago with his wife Bridget, and his three sons Tommy, Johnny, and Sean. All three of their births were recorded for, and played back on, the John Records Landecker radio show.

COMING SOON on www.eckhartzpress.com

Records Truly is My Middle Name, The Soundtrack (CD)

Also Available at Eckhartz Press

The Balding Handbook by David Stern

Cheeseland by Randy Richardson

The Living Wills by Rick Kaempfer and Brendan Sullivan

Down at the Golden Coin by Kim Strickland

ECKHARTZ PRESS

www.eckhartzpress.com